THE UNIVERSITY OF CHICAGO PUBLICATIONS
IN RELIGIOUS EDUCATION

EDITED BY
SHAILER MATHEWS THEODORE G. SOARES
W. W. CHARTERS

CONSTRUCTIVE STUDIES

A SHORT HISTORY OF CHRISTIANITY IN THE APOSTOLIC AGE

THE UNIVERSITY OF CHICAGO PRESS
CHICAGO, ILLINOIS

THE BAKER & TAYLOR COMPANY
NEW YORK

THE MACMILLAN COMPANY OF CANADA, LIMITED
TORONTO

THE CAMBRIDGE UNIVERSITY PRESS
LONDON

THE MARUZEN-KABUSHIKI-KAISHA
TOKYO, OSAKA, KYOTO, FUKUOKA, SENDAI

THE MISSION BOOK COMPANY
SHANGHAI

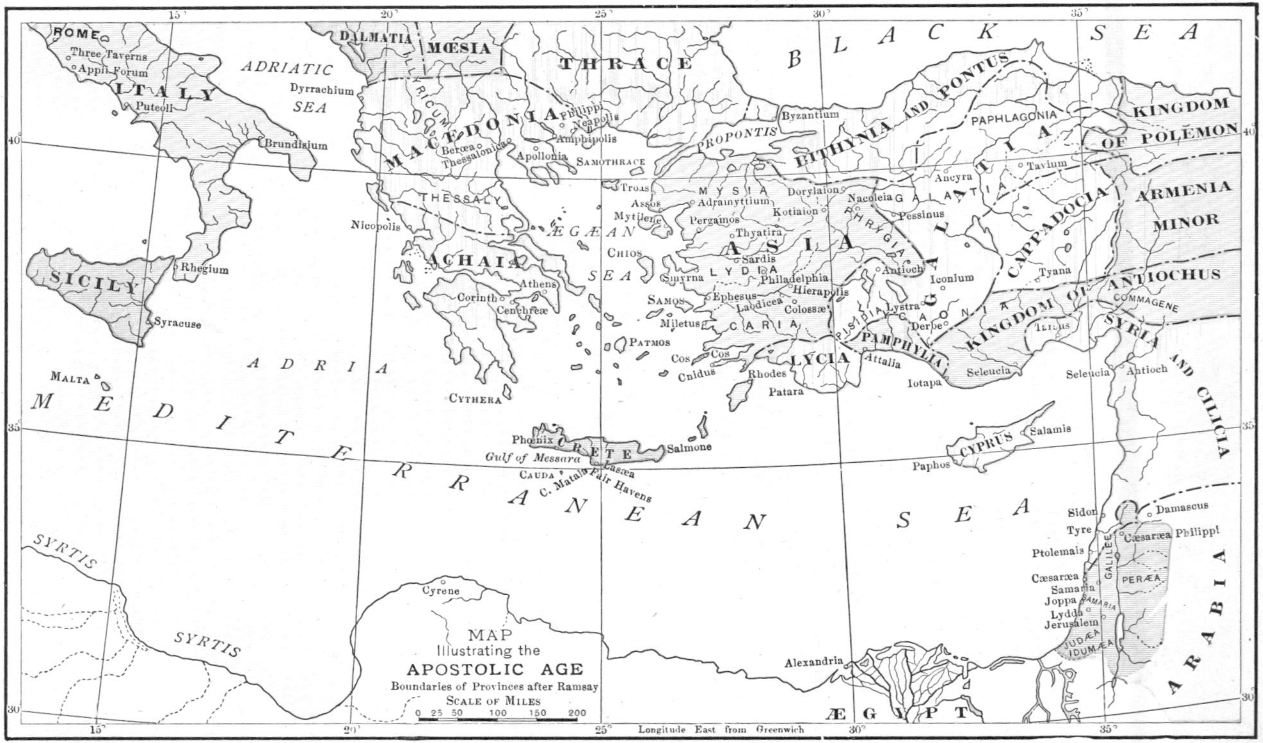
MAP
Illustrating the
APOSTOLIC AGE
Boundaries of Provinces after Ramsay
SCALE OF MILES
0 25 50 100 150 200
Longitude East from Greenwich
BLACK SEA
MEDITERRANEAN SEA
ADRIATIC SEA
ADRIA
ÆGÆAN SEA
ROME
Three Taverns
Appii Forum
ITALY
Puteoli
Brundisium
Rhegium
SICILY
Syracuse
MALTA
DALMATIA
MŒSIA
ILLYRICUM
Dyrrachium
THRACE
MACEDONIA
Philippi
Neapolis
Amphipolis
Berœa
Thessalonica
Apollonia
SAMOTHRACE
THESSALY
Nicopolis
ACHAIA
Athens
Corinth
Cenchreæ
CYTHERA
Phœnix
CRETE
Gulf of Messara
CAUDA
C. Matala
Fair Havens
Lasæa
Salmone
Byzantium
PROPONTIS
BITHYNIA AND PONTUS
PAPHLAGONIA
GALATIA
KINGDOM OF POLEMON
ARMENIA MINOR
CAPPADOCIA
KINGDOM OF ANTIOCHUS
COMMAGENE
SYRIA AND CILICIA
Tavium
Ancyra
Pessinus
Nacoleia
Dorylaion
Kotiaion
MYSIA
Troas
Assos
Adramyttium
Mytilene
Pergamos
Thyatira
CHIOS
ASIA
Sardis
LYDIA
Smyrna
Philadelphia
Hierapolis
Ephesus
Laodicea
Colossæ
SAMOS
Miletus
CARIA
PATMOS
Cos
Cnidus
Rhodes
Patara
LYCIA
PHRYGIA
Antioch
Iconium
Lystra
Derbe
LYCAONIA
PISIDIA
PAMPHYLIA
Attalia
Iotapa
Seleucia
Tyana
Tarsus
Antioch
CYPRUS
Salamis
Paphos
Damascus
Sidon
Tyre
Cæsaræa Philippi
Ptolemais
GALILEE
PERÆA
Cæsaræa
Samaria
SAMARIA
Joppa
Lydda
Jerusalem
JUDÆA
IDUMÆA
ARABIA
Alexandria
ÆGYPT
Cyrene
SYRTIS
SYRTIS

A SHORT HISTORY OF CHRISTIANITY IN THE APOSTOLIC AGE

By

GEORGE HOLLEY GILBERT, PH.D., D.D.

THE UNIVERSITY OF CHICAGO PRESS
CHICAGO, ILLINOIS

Published November 1906
Second Impression April 1907
Third Impression October 1912
Fourth Impression September 1914
Fifth Impression September 1915
Sixth Impression March 1916
Seventh Impression September 1918
Eighth Impression August 1919
Ninth Impression March 1920
Tenth Impression March 1922
Eleventh Impression November 1923
Twelfth Impression August 1924
Thirteenth Impression February 1926

Composed and Printed By
The University of Chicago Press
Chicago, Illinois, U.S.A.

PREFACE

The aim of this book is to furnish Bible students a guide and companion in their investigation of the apostolic age. The author, cherishing that same ideal of thorough, constructive study of the Bible which dominates the former volumes of this series, has endeavored to do for the earliest period of church history what Professors Burton and Mathews have done for the life of Christ. As in that volume, so in this, the needs of students in academies and colleges, and in the advanced classes of Sunday schools, have been constantly regarded.

This work has been done with a conviction that the simple facts about the gospel in the first Christian generation are as interesting as a great imaginative poem, as essential to a liberal education as a knowledge of Greek history in the time of Pericles or of English history in the reign of Henry VIII, and more inspiring, more illuminating as regards the very spirit of Jesus, than the facts of any subsequent period in the long history of the Christian church.

In order that one may get the best results from the use of this book, it is urged that the passages of Scripture referred to in the synopsis at the head of each chapter be read carefully before reading the chapter, and then, after the chapter has been read, be studied again with even more care. The book wishes to be a guide to a certain region of early Christian history, but to the fulfilment of this end the student must enter that region for himself and must *dwell* in it with open eyes and open mind. Teachers who may use this book will, it is earnestly hoped, make plain to their pupils the necessity of securing first-hand acquaintance with the New Testament documents on which it is based.

The book is divided into Parts, Chapters, and Sections, the limits of which are determined by the nature and relations of the events and literature to be studied. Teachers are advised to assign lessons according to their judgment of the ability of the pupils to do the work, always including with the sections assigned for study the questions that pertain to them.

Certain sections and paragraphs have been set in smaller type than the rest of the book. These deal with questions of critical scholarship or matters of detail, and are intended especially for teachers and the more mature pupils. Teachers should exercise their judgment in deciding whether this material should be assigned for study. If it is omitted, the questions referring to it should, of course, also be omitted.

I wish to say frankly, in conclusion, that this volume owes not a little to the numerous suggestions of Professor Ernest D. Burton, of the University of Chicago.

G. H. G.

NORTHAMPTON, MASS.
June 9, 1906

CONTENTS

PART IV

THE LAST YEARS OF THE APOSTLE PAUL

PART V

CHRISTIANITY IN THE LATTER PART OF THE FIRST CENTURY

INTRODUCTION

INTRODUCTION

SYNOPSIS

A. OUR KNOWLEDGE OF THE CHURCH IN THE APOSTOLIC AGE

§ 1. **General Survey of the Sources of Our Knowledge.**—There are two great sources whence we derive our knowledge of the church in the earliest period of its history, viz., the book of Acts and the New Testament epistles and Apocalypse. The gospels also, with the possible exception of John, were indeed written in this period, and are not without value for our view of the development of thought in the first century, though they are directly concerned with the work of Jesus. They throw light, for instance, on the early interpretation of Old Testament prophecy and on the primitive growth of the doctrine of the person of Christ.

Again, there are other Christian writings, notably the *First Epistle of Clement to the Corinthians* and *the Teaching of the Twelve Apostles*, which, though written at the close or even beyond the close of the apostolic age, afford us some help, especially in constructing a picture of the Christian thought of that time.

Finally, the Roman historian, Suetonius, in his *Life of Claudius*, and Tacitus, in his *Annals*, are of value for the light they shed on the earliest persecutions.

But these sources of information, while valuable, particularly for advanced students, are quite subordinate to Acts and the epistles.

§ 2. **The Book of Acts.**—This writing is presented as a continuation of the third gospel, which it calls "the former treatise" (Acts 1:1). Like that it is addressed to Theophilus, a Christian whom the author wished to establish thoroughly in the faith (Luke 1:3). The two books are also intimately bound together by a common literary style of a high order of excellence. It is generally recognized, therefore, that they are the work of the same author. Who this author was the gospel does not at all indicate, but the book of Acts with the letters of Paul gives us valuable hints. For in certain parts of Acts (viz., 16:10–17; 20:5–21:18; 27:28) the narrative is carried on in the first person. In these sections the narrator is a companion of Paul who went with him from Troas to Philippi on the second missionary journey, later from Philippi to Jerusalem, and finally from Cæsarea to Rome. Now only two friends seem to have been with Paul on his eventful voyage to Rome, of whom one was Aristarchus, a Macedonian of Thessalonica (Acts 27:2), and the other, the unnamed author of the account of this voyage. In the letters written by Paul from Rome we seem to get near to this unnamed author. There are five[1] men with Paul, one of whom he mentions as sending greeting to his readers, viz., Aristarchus, then Mark, Epaphras, Luke, and Demas (Col. 4:10–14; Philemon 23, 24), and we naturally look among these men for the author of the description of the voyage to Rome and of the other parts of Acts which are written in the first person. Now four of these five men are excluded from the authorship of the diary. Aristarchus is excluded by Acts 27:2, where he is mentioned by name and distinguished from the writer. Mark is excluded by the fact that he was not with Paul on the second missionary journey (Acts 15:39). Epaphras was a Colossian (Col. 4:12), and as Paul did not labor in the vicinity of Colossæ until the third missionary journey, there is no ground for thinking that Epaphras can have been with him on the second journey. Demas is apparently excluded by 2 Tim. 4:10, for Paul there says that he had forsaken him, having loved this present world. But it is improbable that a man who had continued with Paul in all the perils recorded in Acts 16:21–22; 27; 28 would at last forsake him out of love for the present world. There remains, then, of the five men, who were with Paul when he wrote to the Colossians and Philemon, only Luke, the "beloved physician" (Col. 4:14). We have ground, therefore, for ascribing to him the authorship of the diary which is embedded in Acts.

But it seems most natural to hold that he who wrote this diary wrote also the entire book, since a man of literary ability like that of the author of Acts would scarcely have incorporated in his history, in an unchanged form, the diary of some other man. With a good degree of confidence, therefore, we hold, with the church of the second century, that the author of Acts and of the third gospel was Luke.

[1] Six in Colossians; but the sixth (Jesus called Justus), being wholly unknown, is ignored in the above statement.

In view, moreover, of the identity of the author of Acts and the third gospel, we apply to the composition of Acts what is said in the introductory verses of the third gospel (Luke 1:1–4), and hold that the author's careful investigation of his material furnishes good ground on which to accept the general trustworthiness of his narrative. In the parts covered by the diary he had first-hand knowledge. In other parts, as in the account of the first missionary journey, he needed no other source than Paul. For the history of the founding of the church and of the earliest spread of Christianity, especially for the long addresses of Peter and Stephen, he was probably dependent, at least in part, on the writings of others.

The purpose of Acts, as we may infer from the author's words in the preface to the gospels, was to inform and establish Theophilus, and the specific plan by which this was to be accomplished is suggested in Acts 1:8. It was to narrate the triumphant manner in which men had borne witness to Jesus from Jerusalem to the ends of the earth.

As to the time when Acts was written, those who hold it to be the work of Luke are divided between an earlier date (59–65 A. D.) and a later (75–80 A. D.), the preference now being for the second.

§ 3. **The New Testament Epistles.**—The second main source of knowledge regarding the church in the apostolic age is the New Testament letters. The composition of all these documents, if we except 2 Peter, probably falls within the first century. The authorship of some of them, e. g., 2 Peter and Hebrews, is entirely unknown; that of a somewhat larger number is regarded by many scholars as uncertain—this number including, among others, the two epistles to Timothy and Titus, the epistles of John, and the Apocalypse; but the authorship of the more important half of the whole group of writings is very generally accepted as reasonably sure. This number includes ten letters of Paul and one of Peter.

As compared with Acts these New Testament epistles introduce us to the *teaching* which was current in the apostolic age rather than to the external history of the church. And yet at the same time it is in these letters that we get some of our most vivid pictures of the effects which the new preaching produced. The book of Acts unrolls a large historical canvas before us; the letters contain miniatures.

§ 4. **Limits of Our Knowledge.**—While we know much of the history of the church in the apostolic age, it is wise to remember that our knowledge is limited on every side. Of the work of nine of the apostles whom Jesus chose and trained, and whom he sent out to bear witness even to the end of the earth, we know nothing at all. It is not once mentioned in our sources. Of the remaining two apostles —Peter and John—the latter simply appears a few times as the usually silent companion of Peter. Whether he preached and founded churches, and if so, where, we do not know. Peter is the hero of the early part of Acts, and we have glimpses of his movements until the death of James (Acts 12:2). We also know from Paul a little about his later career (Gal. 2: 11; 1 Cor. 1:12; 9:5); but if he suffered martyrdom in the reign of Nero, as ancient tradition affirms, there is a period in his life of at least twenty years which is to us practically a blank. We know of one short evangelistic tour by him besides his early activity in Jerusalem, but that is all. If he made other and extensive tours, which seems probable (cf. Gal. 2:9), and if he founded churches or had great influence in other ways as the rock-apostle, there is no record of these things.

Thus our knowledge of the work of the original apostles is exceedingly meager. It passed into history largely as an impersonal force. It found no Luke to chronicle it for coming generations.

Paul is the only man of the apostolic age whose labors have been recorded with any fulness, and yet our knowledge even of him is but fragmentary. Thus of the first fourteen years of his Christian activity thirteen are practically unknown. He had worked many years as a foreign missionary before he went out from Antioch on the so-called first missionary journey. He was a great preacher, but we have none of his sermons; at most, five-minute abstracts or reports of a few of them. He was a great organizer and administrator; but though we have important information regarding these phases of his activity, the sources leave us uncertain on some points.

Of the inner history of the church also in Paul's day our information is not complete. We know, e. g., that there were grave misunderstandings between the Jewish and the gentile Christians, but we have no statement of the case from one who fully sympathized with the Jewish position. Again, we know that believers in Paul's time were made acquainted with the life and the teaching of Jesus, but what written accounts of these were in circulation, and how such accounts were regarded in comparison with the Old Testament, no one is in a position to say definitely.

These points may suffice to suggest the limitations of our knowledge regarding the church of the earliest age, and the need of caution in the use of our sources.

B. A BRIEF SURVEY OF THE EXTENSION OF CHRISTIANITY IN THE APOSTOLIC AGE

§ 5. **The Limits of the Apostolic Age.**—The apostolic age began when the disciples became convinced of the resurrection of Jesus. The date of this event can be approximately determined; it probably belongs to the year 30 A. D.; but the close of the period is indefinite. The term itself naturally suggests that the period closed with the death of the last of the apostles whose work and death are known; but the death of the three men of whose labors we have any considerable information, viz., Peter, John, and Paul, is not recorded in the New Testament. A very old tradition puts the death of Peter and Paul in the persecution of the Christians under Nero (64–66 A. D.), and that of John in the time of Domitian, near the close of the first century. Now, since we have no direct information whatever regarding the history of the church from the death of Peter and Paul to the time of Clement of Rome, approximately from 65–95 A. D., it seems more natural to find the terminus of the age in 65 A. D. than in the death of John. But wherever we set the exact limit, it will remain true that the Apostolic Age practically closed some thirty-five years after the great day of Pentecost (Acts 2:1). This is the length of the first creative epoch in the history of Christianity.

It is beyond the scope of the present work to enter into an extended discussion of the chronology of the period. Within the thirty-five years above referred to there are two events to which there are references in contemporary history which enable us to determine their dates with approximate accuracy. These events are the death of Herod Agrippa I (Acts 12:23) and the accession of Festus (Acts 24:27). The former of these events took place in 44 A. D.; the latter probably in the summer of 58 A. D., though some modern scholars date it as early as 55 A. D., and some as late as 60 A. D. Into the chronological framework determined by these relatively fixed points the other events of the period can be fitted with varying degrees of certainty and definiteness. The result, subject to doubt on many points of detail, but at no point very wide of the mark, is exhibited in the following table:

CHIEF EVENTS OF THE APOSTOLIC AGE[1]

27 or 30 A. D. Death and resurrection of Jesus; Pentecost.

32 A. D. The conversion of Paul.

32–35 A. D. In Arabia and Damascus.

35–44 A. D. In Syria and Cilicia.

44 A. D. The planting of the church in Antioch.

45–47 A. D. Paul's first missionary journey.

48 A. D. The conference in Jerusalem.

49–51 A. D. Paul's second missionary journey.

52–56 A. D. Paul's third missionary journey.

56–58 A. D. Paul's two years' imprisonment in Cæsarea.

58–59 A. D. Paul's voyage to Rome.

59–61 A. D. Paul's two years' imprisonment in Rome.

64 A. D. The death of Paul. The death of Peter also probably occurred not far from this time.

70 A. D. The destruction of Jerusalem.

64–100 A. D. A period of relative obscurity; the gospels, the Revelation, and several New Testament letters were written, but of the external events little is known.

§ 6. **The Theater of Action.**—The ministry of Jesus was limited to an area about 100 miles in extent from north to south, and half that distance from east to west. The labors of the apostolic age, so far as known to us, extended across a territory some 2,000 miles from east to west and 700 from north to south. If we leave Rome out of account, the field of apostolic labor is at once reduced to about 1,000 miles from east to west and 500 from north to south. The course of the gospel across this region was along the Mediterranean coast, first northward to Antioch, then westward and northwestward to Troas and Philippi, and finally southward to Corinth. The missionary work of which we have record was confined chiefly to four large cities, viz., Jerusalem, Syrian Antioch, Ephesus, and Corinth, and to seven others of lesser size, of which four were in Asia Minor, viz., Antioch, Iconium, Lystra, and Derbe, and three in Greece, viz., Philippi, Thessalonica, and Berœa. The work of evangelization was extended rapidly from these centers through the surrounding country (see, e. g., Acts 14:7; 19:10), but of this wider work within the period under consideration we know little.

[1] For the sake of completeness we give the approximate date of the death of Jesus. This rests upon grounds of its own which are independent of the Pauline chronology.

References to literature on the subject are given under § 10

§ 7. **The Numerical Result.**—On the day of Pentecost there were 120 believers gathered together in Jerusalem (Acts 1:15), who, although not all of those who had faith in Jesus as the Messiah, probably included the most vigorous elements of the whole company; at the close of the period there were companies of Christian disciples in thirty cities and towns mentioned by name in our sources,[1] besides a considerable number of churches known to have existed though not named (see Acts 9:31; 15:41; 1 Cor. 1:2; 1 Pet. 1:1; Titus 1:5). Furthermore, the fragmentary character of our sources makes it probable that the results of evangelistic effort prior to the year 65 A. D. were considerably more extensive than we are able to point out in detail. It can scarcely be doubted, for instance, that the work of Paul and Barnabas in Cyprus, followed by that of Barnabas and Mark, bore fruit in the planting of a number of churches, and as little can we doubt that the message of Jesus was proclaimed in Alexandria and on the Euphrates before the death of Peter and Paul.

Of the size of the Christian communities of whose existence we have definite knowledge nothing certain can be said. The early development of the church in Jerusalem assumed large proportions, as did that of the churches in the Syrian Antioch, Ephesus, Corinth, and Rome. The riots occasioned by the preaching of the gospel in Philippi, Thessalonica, and Ephesus indicate plainly that the adherents of the new religion had become a power of no small magnitude. But of the total number of disciples won between Pentecost and the death of Paul, it is clearly impossible to speak except in the most general manner. The sources justify us in saying that the country bordering on the north coast of the Mediterranean as far as Corinth and also the interior of Asia Minor were thoroughly leavened by the gospel.

§ 8. **The Relation of the Jewish Church and the Roman Government to Christianity.**—From Pentecost to the Neronian persecution the authorities of the Jewish church opposed the work of Christian missions both among the Jews and the gentiles, but the

[1] Damascus, Jerusalem, Samaria, Lydda, Joppa, Cæsarea, Ptolemais, Tyre, Sidon, Antioch (S.), Antioch (P.), Iconium, Lystra, Derbe, Ephesus, Colossæ, Troas, Philippi, Thessalonica, Berœa, Athens, Corinth, Puteoli, Rome, Smyrna, Pergamum, Thyatira, Sardis, Laodicea, Philadelphia.

Roman government took no notice of these missions as a religious movement. There were Christian martyrs in this period, but they fell before religious fanaticism, not as victims of political persecution. The power which had brought Jesus to the cross sought from the first to stamp out the movement instituted in his name. Apostles were imprisoned and beaten, and one was beheaded; the first of the "seven" was stoned, and at one time the persecution was so hot in Jerusalem under the leadership of Paul that most Christians appear to have been driven from the city. Saul had no successor in the work of persecution of zeal and ability equal to his own, but the spirit of the Jewish authorities remained unchanged throughout the apostolic age, and wherever the gospel was preached the great majority of the Jews opposed its spread. But, while this is true, we should remember that a few Jews accepted it, and that from among these few came the greatest of the missionary workers—Paul and Barnabas, Stephen and Philip, Aquila and Apollos and Silas. The spread of the new religion in the apostolic age, though chiefly successful among the gentiles, was carried on by Christian Jews.

The state, as we have said, took no notice of the Christian missionaries as religious teachers during this first period. It was as safe to be a Christian as to be a Jew or an idolater, so far as the Roman government was concerned. Paul was apprehended and brought to trial, but only on one occasion was it made a ground of accusation against him that he was a follower of Jesus (Acts 24:5), and Felix, the Roman procurator, paid no attention to the charge. When the successor of Felix sent Paul to Rome to be tried before the emperor, he confessed that he had no definite charge to send with him though he knew that Paul differed religiously from the Jews. Whatever opposition, therefore, the Christian missionaries experienced from the Roman government in the apostolic age—and it was slight—was due to other causes than their religious faith.

§ 9. **Questions and Suggestions for Study.**—(1) Name the two chief sources of our knowledge of the apostolic age. (2) What value have the gospels in this connection? (3) What other writings bear on the subject? (4) How is Acts related to the third gospel? (5) What light do Acts and the epistles throw on the authorship of the diary? (6) What may we infer from Luke 1:1–4 regarding the historical character of Acts? (7) What are the purpose and specific plan of Acts? (8) When was Acts written?

(9) What New Testament letters are widely accepted among scholars as of known authorship? (10) How do the epistles compare with Acts as sources for the history of the apostolic age?

(11) How complete is our knowledge of the work of the original apostles? (12) What notable gaps are there in our knowledge of the career of Paul? (13) Illustrate the incompleteness of our knowledge of the internal history of the apostolic church.

(14) Define the apostolic age chronologically. (15) Describe in general the theater of Christian activity in the apostolic age. (16) How many cities and towns are mentioned in our sources in which the gospel was planted in the apostolic age? (17) What bearing has the fragmentariness of our sources on the question of the extension of the gospel in the apostolic age?

(18) What was the general attitude of the Jewish church toward Christianity in the apostolic age? (19) Of what nationality were most of the great missionaries of that time? (20) What was the general attitude of the Roman government toward Christianity in the apostolic age?

§ 10. **Supplementary Topics for Study and References to Literature.**[1]—1. From the study of the diary, the so-called "we-sections" (Acts 16:10–17; 20:5—21:18; 27:1—28:31), make a narrative of the experiences that the author of Acts shared with Paul.

2. On the sources of our knowledge of the apostolic age, see especially the recent works on New Testament introduction, as those of Salmon, Godet, Holtzmann, Jülicher, and Bacon.

3. On geography look up in any standard atlas the location of the cities mentioned in § 7.

4. On the attitude of the Roman government toward Christianity, see:

Ramsay, *The Church in the Roman Empire*, pp. 346–60.

[1] The literature referred to in all the paragraphs with this heading will be in English. The aim of the references is simply to *start* the student in his collateral reading, and hence the number of references will not be large.

5. On the chronology of the apostolic age, see:

Schürer, *Jewish People in the Time of Jesus Christ*, Div. 2, Vol. II, pp. 163, 182 ff. ,Burton *Records and Letters of the Apostolic Age*, pp. 201 ff., McGiffert, *The Apostolic Age*, pp. 356 ff., 673; Turner, in Hastings' *Dictionary of the Bible*, article on "Chronology of the New Testament;" Mathews, in *Biblical World*, Nov., 1897, pp. 353 ff.

PART I

THE PRIMITIVE JEWISH CHURCH IN JERUSALEM

CHAPTER I

THE DISCIPLES RALLIED AND WAITING FOR THE SPIRIT

SYNOPSIS

§ 11. **The reality of the resurrection.** **Acts 1:1–5; also Gal. 1:15–17; 1 Cor. 15:4–8; Matt. 28; Luke 24; John 20, 21**

§ 12. **The ascension.** **Acts 1:6–11; Luke 24:51; John 20:17; 21:19–22; Rom. 8:34; Eph. 4:9, 10**

§ 13. **The gathering in Jerusalem.** **Acts 1:12–14; Luke 24:52, 53**

§ 14. **The choice of Matthias.** **Acts 1:15–26**

§ 11. **The Reality of the Resurrection.**—The book of Acts and the apostolic age do not begin with Pentecost, but with the resurrection. There would have been no gathering of disciples in the upper chamber and no Pentecost, had they not previously been convinced that their Master was alive. With any difficulties that stand in the way of our forming a clear conception of the resurrection of Jesus it is not our present task to deal. We are concerned here with a simple fact of history, viz., that the makers of the apostolic age were convinced of the reality of the resurrection of Jesus. The author of Acts begins his record of the great period with this event. We must do the same, for the apostles themselves and their deeds can not be understood unless we hold that the resurrection of their Master was an absolute reality to them. We see a stream of creative power flowing on through the apostolic age, and though we can not observe the sources of that power and explain them, we can not fail to see that the actors in this period believed that the power came from the resurrection of Jesus and the Spirit of God. And whatever mystery may remain around this double source of the transforming power manifested in the apostolic age, we do not know of any other adequate explanation of the fact than that which we find in the earliest records.

The mode of the resurrection of Jesus and the nature of his appearances to the disciples may never become altogether clear, but no fact of history is better established than that the disciples were convinced of having met the risen

Palestine Exploration Fund

THE MOUNT OF OLIVES AS SEEN FROM JERUSALEM

Lord face to face. Moreover, it seems impossible to account for this conviction without accepting a real return of Jesus to them, whatever may have been the nature or form of that return. For the conviction of his resurrection arose when the disciples were overwhelmed with sorrow; it persisted to the end of their lives; it was the fundamental fact in their testimony; and their testimony founded the Christian church.

§ 12. **The Ascension.**—Luke is the only New Testament writer who speaks of a definite historical ascension of Jesus, and he does this only in Acts. The last that he says of Jesus in the gospel is that, having blessed the disciples on the Mount of Olives, he "parted from them." The ascension described in Acts took place forty days[1] after the resurrection; it took place on the Mount of Olives in the presence of the apostles, and was a visible phenomenon (Acts 1:9, 10). The event is evidently thought of as concluding the series of manifestations of the risen Lord to the disciples who had known him in the flesh, preceding his taking his seat at the right hand of the Father. It could hardly be otherwise than that the last of these appearances should be looked upon as ending in the departure of Jesus to heaven (cf. 1 Thess. 1:10).

The language recording the ascension is, of course, that of appearance, expressing in the forms of thought which were natural to the early Christians (according to which, e. g., heaven was *above* them) their interpretation of their experiences. The resurrection and the exaltation, between which the narrative of the ascension furnishes a link of connection, are conspicuous in the faith of the early church as reflected in the New Testament, but the ascension, as we have seen, is directly mentioned only once as a fact of history. Our belief in Jesus as the risen and reigning Savior would be the same had Luke not written Acts 1:9–11. That Jesus rose from the dead and was exalted to a throne of power were fundamental elements of early Christian faith; but how he finally passed into the unseen world, at what time, or in what place, these questions are plainly unimportant.

§ 13. **The Gathering in Jerusalem.**—The disciples were scattered by the death of Jesus. The Gospel of Mark records that Jesus

[1] The number forty is sometimes used *symbolically* both in the Old Testament and the New Testament (e. g., Ex. 34:28; 1 Kings 19:8; Mark 1:13), and that is probably its use in the present case. The period of forty days that preceded the public ministry of Jesus was naturally followed by a period of equal length at the close of that ministry. The latter period like the former may have been regarded as one of trial, because the risen Lord during these days was not yet seated at the right hand of God in glory and power.

had foreseen that this would be the case (Mark 14:27). When he was arrested, all the eleven fled, and only one or two of them are seen again until we come to the narrative of the appearances of the risen Lord. It was doubtless the appearance of Jesus after his resurrection which reunited the apostles, as it was that which lifted them up out of the weakness and despair into which his death plunged them. Though we should perhaps gain a different impression as to the places of this reunion from the third and fourth gospels, taken alone, the decisive experience seems to have taken place in Galilee (Mark 14:27, 28; 16:7; Matt. 26:31, 32; 28:10). It was there amid the scenes of the most fruitful labors of Jesus that we are to put that appearance of him to more than five hundred disciples at once, of which Paul makes mention (1 Cor. 15:6).[1]

But though the apostles had a decisive experience in Galilee which fulfilled the word that Jesus had spoken before his arrest, they returned to Jerusalem before they began their great work. At what time exactly and under what motives they left Galilee and went up to the city where their Lord had been crucified, it is not possible to determine. The simple fact that they went is evidence that they had something of the spirit of the Master, for they probably had not forgotten his word that their way, like his, was to be one of suffering at the hands of their countrymen (e. g., Matt. 10:24, 25; Mark 13:9).

§ 14. **The Choice of Matthias.**—In the interval between the return of the apostles to Jerusalem and the first great public act of their ministry, which interval appears to have been brief, the book of Acts puts two significant events, to wit, a private gathering of certain disciples for prayer, and the appointment of a man to the vacant place of Judas.

It is noticeable that in the days immediately following the ascension, the apostles, according to Luke's gospel (24:53), were "continually in the temple, blessing God," while the event of which Acts speaks, in the same situation, is a private gathering for prayer. These events are certainly not to be identified. We know of no "upper room" in the temple for private religious assemblies, and it is altogether improbable that, had there been such a room, it would have

[1] See Gilbert, *Student's Life of Jesus*, pp. 328, 329.

Palestine Exploration Fund

THE MOSQUE OF OMAR, ON THE SITE OF THE ANCIENT TEMPLE

been at the disposal of a company of Galilean fishermen whose teacher had just been crucified at the instigation of the religious authorities who had charge of the temple. We think of the meeting therefore, as in some private house, not unlikely in that room in which the Last Supper had been celebrated, which may have been in the home of Mary, the mother of Mark.

The disciples went to the temple from day to day as pious Jews; they met together for prayer in a private room as disciples of Jesus, for we can not doubt that it was his example which led them to this simple informal act of worship. As to the object of their prayer, the situation suggests that their thought was occupied with the coming kingdom and their relation to it.

The second significant event which fell in this interval was the choice of a twelfth apostle. This act shows that the eleven had recovered their presence of mind, and also that they were conscious of a mission. In appointing, as a successor to Judas, one who had personal knowledge of the ministry and the resurrection of Jesus, they were evidently anticipating a work of bearing witness to that resurrection and that ministry. It accords with what the gospels tell us of Peter, that he was the one to suggest this choice; it accords with the principle of brotherhood found in the gospel that the whole company of believers participated in this first appointment in the church; and it accords with the new conception of God that the disciples did not proceed to make use of the ancient mode of giving lots until they had first prayed the Lord to show them his will by means of this device. It illustrates the meagerness of our knowledge of the men who had walked with Jesus that these two who were thought worthy even of a place with the eleven apostles are not mentioned in the gospels or elsewhere in the New Testament.

§ 15. **Questions and Suggestions for Study.**—(1) With what conviction did the apostolic age begin? (2) To what two sources must we attribute the power of the apostles and other disciples?

(3) Which of the evangelists make no reference to an ascension of Jesus? (4) Describe the last appearance of Jesus recorded in Matthew, Luke, John 20 and John 21. (5) Describe his last appearance according to Acts 1:6–12. (6) What is the important thought in the ascension? (7) How does the mode of Jesus' departure from

the earth compare, in the importance assigned to it in early Christian thought, with his resurrection and sitting at God's right hand?

(8) What immediate effect did the death of Jesus have on his disciples? (9) Where, according to Mark and Matthew, were the disciples to expect a vision of Jesus after his resurrection? (10) Where is it most probable that his appearance to more than five hundred disciples took place? (11) What gave new life to the apostles and reunited them? (12) What spirit did they show by returning to Jerusalem?

(13) What significant events fell between the return of the apostles to Jerusalem and the great day of Pentecost? (14) Where did the apostles spend much time after they had returned to Jerusalem? (15) What reasons are there for thinking that the meeting for prayer was in a private house? (16) In whose house may this meeting have taken place, and what other events may have occurred in the same room? (17) What did the choice of a twelfth apostle show in regard to the state of mind of the eleven? (19) What constituted a man fit to become the successor of Judas? (20) What candidates were put forward by the company of believers? (21) By what means did they seek to find out whom the Lord had chosen?

§ 16. **Supplementary Topics for Study and References to Literature.**

1. From the study of Acts 1:2–26; Luke 24:44–53, write a chapter introductory to the history of the Jewish church in Jerusalem.

2. Search out and read carefully the various addresses of Peter in Acts 1–12.

3. Read the addresses ascribed to Peter in Acts, and then with these in mind read 1 Peter.

4. Among the recent general works on the apostolic age mention may be made of the following:

Weizsäcker, *The Apostolic Age of the Christian Church*, 2 vols. 1894, 95; McGiffert, *A History of Christianity in the Apostolic Age*, 1897; and Bartlet, *The Apostolic Age: Its Life, Doctrine, Worship and Polity*, 1899.

5. Of works which treat of particular features of Christianity in the apostolic age, the student is referred to:

Ramsay, *The Church in the Roman Empire*, 1893, and Harnack, *History of Dogma*, Vol. I, pp. 41–212.

CHAPTER II

THE DAY OF PENTECOST

SYNOPSIS

§ 17.	**The coming of the Spirit.**	**Acts 2:1–13; also Acts 10; 19:1–7**
§ 18.	**The sermon of Peter.**	**Acts 2:14–36**
§ 19.	**The conversion of three thousand.**	**Acts 2:37–41**
§ 20.	**The disciples in peace and favor.**	**Acts 2:42–47**

§ 17. **The Coming of the Spirit.**—At one of the private meetings for prayer (see Acts 1:14), that one, namely, which fell on Pentecost, the fiftieth day from the first day of the Passover (Lev. 23:15, 16), hence about seven weeks after the crucifixion of Jesus, something great and decisive took place in the little circle of Christian disciples. They all came into a new and vital sense of communion with God; they were "filled with the Holy Spirit." An evidence of this new consciousness of the presence of God with them, indeed, the plainest evidence that could be given, is the fact that on this day and in the days following, the disciples bore witness regarding Jesus with such power that their numbers were largely and steadily increased. These are essential facts of Pentecost and its results.

The first of these facts—the being filled with the Spirit—is set forth in Luke's story with various details of a miraculous character. First, the house where the disciples were gathered was suddenly invaded by a sound from heaven, which was like the rushing of a mighty wind. Then there appeared to the company something like tongues of fire, and one of these bright objects rested on the head of each one present. Straightway all began to speak with "other tongues."

This last detail is to be especially noticed. It is plain from vss. 5–12 that Luke meant a speaking in foreign languages. It was, therefore, unlike the ecstatic speech which we find in Cæsarea, Ephesus, and Corinth (Acts 10:46; 19:6; 1 Cor. 14). This was called speaking "with tongues" or "in a tongue." It was a speaking to God, and was not understood without an interpreter (1 Cor. 14:2), while the Pentecostal speech was to men and was understood by the hearers.

The speaking with "other" tongues was, according to Luke, not only supernatural, it was also temporary. For when Peter stood up and spoke to the crowd who had come together, he addressed all the different nationalities at once, and there is no suggestion that he spoke any language except his own mother-tongue. In his later ministry, according to Papias, Peter had Mark as an interpreter, another evidence that he had no supernatural gift of speech in foreign languages.

Now as against the view of the text, it may be said that there is no adequate purpose for the miracle. According to vs. 12 the people were simply amazed and perplexed by the strange speaking. It did not convert them. That was done by Peter's sermon in Aramaic, which all the people apparently understood. Nor was the alleged miracle needed to teach that the gospel of Jesus was for all mankind. Jesus himself had plainly declared as much (see, e. g., Mark 14:9), and the truth of his word did not require the confirmation of a spectacular miracle.

It is, in fact, probable that the difference between this event and those which are so explicitly described by Paul in his letter to the Corinthians lay not in the facts themselves, but that the peculiar feature of this narrative, according to which the disciples spoke foreign languages understood by the hearers, crept into the tradition as a misunderstanding of the fact in the process of transmission from the event to the time when the story reached Luke. Indeed, even the narrative of Luke contains a clear hint of the nature of the historical event. For it was charged against the apostles that they were filled with new wine. But this charge does not accord with the rest of the narrative. When a man speaks in a foreign tongue, even those who do not understand him do not get the impression that he is drunk. If, however, the phenomenon was ecstatic speech, the charge was quite natural, as we may see from the words of Paul (1 Cor. 14:23).

The value of Luke's narrative is not lessened for us in modern times, but rather heightened, if the underlying reality was not a speaking in foreign tongues, but ecstatic speech, the expression of an almost boundless enthusiasm. That the men whose Master had recently been crucified were now overwhelmed with feelings of joy and gratitude so deep that their attempts to express themselves on "the mighty works of God" were momentarily unintelligible, is surely a striking proof that the kingdom of this Master was the great reality for them.

§ 18. **The Sermon of Peter.**—What Luke gives us as the sermon of Peter on this great occasion is easily read in three minutes. This fact of itself suggests that what we have is at best a short abstract or epitome of what the apostle said. We may suppose that a brief version had been handed down through the forty or fifty years that elasped before the composition of the book of Acts, or that the sermon, having been preserved in fuller form, was epitomized by Luke. Not only is it natural to suppose that the substance of a sermon which had such important results was long preserved in Jerusalem, but the close relation of the sermon to the epistle of Peter, especially to the first chapter of that epistle, goes far toward confirming what appears in itself wholly natural. And to this fact may be added the distinctly Petrine tone of the sermon—its boldness, aggressiveness, and loyalty to Jesus. What some of the onlookers ascribed to drunkenness he declared was the fulfilment of a sublime prophecy. He did not hesitate to charge his hearers once and again with the crucifixion of Jesus. And he emphasized both the greatness of Jesus as seen in his earthly life and his present exaltation and power.

The first sermon of the apostolic age strikes the keynote of all its preaching, viz., that Jesus is Christ and Lord. What Peter and the others had said in the house where they became conscious in some new sense of the presence of the spirit of God, we do not know, but when he faced the throng outside, he gave a plain, straight testimony regarding Jesus. He bore this testimony with an inspiring sense that the "last days" had come, i. e., the time of the fulfilment of the purposes of God, the time immediately preceding the second coming of Christ and the restoration of all things (see Matt. 19:28; Jas. 5:3). This period was now inaugurated by the outpouring of the Spirit of God on the whole company of believers.

The testimony of Peter culminated in the assertion of the messiahship of Jesus, and included three main points: (1) Jesus in his early life had been manifestly approved of God, i. e., approved as the Messiah; (2) God had raised him from the dead, which event the Scriptures had before announced; and (3) the Spirit which filled the disciples had come through him. The first two points fell within the personal observation of Peter; the last was, of course, a matter of Christian faith. Peter and the other disciples were conscious of the presence of the Spirit; but that it was Jesus who had given the Spirit was not based on direct personal knowledge, though, according to Luke (24:49), Jesus had spoken a word that justified the conclusion of Peter.

From the standpoint of the hearers probably nothing in Peter's argument was more impressive than the simple spectacle of Peter himself and the other disciples, who said that the Spirit of God had come upon them. Their appearance and Peter's living words were an evidence of the resurrection of Jesus, and also of a new wondrous spiritual power.

It is worthy of notice that Peter mentioned the mighty works of Jesus as the great evidence of God's approval of him (Acts 2:22). These works that struck the senses were to him a clearer proof of the messiahship of Jesus than was his teaching. It seems obvious, however, that as the church becomes more mature, this order is inverted, and the highest evidence of the messiahship of Jesus is seen in his teaching, especially in his revelation of God.

§ 19. **The Conversion of Three Thousand.**—Peter's sermon had an immediate and deep result. Many of his hearers were conscience-smitten and grieved at the fate of Jesus, and more than this, they were convinced of the truth of Peter's claim. It is not possible to say just what in his sermon wrought so powerfully upon them. They themselves may not have been able to say, and different ones would probably have given differing answers. Peter's appeal to the facts of the life of Jesus, his assertion that he and others were personal witnesses of the resurrection, and that the resurrection was in accord with Scripture, were elements adapted to convince the intellect of the hearers. But we can not hold that these arguments, however forcible, were the ultimate power involved in producing the result. The analogy of other great religious movements suggests that, after all, the decisive factor was something intangible, spiritual, mysterious, in short, the presence and the power of God.

The personal and practical counsel of Peter is no less remarkable than his demonstration of the messiahship of Jesus. He describes the way of salvation in the simplest terms. It is repentance for sin and baptism in the name of Jesus, this baptism resting on the belief that Jesus is the Christ. It is to be noticed that Peter speaks of baptism into the name of Jesus Christ, not, as in Matt. 28:19, into the name of the Father and of the Son and of the Holy Spirit. Baptism into the name of Jesus is the only form mentioned in the book of Acts and the New Testament epistles.

In connection with the number of conversions, which Luke puts approximately at 3,000, it is to be remembered that according to vss. 5–11 the Jews from abroad were largely represented at Pentecost, and there is reason to believe that they were more open to the appeal of the gospel than were the Jews of the homeland. An illustration of this may be seen in the fact that, while we know definitely[1] of but one Jewish-Christian community in Palestine in the apostolic age, viz., that in Jerusalem, we find evidence of an influential Jewish element in most of the great churches abroad, as in those of Antioch in Syria, Ephesus, Corinth, and Rome.

§ 20. **The Disciples in Peace and Favor.**—Between the day of Pentecost and the healing of the lame man at the door of the temple lay a period of uncertain length. The life of the disciples during this time is broadly sketched by Luke in a half-dozen verses that are surcharged with interest. His account breathes the spirit of the gospel.

As was natural, the men who had known Jesus were the first teachers of the little community, and the picture of Luke suggests some of their teachings. Thus, in characterizing the disciples as those who "believed," i. e., believed that Jesus was the Messiah, the narrative doubtless intimates what was central in the apostles' teaching. To accept this one article of faith and to hold it in love was to be "saved" (vs. 47). The account also gives prominence to the fellowship of those who had come to believe in Jesus, and this feature of their life, reflecting a fundamental element of the gospel, may be taken as suggesting another subject of apostolic teaching in those days. The spirit of this fellowship is seen in the rare generosity with which the disciples used their possessions for one another's need. The distinction between mine and thine was lost in an overflowing love.

How far this fellowship led the disciples to live together and to eat together, to be a community wholly by themselves, after the fashion of the Essenes, it is not possible to say. If the "breaking of bread" refers to a common meal together, as some scholars have held, it obviously suggests that the other daily meals were not taken in common, but this understanding of the phrase is extremely doubtful. We are rather to take it as referring to the memorial supper. For (1) the breaking of bread is mentioned in the midst of spiritual features—prayer, Christian fellowship, and "apostles' teaching"—which leads us to think that it stands for something more than a meal for the satisfaction of hunger; and (2) Luke elsewhere once uses the same expression, where it plainly has a religious significance (Luke 24:35), and also employs very similar language which it is impossible to refer simply to a common meal (Acts 20:7, 11). Further, it is

[1] Paul refers in a general way to "churches" of Judea, Gal. 1:22; 1 Thess. 2:14

to be noted that Paul, of whom Luke was a disciple, gives prominence to the breaking of the bread in the Lord's Supper (1 Cor. 10:16; 11:24). It seems, therefore, most probable that the phrase designates the memorial supper. This explanation suits vs. 46, where "breaking bread at home" is parallel to "continuing in the temple;" but continuing in the temple was, of course, for worship, and hence the breaking of bread is naturally understood of a religious act. It will be observed that this breaking of bread was "day by day," which suggests that the supper was relatively more conspicuous than it is now; and it will also be noticed that it was a home observance. The language allows us to think that it was even a family celebration, but the impulse to fellowship, which was so prominent a feature, makes it more likely that companies larger than a single family usually kept it together.

This observance, then, was a subject on which of necessity the new converts must receive instruction from the apostles. Another subject may have been that of prayer. As praying had characterized the disciples before the day of Pentecost (cf. Acts 1:14, 24), so it continued to characterize the larger fellowship in the days immediately succeeding. And the reference here (vs. 42) is probably not to participation in the temple service, but to a distinctive Christian feature of the life of the disciples.

§ 21. **Questions and Suggestions for Study.**—(1) When did the feast of Pentecost occur? (2) What are the essential facts in the story of the great day of Pentecost as told in Acts, chap. 2? (3) What historical evidence have we that something extraordinary took place among the disciples on that day? (4) What promise was fulfilled by the "coming of the spirit"? What are the miraculous details in Luke's narrative of Pentecost, Acts 2:1–6? (5) How did the speaking with "other tongues," as described in Acts, differ from the speaking "with tongues," as spoken of by Paul in 1 Cor.? (6) What was the effect of speaking with other tongues on Pentecost? (7) By what were the people converted? (8) Are we to suppose that the disciples were given power to speak foreign languages on the day of Pentecost as a sign that the gospel was for all mankind? (9) What is the most probable explanation of the origin of this narrative? (10) How is its value for us affected if we regard the underlying event as nothing else than ecstatic speech?

(11) What reasons are there for thinking that we have in Acts 2 the substance of Peter's sermon? (12) What is the keynote of the sermon? (13) Mention three main points. (14) What prophecy did Peter see fulfilled in the experience of the disciples on the day of

Pentecost? (15) In what did Peter see the chief evidence of God's approval of Jesus? (16) On what element do we lay greater stress at the present time?

(17) What was the immediate effect of Peter's sermon? (18) What was the decisive factor in producing that effect? (19) How did Peter define the way of salvation? (20) Into what name did he baptize? (21) What helps to account for the large number of converts on the day of Pentecost? (22) What were some of the subjects of apostolic teaching? (23) In what way was the spirit of fellowship manifested? (24) What did Luke mean by the "breaking of bread"? (25) What noticeable features of the early observance of the Lord's Supper does this passage suggest?

§ 22. **Supplementary Topics for Study and References to Literature.**

1. Write a chapter on the day of Pentecost making special study of Peter's sermon and of the facts regarding Christ on which the early church laid special emphasis.

2. What was Paul's estimate of speaking with tongues?

3. Where do we meet with this phenomenon in the New Testament church?

4. What two words constituted the essential creed of the apostolic age?

5. What distinguished Jewish-Christians of the apostolic age belonged to the Dispersion?

6. The Jews of the Dispersion: the countries through which they were scattered; their number and standing; the influence exerted by them on the Greeks and Romans and by the latter on them.

CHAPTER III

THE GROWTH OF THE CHURCH IN JERUSALEM

SYNOPSIS

§ 23.	**A lame man healed by Peter.**	**Acts 3:1–10**
§ 24.	**Peter's address in Solomon's porch.**	**Acts 3:11–26**
§ 25.	**The first attempt to suppress the new movement.**	**Acts 4:1–31**
§ 26.	**The union and communion of believers.**	**Acts 4:32–36**
§ 27.	**Ananias and Sapphira.**	**Acts 5:1–11**
§ 28.	**Signs and wonders wrought by the apostles.**	**Acts 5:12–16**
§ 29.	**The second attempt to suppress the new movement.**	**Acts 5:17–42**

§ 23. **A Lame Man Healed by Peter.**—The "many wonders and and signs done through the apostles," to which Luke referred at the close of the last chapter, are represented by a single case, which may have been remembered because of its important consequences. This is the first recorded sign wrought by an apostle and the only one ascribed to the earliest period of which any particulars are given.

According to the gospels, miracles of healing were wrought by the apostles during the life of Jesus, but no details of such miracles have been preserved. In the apostolic age, even at the first, miracles of healing are far less conspicuous than in the gospels. The book of Acts mentions but three signs done by any of the twelve apostles, and these were all wrought by Peter. It is doubtful, therefore, whether many specific instances had been preserved to the time when Acts was composed.

It is on the occasion of this first recorded sign in Acts that a second apostle comes forth into a certain prominence by the side of Peter, viz., the apostle John. He continues to be associated with Peter until the conversion of Samaria (Acts 8:14), after which time Peter appears alone. No other of the twelve is mentioned by name in Acts after the first chapter except James (Acts 12:2).

The story of the healing of the lame man is of importance in itself because it indicates how the apostles wrought their signs. We do not know what words, if any, they had spoken in connection with healing when sent out two by two in Galilee; but now when Peter looks on the lame man and bids him walk, it is "in the name of Jesus Christ." That name is in some way the secret of his cure. Jewish exorcists used various names, sometimes even that of Jesus (Acts 19:13). Peter also used the name of Jesus, but used it in faith. He declares explicitly that the healing was due to faith. That which he "has" and which he can give to the lame man (vs. 6) is the benefit of his own strong faith in the name of Jesus, i. e., in Jesus himself. Yet he does not regard this faith as the final explanation of the healing. He traces the miracle to the power of the covenant God of Israel, and evidently regards his faith in Jesus as the human means by which that power had been appropriated.

§ 24. **Peter's Address in Solomon's Porch.**—The first recorded Christian sermon was in or near a private house (Acts 2:2, 6, 11); the second, which we are now considering, was within the precincts of the temple (Acts 3:11), viz., in the eastern colonnade. The healing also had been on this side of the outer court, and the location both of the healing and the subsequent address led easily to a conflict with the temple authorities.

Peter made four statements that must have been particularly obnoxious: (1) He charged that his hearers and the rulers, in condemning Jesus, had been guilty of an especially flagrant violation of law, for they had overridden the judgment of Pilate who was determined to release Jesus. They had also asked the life of one who was known to be a murderer, thus aggravating their sin. (2) Peter asserted the resurrection of Jesus, claiming that he and others had been personal witnesses thereof. (3) He claimed that the name of this crucified Jesus had made this lame man strong. And (4) he declared that Jesus, who was the Christ and the "Servant" of Old Testament prophecy, would come again from heaven. His arraignment of the Jews on account of the death of Jesus, although somewhat softened by the thought that they had acted in ignorance, was more severe than that of his first sermon (Acts 2:23), and his exaltation of Jesus was more varied and emphatic.

Thus the character of Peter's address was obviously such as to arouse the opposition of the rulers, while at the same time its bold and aggressive tone was fitted to awaken the interest of the multitude and to draw them to him. The stress which he laid on the future appearing of Jesus not only helped to offset the humiliation of the cross in the minds of the hearers, but also served to kindle their hope.

§ 25. **The First Attempt to Suppress the New Movement.**—We have seen that Peter's address was fitted to make a deep impression and when, therefore, we are told that the number of believers came to be about 5,000 men (Acts 4:4), we are prepared to see in this an approximate estimate of the sudden increase.

We need not suppose that anyone counted the new converts that night after Peter had finished speaking, or that the converts all declared themselves at once; but we may hold as historical that the words and deed of Peter bore abundant fruit in the immediate future.

It is not surprising that the apostles were interrupted by the temple authorities, and were put in ward. Nothing less could have been expected, for though they were still pious Jews, they were Jews who saw the fulfilment of Judaism in Jesus whom the rulers had put to death as a false Messiah. The imprisonment of the apostles was only until the next day, when a formal trial could be held. They were locked up merely for safe keeping, lest they should escape, or their friends should combine and make their arrest difficult. In the procedure against them the Sadducees appear to have been prominent, their opposition, according to Luke, being due to the fact that the apostles proclaimed the resurrection of the dead, a doctrine which they rejected (Matt. 22:23).

The seriousness of the situation which the deed and words of Peter had created is reflected in the fact that at the hearing of the apostles, the highpriestly family was fully represented (vs. 6). Annas and Caiaphas were present—the former being called the highpriest because he had previously held the office, though it was now held by his son-in-law, Caiaphas. John and Alexander never filled the highpriest's office.

The apostles were twice brought before the council. At their first appearing they were asked to account for the healing of the lame man, and Peter made answer, with a boldness and ability which amazed them, that the man had been healed in the name of Jesus, the only name, he added, in which there is messianic deliverance. At the second appearing of the apostles, they were strictly commanded not to teach at all in the name of Jesus, and when they declared that they must continue to teach what they had seen and heard, they were threatened and dismissed.

The rulers were perplexed. They saw in these men the same spirit which they had seen in Jesus, and the deed of healing was one which could not be denied. These things were freely admitted in their council, as also their fear that this new teaching would spread further among the people. But the most that they dared to do was to threaten the apostles—an evidence that the popular sentiment was strongly with the Christian movement.

The failure of the attempt to silence Peter and John, when reported to the remaining apostles or to these in company with other believers, made a deep impression. With one accord they turned to God in a prayer which was marked by an increase of holy boldness. It was plain to all that the recent opposition to Jesus and the present opposition to his disciples was a fulfilment of the second Psalm, and therefore part of a divine plan. The threatenings of their enemies could not avail against him who made the heaven and the earth and the sea. The narrative closes with the significant statement that all the company showed that boldness which they had sought from God in prayer, which is a proof that they were filled with the Spirit. The shaking of the earth, which is said to have accompanied their inner experience, may be regarded in the same way as the "sound" that filled the house on the day of Pentecost.

§ 26. **The Union and Communion of Believers.**—As the first critical event in the relation of believers to the world, viz., the event of Pentecost, is followed in the narrative by a reference to the remarkable condition of believers in their relation to each other, so also is the second critical event. The picture of the inner condition is now drawn with somewhat more of detail and with greater vividness, but its essential thought remains the same. The entire company of believers were still animated with such a spirit of brotherhood that they had all things in common. The poor were not suffered to feel any lack. Apparently there were not a few who needed help, for houses and lands were sold from time to time that distribution might be made. This readiness to share with the brother in need was rightly regarded as evidence that the favor of God was signally bestowed on the community. There were, indeed, some among them who did not possess this spirit (e. g., Acts 5:1–11), and some, probably the majority of those who did possess it, did not dispose of all their prop-

JERUSALEM AND THE
TEMPLE OF HEROD
FROM THE NORTH EAST

From *Sacred Sites of the Gospels*, by Sanday and Waterhouse. By permission of the Clarendon Press, Oxford.

The colonnade on the upper edge of the picture represents the Royal Porch which bounded the great Court of the Gentiles on the south. Solomon's Porch, a colonnade of similar character, bounded this court on the east, and is shown at the left-hand side of the picture. The buildings in the center are the Court of the Women, the Court of the Gentiles, the Court of the Priests, and the Sanctuary proper with their surrounding chambers. Cf. diagram on page 184.

erty. What Barnabas sold was a field; presumably he did not sell his house. And we learn incidentally that Mary, the mother of John Mark, did not sell her house (Acts 12:12). The language of Luke in vs. 34 is general and there is no reason to suppose that believers, at least as a rule, sold the houses in which they lived. They were possessed by the spirit of love, but not by the spirit of unreason.

§ 27. **Ananias and Sapphira.**—The story of Ananias and Sapphira is introduced not as an exception to the general rule in Acts 4:34, and not for the sake of the contrast it presents to the case of Barnabas, but because of its effect (Acts 5:11). The incident, while showing, indeed, that the fair picture of the preceding verse was not without dark shadows, contributed in its way to the prestige of the apostles, to a wholesome sense of the seriousness of membership in the new community, and so to the growth of the Christian body.

The sin of Ananias and his wife was hypocrisy, that sin against which Jesus had spoken oftener than against any other. They wished the honor of complete devotion to the brotherhood without paying the full price. They agreed to deceive Peter and the rest in regard to the sum of money which their land had brought. It is plain, therefore, that they, like Simon of Samaria (Acts 8:9), had only the most superficial apprehension of the character of the gospel. They had simply been taken in its net, which then, as in all subsequent times, gathered bad fish with the good.

The relation of Peter to the case of Ananias and Sapphira appears to be plain. We are not told how he knew that Ananias was lying. We should assume, therefore, that he read it on his face and in his manner. When he exposed the man's inner thought and purpose, declaring that his attempt to deceive was an attempt to deceive God rather than men, Ananias fell down dead. It is to be noticed that Peter spoke no word of judgment. He only uncovered the sin. We have no reason to think that he had any idea that death was about to fall on the man before him.

But when, three hours later, Peter heard from Sapphira the same lie which her husband had acted, it was natural that he anticipated for her the same fate which had befallen him. He did not assume to pass sentence of death in her case any more than in that of her husband. Though his declaration to her may have so affected her mind as to have contributed to cause her death, it was evidently not uttered with this intent. Rather is his confidence that she would straightway fall a prey to death evidence that he regarded the death of Ananias as a supernatural judgment. So also was it probably regarded by Luke. But whether this explanation of the event is the correct one is a fair question to raise. We have no right to assume that the cause of death was supernatural if it can be accounted for on natural grounds. A death is plainly not supernatural merely because it is sudden and seemingly opportune. Many a man has dropped dead in circumstances apparently less awful for heart and conscience than were those which suddenly confronted Ananias. The improbability that his wife would succumb just as he had is doubtless very great, but obviously it can not be said to be impossible that one explanation should cover both cases.

It need scarcely be pointed out that the view of the death of Ananias as a supernatural divine judgment accords neither with the method of Jesus in dealing with the sin of hypocrisy nor with the character of God as revealed in Jesus.

§ 28. **Signs and Wonders Wrought by the Apostles.**—To the growth of the church, according to Acts, the mighty works of the apostles contributed in a conspicuous manner, although, as already pointed out, the author specifies only three miracles as wrought by the original apostles. For some time after the arraignment of Peter and John, the apostles and other believers were allowed to meet in Solomon's porch, where we may suppose that they bore their powerful witness of the resurrection of Jesus (Acts 4:33), and where, it may be, some of the signs mentioned in Acts 5:12 were wrought.[1] That their activity here must constantly have been hateful to the temple authorities is self-evident. It was tolerated for a time because of the extent of the popular favor.

In this period of relative quiet considerable numbers of men and women were added to the Lord, i. e., by baptism into the name of Jesus, and Peter became more prominent than ever as a healer of disease. Enthusiasm for him ran so high that some people believed his shadow would effect cures—a superstitious veneration parallel to that of the woman who touched the garment of Jesus (Mark 5:28), and to that of the Ephesians who took aprons and handkerchiefs which had been in contact with the body of Paul and carried them to those who were sick (Acts 19:12). It is to be remembered, however, in considering this incident, that even superstitious ideas may be the channels of divine blessing. Men may have been helped by the shadow of Peter as well as by the garment of Jesus. The mingling of superstition with faith does not destroy its value.

[1] The verbs in 5:12–16 are imperfects, descriptive of what took place through an indefinite period.

§ 29. **The Second Attempt to Suppress the New Movement.**—The interval between the imprisonment of Peter and John and the imprisonment of all the apostles was probably short, for the apostles, by disregarding the threats of the temple authorities as well as by their increasing and successful activity, were daily becoming a more formidable power, and the instinct of self-preservation would not have allowed the rulers long to postpone their second attempt to check the dangerous movement.

The attitude of the rulers had grown more determined, for they now believed that the aim of the apostles was to get revenge for the death of Jesus, and they saw that the new teaching had filled Jerusalem (vs. 28). This more determined attitude is seen (1) in the fact that all the apostles were seized, and not merely Peter and John; and (2), in the fact that they were beaten, and not simply threatened.

The opposition now as in the earlier case was headed by the Sadducees, while the man whose counsel prevailed, and who, humanly speaking, saved the lives of the apostles, was a Pharisee (vs. 34). The apostles were put in prison over night, but when wanted the next morning they were found not in the prison, but in the temple. Of the circumstances of their deliverance we have no certain information. Luke appears to have regarded it as miraculous, ascribing it to an angel of the Lord. It is not clear, however, why they should have been delivered by a miracle only to be rearrested at daybreak.

The apostles when brought before the council were charged with complete disregard of the commandment which had been laid upon them (Acts 4:18), and frankly admitted that the charge was true. At the same time they claimed to have obeyed God. They might have stopped at this point, but they regarded the occasion as an opportunity to bear witness of the resurrection which they could not let pass.

The result of Peter's words—for he spoke for the apostles—was that the rulers were inflamed with rage, and would have proceeded to extreme measures had not Gamaliel intervened. The weight of his influence checked the purpose to slay the apostles, and they escaped with merely a beating.

Gamaliel thought it possible that God was in this religious movement, and therefore favored a policy of non-intervention. If, however, God was not in it, then, he argued, it would come to naught of itself, as their own history taught.[1] The counsel of Gamaliel was accepted, though in a somewhat modified form, for the beating of the apostles was inconsistent with the spirit of that counsel. Thus the second attempt of the authorities to suppress the new movement failed, and even the temple itself was not closed to the preaching of the apostles.

§ 30. **Questions and Suggestions for Study.**—(1) What was the first sign wrought by an apostle of which we have any details? (2) To what may we attribute the preservation of this story? (3) How many signs by the twelve apostles are recorded in Acts? (4) What apostle appears with Peter in connection with this first sign, and when does he disappear from the story? (5) Wherein does the importance of the story chiefly lie? (6) How did Peter use the name of Jesus? (7) To what power did he ascribe the healing? (8) What part did his faith in Jesus have in the deed?

(9) Locate the place of delivery of Peter's first and second sermons. (10) Name four statements in his second sermon that must have been obnoxious to the rulers. (11) What was the tone of Peter's address? (12) What was its effect on the multitude?

(13) What sect was prominent in the first attempt to suppress the apostles? (14) Name four leading members of the Sanhedrin. (15) Describe what took place at each of the two appearances of the apostles before the rulers. (16) Why were the rulers perplexed by the situation? (17) What effect did the apostles' report of their trial have on the company of believers?

(18) What was the internal condition of believers in the days subsequent to the imprisonment of Peter and John? (19) How is the

[1] According to Luke's report, Gamaliel cited two instances in support of his position, that of Theudas and that of Judas of Galilee. He placed Theudas first in time. Now Judas of Galilee, or of Gaulonitis (cf. Josephus, *Antiq.*, 18.1.1), perished because of his opposition to the census of the year 7 A. D., and we have no knowledge of a revolutionist by the name of Theudas who lived before this. Josephus tells of a Theudas who lived in the procuratorship of Cuspius Fadus, which began in 44 A. D., and what he says of him agrees with the statement in Acts (cf. *Antiq.*, 20.5.1). We are then obliged to assume that there were two men by the name of Theudas who played the same rôle and met the same fate, or, what is more probable, that the incident of Acts 5:36 is an addition to the speech of Gamaliel.

statement to be understood that so many as had houses or lands sold them? (20) For what purpose was the story of Ananias and Sapphira introduced? (21) What was their sin? (22) How did Peter probably detect this? (23) How did his relation to Sapphira differ from his relation to Ananias? (24) How did he regard the fate of Ananias and Sapphira? (25) What are some of the reasons for accepting another explanation?

(26) To what extreme did enthusiasm for Peter run? (27) How were those on whom his shadow fell healed? (28) How long an interval separated the first and second imprisonment of the apostles? (29) What was the attitude of the rulers at the time of the second imprisonment? (30) Who still led the opposition? (31) What charge was brought against the apostles, and how did they meet it? (32) What effect did Peter's words have on the rulers? (33) What was the argument of Gamaliel? (34) What was the outcome of the second attempt to suppress the gospel?

§ 31. **Supplementary Topics for Study and References to Literature.**

1. Write a chapter on the growth of the church in Jerusalem, using, perhaps, the following outline:

a) Peter's success in preaching and healing.

b) The fellowship of the church.

c) The attempt to suppress the new movement.

2. What does Josephus say about the Pharisees (*Antiq.*, 18. 1. 3)?

3. What does he say about the Sadducees (*Antiq.*, 18. 1. 4)?

4. Where in Acts is the word "church" first used, and what does it mean?

5. What does Josephus say about the Zealots (*Antiq.*, 18. 1. 6)?

6. For list of the highpriests see:

Schürer, *The Jewish People in the Time of Jesus Christ*, Div. 2, Vol. I, p. 197–200.

7. On the relation of the "Senate of the Children of Israel" to the Sanhedrin see:

Schürer. *op. cit.*, Div. 1, Vol. II, p. 167.

CHAPTER IV

THE APPOINTMENT OF THE SEVEN AND THE MARTYRDOM OF STEPHEN

§ 32. **The appointment of the Seven.**	Acts 6:1–7
§ 33. **The martyrdom of Stephen.**	Acts 6:8—8:1*a*

§ 32. **The Appointment of the Seven.**—The narrative of the appointment of seven[1] men to have charge of the charities of the church, while serving as an introduction to the story of the first Christian martyr, has a value of its own. Thus, in the first place, it shows that the new spirit of brotherhood was not yet strong enough to obliterate the old prejudice of the Hebrews against the Grecian Jews. Those designated "Hebrews" were residents of Palestine, and hence spoke the Aramaic language, while the "Hellenists" were Jews from abroad who spoke Greek and who in greater or lesser degree had been affected by Greek civilization. Natives of the Holy Land, who had not come into any close contact with the gentiles, naturally looked askance at their brethren from abroad who in various particulars bore the stamp of a non-Jewish nationality. This prejudice showed itself within the church. Those who had in hand the distribution of food or money discriminated against the Hellenists—a procedure which may have been rendered relatively easy by the meagerness of the funds at their disposal. Because of this discrimination the Hellenists made complaint on behalf of those of their number who needed aid but did not receive it.

Again, this narrative has a value of its own, inasmuch as it shows that in the settlement of the first trouble in the apostolic church, a democratic spirit prevailed. The multitude were called together, the multitude approved the suggestion of the apostles, and the multitude chose the men who should henceforth have the care of the

[1] The work for which the Seven were appointed corresponded to that which was assigned at a later day to those who were called "deacons." Nevertheless, Luke does not give them this name, and there is no indication in the New Testament that they were a permanent part of the organization of the church in Jerusalem. Uhlhorn, *Christian Charity in the Ancient Church*, 1883, supposes that they developed into elders as the apostles withdrew from Jerusalem.

poorer brethren. The apostles, as the oldest in Christian experience and as those who, in their acquaintance with Jesus, had enjoyed special opportunity of knowing his mind, had a moral right and duty to tell what sort of men should be selected (vs. 3), and after the choice had been made, to consecrate the men unto their work by a religious service (vs. 6). They did not themselves choose the seven men on the ground of their apostolic dignity, nor did they reject any of those whom the multitude had named. They assumed that the whole body of believers was qualified to judge whether a man was full of the Spirit and of wisdom. They did not question the choice of the multitude: they simply approved it.

The act of laying hands on the men who had been chosen was an ancient Jewish custom (e. g., Deut. 34:9), common also in the various ordinations in the synagogue. It was symbolic of the bestowal of blessing, either physical or spiritual (Mark 7:32; Matt. 19:13).

It is significant that the names of the seven men are all Greek. It does not follow, of course, that all the men were Hellenists, for Palestinian Jews, as in the case of the apostles Andrew and Philip, sometimes had Greek names; but the fact that all seven names are Greek favors the view that the Hellenists were largely represented on the board of charities. The appointment of Nicolas, who was not only a Hellenist, but also a proselyte, indicates that the prejudice of the Palestinian Jews was not shared by the multitude; in other words, when taken together with the fact that the seven names are all Greek, it may suggest that the believers at this time were largely Hellenists.

The rapid increase of the church in the days when the board of charities was established seems to have been regarded by Luke as connected with that fact. And the appointment of the Seven may, indeed, have helped in two ways: (1) The apostles were thereby released from all care of the poor, and were able to give themselves wholly to prayer and the word, and (2) the spiritual power of the brotherhood of believers as a whole may well have been increased by the removal of that which had been a source of hard feeling. Thus by the failure of the rulers to check the new movement and by the better administration of the internal affairs of the church, the way was prepared for a triumph of Christian testimony even among the priests (Acts 6:7).

§ 33. **The Martyrdom of Stephen.**—The dramatic story of Stephen, in the course of which we are introduced to Saul of Tarsus, falls into three parts: (*a*) his arrest (6:8–15); (*b*) his defense (7:1–53); and (*c*) his death (7:54—8:1*a*).

a) *The arrest of Stephen.*—Stephen was chosen to "serve tables," but he soon proved himself a veritable apostle. The language employed to describe his deeds is stronger than that with which Luke refers to the deeds of the Twelve. He was a man of power, not merely of power to work wonders and signs, but of intellectual power to present and defend the gospel, and of spiritual insight into the essential nature of the new doctrine of Christ; a man who also possessed the power that comes from sublime courage. His career soon aroused a more bitter opposition than had been provoked by Peter.

The opposition to Stephen came from the Hellenists, particularly from members of five[1] synagogues. First of these was the synagogue of the Libertines, that is, probably, of Jews who had once been Roman slaves or of the descendants of such. Cyrene, half-way between Carthage and Alexandria on the north coast of Africa and directly south of Greece, was the home of those Jews who formed the second synagogue. The third was composed of Jews from Alexandria, the fourth of Jews from Cilicia, Saul's native province, and the fifth, of Jews from the province of Asia, whose capital was Ephesus. The fact that so many Hellenistic synagogues were involved in the opposition to Stephen testifies to the extent of his influence. We may suppose that he had visited these synagogues and borne his testimony in them.

The ground of the opposition can not be definitely made out. The witnesses whose testimony is introduced by Luke are said to have been false, and yet we may probably infer from their words the general character of Stephen's offensive utterances. It is not unlikely that, influenced by the words of Jesus, he spoke of the destruction of the temple, though he can scarcely have declared that this would be directly by Jesus, i. e., at his second advent. Then, remembering how Jesus had laid stress on the inward rather than the outward, and remembering also his words about the fulfilment of the law,

[1] The view that this passage refers to five synagogues, though not necessarily required by the Greek, appears on the whole preferable.

Stephen may well have said that the customs of Moses were not essential to salvation.

The appearance of Stephen when brought before the Sanhedrin on the charge of blasphemy was, according to the language of Luke, something extraordinary, but not necessarily supernatural. We may believe that his face was strikingly transfigured by the confidence he had in Jesus and by the conviction that what he had said was true.

b) The defense of Stephen.—The longest speech which has been preserved from the apostolic age is also in respect to its content one of the most remarkable.

Its relation to the Old Testament in particular, is worthy of notice, for it diverges at many points and widely. This divergence is the more worthy of notice because of its bearing on the genuineness of the speech. The more important instances are as follows: (1) Stephen speaks of an appearance of God to Abraham while he yet dwelt in Mesopotamia, before he migrated to Haran. The Old Testament knows nothing of this. The first divine commandment to Abraham is that which was given in Haran (Gen. 12:1). (2) Words that according to Ex. 3:12 were spoken to Moses are introduced by Stephen as spoken to Abraham. (3) Stephen gives the number of people who went down into Egypt as seventy-five, in this point agreeing with the Greek translation of the Old Testament, but differing from the Hebrew Old Testament, where the number is always seventy (Gen. 46:27; Ex. 1:5; Deut. 10:22). (4) Stephen confounds Abraham's purchase of a field from Ephron, the Hittite, in Machpelah near Mamre, with Jacob's purchase of a parcel of ground from the sons of Hamor in Shechem (Gen. 23; 33:19–20; 50:13). (5) The Old Testament says that Moses was eighty years old when he stood before Pharaoh (Ex. 7:7), and also says that he was "grown up" at the time when he slew the Egyptian and fled into Midian (Ex. 2:11); but it is Stephen who divides the eighty years into two equal parts. (6) The view that the angel who appeared to Moses in the bush was also with him in Egypt (Acts 7:35), the statement that an angel spoke to Moses on Mount Sinai (Acts 7:38), and also the statement that the law was ordained by angels (Acts 7:53), are all peculiar to Stephen. They are not found in the Old Testament. (7) The Old Testament makes no reference to the worship of Moloch or of Rephan by Israel in the wilderness. Stephen gets these names from the Greek translation of the Old Testament as does he also the name Babylon, where Amos 5:27 has Damascus.

Now these points of divergence from the Old Testament favor the genuineness of the speech, for they are more readily understood as occurring in an extempore address of a Jew accustomed to the Septuagint, the Greek translation of the Old Testament, and acquainted with Jewish tradition, than as part of an imaginary reproduction of Stephen's speech made by Luke who was not a Jew.

Stephen's speech is called a defense. It was also an arraignment of his accusers, its central thought being that they were resisting the Holy Spirit as their fathers had done before them.

Abraham, indeed, was spiritually minded, but the sons of Jacob withstood the Spirit of God, and yet more plainly did the Israel of Moses' day. They resisted him in Egypt and all through the journey of the wilderness. Moreover, at a later day, in thinking of God as an earthly king, one who dwells in temples made with hands, they resisted the Spirit that spoke through the prophets (e. g., Is. 66:1--2).

This speech furnishes no ground for the charge of blasphemy against Moses (Acts 6:11), or that Stephen had spoken against the temple. And yet, since it exalts the spiritual above the material, after the manner of the prophets, it shows clearly enough that Stephen may have made statements regarding Moses and the temple which to the legal ritualistic Jews would have seemed blasphemous.

c) The death of Stephen.—It appears obvious that Stephen did not finish his speech. As a Christian full of the Spirit and of wisdom he had more to say about Jesus than that he had been betrayed and murdered by the rulers. He had a positive message as well, of which we have a hint in the exclamation that came from his lips when it was apparent that his auditors, instead of listening longer to his words, would put him to death (vs. 56).

Now the rage of the rulers which broke in upon the speech of Stephen is to be attributed to his personal charges against them rather than to anything he had said about Moses (vs. 54). They are accused of resisting the Spirit and of murdering Jesus. For this they gnash upon him with their teeth; and when Stephen declares that he sees Jesus at the right hand of God, they stone him. He is sacrificed, therefore, not only because he holds heretical views regarding Moses and the temple, but especially because of the charge of dreadful guilt which he brings against his judges, and because of the vivid testimony he bears to the messiahship of that Jesus whom they had recently caused to be crucified.

The death of Stephen was apparently accomplished not only without the sanction of the Roman governor, which the law required, but also without any formal sentence of the Sanhedrin. It was a passionate and lawless deed. That Stephen, rather than Peter, was the first Christian martyr was probably due to the temper and ability of the man, more than to the substance of his teaching. If he was also a Hellenist, his accusation of the Jerusalem authorities would have been especially offensive.

§ 34. **Questions and Suggestions for Study.**—(1) Define the meaning of "Hebrew" and "Hellenist." (2) What caused the Hellenists among the Christians to murmur? (3) What spirit was manifested in the method of the appointment of the Seven? (4) What part did the apostles have in this appointment? (5) What is suggested by the names of the Seven? (6) In what ways may the appointment of the Seven have furthered the success of the gospel?

(7) Into what parts does the story of Stephen fall? (8) Whence did the opposition to Stephen come? (9) Define the sources from which the members of the five synagogues of Acts 6:9 came. (10) What was the probable ground of the opposition to Stephen? (11) Name seven points in which the speech of Stephen departs from the Hebrew Old Testament. (12) What bearing do these points have on the genuineness of the speech? (13) What is the central thought of the address of Stephen? (14) In what general manner does the speech lend support to the charges against Stephen? (15) What ground is there for thinking that Stephen was not allowed to finish his speech? (16) What were the chief reasons why he was stoned? (17) Wherein was his death illegal?

§ 35. **Supplementary Topics for Study and References to Literature.**

1. Write a chapter on the appointment of the Seven, using, perhaps, the following outline:

a) The need of such appointment.

b) The apostles' action in the matter.

c) The accusation against Stephen.

2. On the "Dispersion" consult:

Schürer, *History of the Jewish People*, Vol. II, p. 31; Mathews, *A History of New Testament Times in Palestine*, pp. 157, 158, and Gilbert, *Student's Life of Paul*, pp. 3–8.

3. On the Greek translation of the Old Testament read:

E. Nestle in Hastings' *Bible Dictionary*, article on "Septuagint."

PART II

EXTENSION OF THE GOSPEL TO THE GENTILES, OCCASIONED BY PERSECUTION

CHAPTER V

THE WORK OF PHILIP THE EVANGELIST

SYNOPSIS

§ 36. **The Church in Jerusalem Scattered by Persecution.**—The period between Pentecost and the persecution which broke out with the death of Stephen may be roughly estimated at two years, that is, from 30 to 32 A. D., assuming that Pentecost was in the year 30. Accordingly the movement of events in the first seven chapters of Acts must be thought of as rapid, a conclusion which, of course, suits the nature of those events. This time of relatively quiet development was due to the fact that the new movement was wholly loyal to the temple and to Jewish law. But when a man arose who not only saw the inner nature of this outgrowth from Judaism, but who also clearly declared it, the effect of his words was immediate and far-reaching.

The first general persecution of the disciples of Jesus, though it originated with the Hellenists and though its leading spirit was a Cilician Jew, was authorized by the rulers in Jerusalem (cf., e. g., Acts 9:2), and was doubtless heartily furthered by them. Once, at least, they had thirsted for the blood of the apostles (Acts 5:33), and later circumstances must have kept their spirit of opposition at the fever point (e. g., Acts 5:42; 6:7). The death of Stephen, although lamented by some of the Jews, was a welcome signal for a general crusade against the believers in Jesus—a crusade which, even had there been no Stephen, must soon have been set on foot.

In this persecution men and women were committed to prison (Acts 8:3); they were beaten in the synagogues to the end that they might blaspheme the name of Jesus (Acts 26:11), and some were put to death (Acts 26:10). Many fled for their lives, perhaps remembering the word of Jesus that when persecuted in one city they should flee to the next (Matt. 10:23). The statement that *all* were scattered abroad except the apostles is obviously general in its nature; even vs. 3 shows that many remained in Jerusalem, hoping to escape the storm by keeping quiet in their houses. Those who fled were in some cases followed by the persecutors to towns more or less distant from Jerusalem (Acts 26:11).

§ 37. **The Work of Philip in the City of Samaria.**—The effort to stamp out the Christian movement resulted in its vigorous promotion. Many of those who fled from Jerusalem became, for a time at least, evangelists, and preached the word in Judea, Samaria, Phœnicia, Cyprus, and Antioch (Acts 8:1; 11:19). It is probable that most of the fugitives lived outside of Jerusalem, and when the persecution broke out they simply started for their old homes.

Philip, one of the Seven, afterward called an evangelist (Acts 21:8), whose home was in Cæsarea (Acts 8:40; 21:8), was apparently on his way home when he preached in Samaria, for this city was on the main thoroughfare between Jerusalem and Cæsarea. It was the chief city in Samaria, and from the time of Herod the Great, to whom it had been given by Augustus, it bore the name "Sebaste,"[1] in honor of the royal donor. It was some three hours' walk from Sebaste to the village of Sychar, where, according to John, Jesus had once stopped and had been welcomed by the Samaritans. Whether the ground had been prepared for Philip by this sojourn of Jesus we can not say. It certainly is not necessary to assume such a preparation in order to explain the evangelist's success, for he is represented as a man of power, like Stephen, both to preach (Acts 8:26–39) and to work signs (Acts 8:6–7).

Among those whom Philip baptized was a man who had long been well known in Samaria, and who was destined to become widely known in the church, an adept in sorcery like that Bar-Jesus whom Paul encountered in Paphos (Acts 13:6). He was regarded as an incarnation of divine power, and, indeed, as the pre-eminent incarnation. Therefore it was a notable triumph when Philip turned many away from Simon to Christ, and a triumph also, though less significant, when Simon himself submitted to baptism.

Simon evidently regarded Philip as a brother sorcerer who had

[1] From the Greek word having the same meaning as Augustus.

RUINS OF THE CITY OF SAMARIA

some secrets which he himself did not possess. He therefore continued with Philip in the hope of learning these secrets. He too would like to be able to cast out demons, to heal the palsied and lame, not thereby to extend the kingdom of Christ, of which he appears to have had no true conception, but solely to promote his own glory. His amazement at Philip's signs became greater when he saw the effects produced by the laying-on of the apostles' hands, of which effects one may have been the gift of ecstatic speech (Acts 19:6).

As Simon himself had been baptized, and was to all outward appearances a true believer, there is no reason to think that the apostles passed by him when they laid their hands on the new converts. It is not to be supposed, however, that if they laid their hands upon him, he experienced any spiritual uplifting from the act, for he had no true faith in his heart. But his failure to experience any strange effect from the apostolic touch did not blind his eyes to the effects produced in others, and accordingly he made the apostles a cash offer for their powerful secret. He did not covet the Spirit for himself, but only the ability to confer it on others. It is therefore plain that, as Peter said, he had no part or lot in the gospel (vs. 21). He regarded it all as a superior kind of sorcery, and just for that reason he was intensely interested in it. As the curtain falls upon him, he is still Simon the sorcerer, for he is asking Peter to use his influence to protect him from any evil to which his temerity might have exposed him.

It is to be remembered that this narrative was written a good many years after the events which are described. In that interval the name and importance of apostles had been magnified in the church. They were now thought of as an official body, without whose sanction the work of the new kingdom could not be consummated. Ideas current when Luke wrote are reflected to some extent in the story of a time before those ideas arose. Thus, at Pentecost, and again in the time of Paul's conversion, the gift of the Holy Spirit was plainly not thought of as dependent upon an act of the apostles (Acts 2 : 39; 9 : 17).

§ 38. **Philip and the Ethiopian Treasurer.**—The essential part of this narrative is plainly the meeting of Philip with the Ethiopian. Just how this meeting was brought about, and where, are questions on which Luke does not enable us to arrive at definite conclusions. He appears to have regarded them as incidental.

A message of some sort reached Philip while in Samaria, calling him to go to a road that ran from Jerusalem to Gaza, and perhaps directing him to station himself at the ruins of old Gaza, a little north of the new town. Responding to this message[1] he met or overtook the Ethiopian on the road.

This man, since he had come to Jerusalem to worship, must have been a proselyte, and the fact that he was meditating on Isa. 53 gives some color to the view that he had heard of Jesus while in Jerusalem, and was now searching the Scriptures with reference to the Messiah. While thus engaged, he drove near the spot where Philip was waiting; and he, recognizing that this was the opportunity for which he had journeyed from distant Samaria, ran to the chariot and entered into conversation with the man who was reading. The outcome was that the Ethiopian, at his own request, was baptized by the wayside. The men then parted, and Philip started again for Cæsarea. In the towns through which he passed, as Jamnia and Joppa, he preached the gospel, just as before he had stopped to preach in Samaria.

This story of Philip and the Ethiopian is valuable, not only for the light it throws on the methods of an early evangelist, but also, and especially, for its suggestion that the seed of the gospel was widely scattered, even from the first, by means of foreign Jews and proselytes who came to Jerusalem to worship.

§ 39. **Questions and Suggestions for Study.**—(1) About how long a time intervened between Pentecost and the first persecution of disciples? What fact accounts for the relatively undisturbed development of this period? (2) With whom did the first general persecution of the disciples of Jesus originate, and what was the attitude of the rulers toward it? (3) What was done with believers who were seized? (4) How is the statement to be taken that all were scattered except the apostles? (5) How did the persecution pro-

[1] The meaning of the message is not wholly clear. Thus was Philip to go *at noon*, or go *southward?* Was it the road or Gaza itself that was "desert"? The obscurity that covers the messenger and attaches also to the message may have come from the fact that Philip's life would have been in danger if the persecutors in Jerusalem had known his whereabouts. It is plain that whoever brought him the message knew of the movements of the Ethiopian treasurer, and considered Philip the best man to approach him with the offer of the gospel.

mote the Christian movement? (6) Who was Philip, and where was his home? (7) Where was the city of Samaria? (8) How near to it had Jesus labored? (9) What was Simon of Samaria, and how was he regarded by the people? (10) How did Simon regard Philip? (11) What did Simon think of the gift of the Spirit?

(12) What is the essential fact in the narrative of Philip and the Ethiopian? (13) Whither was Philip called? (14) Who was the Ethiopian, and why was he in Jerusalem? (15) What was he reading when he passed Philip? (16) To whom does the prophet's language in this chapter refer? See Isa. 52:13. (17) Of whom did the early church find in this passage a description? See vs. 35 and compare Acts 3:26. (18) What conception of the Messiah does this involve? (19) What was the outcome of Philip's teaching? (20) Mention other instances in which the gospel message was brought to a single person. (21) Whither did Philip go after his meeting with the Ethiopian? Through what prominent towns did his road pass?

§ 40. **Supplementary Topics for Study and References to Literature.**

1. Write a chapter on Philip, having an outline somewhat as follows: His home; his work in Jerusalem; his work in Samaria; his journey to Gaza to preach to a single soul; the character of his message to the Eunuch.

2. Look up the references to the Samaritans in the gospels.

3. How far were Phœnicia and Cyprus from Jerusalem, and what were their chief cities?

4. On Simon as a false Messiah read:

McGiffert, *The Apostolic Age*, pp. 90, 100.

5. What was the capital of Ethiopia, and how far was it from Jerusalem?

6. Regarding proselytes consult:

Schürer, *The Jewish People in the Time of Christ*, Div. 2, Vol. II, pp. 291–327.

CHAPTER VI

THE LIFE OF PAUL BEFORE HIS CONVERSION

SYNOPSIS

§ 41. **His Family and Political Status.**—Our knowledge regarding the family of Paul is very slight. He himself never mentions father or mother, brother or sister. He was born in Tarsus, but was of pure Jewish descent. This is implied in his saying that he was a Hebrew of Hebrews (Phil. 3:5), and is implied also in the fact that he was a member of the Sanhedrin (Acts 26:10), for none but pure Jews could sit in that court (cf. Schürer, *Jewish People*, etc., Div. 2, Vol. I, p. 176). We know from Paul's word to the chief captain in Jerusalem that his father was a Roman citizen (Acts 22:28); but we can not infer from this that his family was wealthy, even moderately so. The bestowal of Roman citizenship on Jews was not dependent on the amount of their property. On the other hand, the fact that Paul learned a trade (Acts 18:3) is no evidence that his father was poor, for the rabbis taught that it was every man's duty to teach his son a trade. Nor should we see a proof of wealth in the fact that Paul was educated in Jerusalem, for near relatives of his family may have lived there (cf. Acts 23:16), and in any case the cost of instruction was probably small.

The word of Paul to Agrippa that he had lived after the straitest sect of the Jews' religion (Acts 26:5), also his saying before the Sanhedrin: "I am a Pharisee, a son of Pharisees" (Acts 23:6), and the character of the man when we first meet him in Acts, suggests that in his father's house there was a zealous observance of the law. We may also safely infer from these facts that he was carefully instructed in the Scriptures from earliest youth. What Josephus says of the training of all Jewish children, though manifestly somewhat exaggerated, may well have been applicable in a good degree to Paul. He says that the children learned the law as soon as they became sensible of anything, and had it engraven on their souls, so that they could tell the whole of it more easily than they could tell their own names.

By the side of Paul's Pharisaic descent stands next in order of importance the fact that he was born a Roman citizen (Acts 22:28). This would have meant a good deal to him even if he had passed his life in Tarsus; it meant more to him in his world-wide travels as a Christian missionary. The chief privileges of Roman citizenship were three: trial by Roman courts, freedom from dishonorable punishments, like scourging and crucifixion, and the right of appeal to Cæsar. It is true Paul suffered much injustice, chiefly at the hands of the Jews, in spite of the fact that he was a Roman citizen, but it is also true that his citizenship saved him from much injustice. We know that it secured his honorable release from prison in Philippi, that it saved him from scourging in Jerusalem, and that it delivered him at last from the plots of the Jews by taking him to Cæsar's bar.

§ 42. **His Early Environment and Education in Jerusalem.**— Paul was proud, not only of his Roman citizenship, but also of the fact that he was a citizen of Tarsus. This city was on the Cydnus River in level Cilicia, twelve miles from the Mediterranean coast and about 515 miles northwest from Jerusalem. For a century before Paul's birth Tarsus had been free, and therefore possessed important rights and privileges. It controlled its own finances, had jurisdiction over its own citizens and over foreigners while they sojourned there, and enjoyed freedom from the Roman land-tax and from a Roman garrison.

Tarsus ranked with Athens and Alexandria as a center of education and culture. Strabo who studied in Tarsus a little before the time of Paul ranked it above these cities in philosophy and general education, and he also says that in his day Rome was full of learned men from Tarsus and Alexandria. It was the home of the poet Aratus (270 B. C.), from whose words Paul quoted in the Areopagus address (Acts 17:28). On an ambitious and alert mind like Paul's the passing of boyhood in a large city which was famous the world over for its devotion to letters, a city in which the Greek language was spoken and where one saw something of the best civilization of the age, can hardly have been without deep and abiding influence. It may be taken as a matter of course that he acquired a knowledge of Greek in Tarsus, the language through which he was to enrich the religious literature of the world, and also that the impressions derived from the life of the city were of an informing and mentally stimulating character. They helped to make him, in the best sense of the word, a man of the world.

But Paul was destined to become a rabbi, and therefore was sent at an early age to study at Jerusalem. How old he was at this time we can not tell definitely, yet the language which he used on two occasions seems to imply that he had not passed out of boyhood (Acts 22.3; 26:4).

Paul was fortunate in his teacher. Gamaliel I was the most illustrious representative of the school of Hillel, of whom, according to some scholars, he was a grandson. He was one of the four teachers to whom the Mishna gives the most honorable title of "rabban." Tradition represents him as humble-minded, one who served those who were inferior to him in rank. In Acts Gamaliel appears as a man of courage and independence, not afraid to advocate an unpopular cause; a man of cool dispassionate temper, and perhaps of a somewhat liberal mind, for he appears to have thought it possible that God was in the religious movement whose leaders were on trial.

We can form only a general idea of the substance and method of the education which Paul received in the school of Gamaliel. The rabbis met their pupils in the courts of the temple. The work of the school was chiefly memorizing. The teacher repeated again and again an explanation of a Scripture passage until the scholars also could repeat it. Hence it came to pass that the word "repeat" meant to teach. The ideal of the student was to be like a well-plastered cistern, which loses no drop of water that is put into it.

The content of rabbinic teaching was, theoretically, the law of Moses, but in reality it was the traditional interpretation of that law, which was regarded as of even greater value. There was no place in the curriculum for the history and literature of any gentile people, no place for art or for such knowledge of science as was then extant among the Egyptians and Greeks. A Hellenist like Paul may have read Greek literature while studying in Jerusalem, but as a pupil of

Gamaliel his one subject of study was the law and its traditional interpretation, and the language used was the Aramaic.

How long Paul sat at the feet of Gamaliel, and whether he himself obtained a license to teach, are questions which must remain unanswered. It is probable that he returned to Tarsus and remained there some time prior to his appearance in the book of Acts at the martyrdom of Stephen. It is most natural to think that he learned his trade of weaving goat's hair in his native city, for this was a Cilician industry, and it is doubtful whether he could have found opportunity in Jerusalem to learn it. Moreover, it seems improbable that he was in Jerusalem during the public ministry of Jesus, for had he been, it is likely that he would have seen the prophet over whom the religious authorities were so much excited. If, however, he had seen Jesus, it is probable that we should have some sort of allusion to the fact in his writings; but there is none, for 2 Cor. 5:16 refers only to a false judgment of Jesus which Paul had formerly entertained.

Though it is not easy to believe that Paul was in Jerusalem during the public ministry of Jesus, it seems probable that he had been there some time before the death of Stephen. His language in Acts 26:10 implies that he was a member of the supreme court, and this fact in turn seems to imply that he had already distinguished himself in Jerusalem. It is possible that he had come back to the city as the rabbi of the Cilician synagogue, and in that capacity had come into prominence.

§ 43. **His Career as a Persecutor.**—There is no reason to doubt that Paul persecuted the followers of Jesus with a good conscience (Acts 26:9), and thought that he was thereby offering acceptable service unto God (cf. John 16:2). He threw himself wholly into the work because he was wholly bent on pleasing the Lord. His motive was purely religious.

It is plain that Paul had the support of the Sanhedrin as a whole (Acts 9:2; 22:5; 26:10), though his course can hardly have had the approval of Gamaliel. On what grounds the Roman procurator was moved to sanction the death of disciples of Jesus we are not told. It is not unlikely that he did it for the same reason that Agrippa, at a later day, seized Peter with the intention of putting him to death, that is, because it was a policy that pleased the leading Jews.

The success of Paul in Jerusalem was obviously very marked. Luke speaks of the persecution as "great" and as a "wasting of the church" (Acts 8:1, 3), in consequence of which many believers fled; and Paul's own language is equally strong. He declares that he persecuted the church beyond measure and made havoc of it (Gal. 1:13). The report of his doings had reached Damascus before him, and had caused believers to tremble (Acts 9:13–14). But though the persecution checked the Christian movement in Jerusalem for a time, it seems not long to have survived the departure of Paul. When he returned, after about three years, he found the apostles in Jerusalem, and at that time, according to Luke, Peter was making tours through Judea undisturbed (Acts 9:32).

§ 44. **Questions and Suggestions for Study.**—(1) Where was Paul born? (2) What implies that he was of pure Jewish descent? (3) To what sect did his family belong? (4) What instruction is it likely that he had in his home? (5) What was his political status? (6) What were the chief privileges of Roman citizenship? (7) In what signal instances did his Roman citizenship benefit him?

(8) Describe the location of Tarsus and its political privileges. (9) How did Tarsus rank in education? (10) What did the passing of childhood and early youth in Tarsus probably mean to Paul? (11) At what age did Paul go to Jerusalem? (12) Who was his teacher there? (13) What was the method of rabbinic teaching? (14) With what subjects did it deal? (15) What reasons are there for thinking that Paul returned to Tarsus for a time after his studies in Jerusalem?

(16) What reasons are there for thinking that he had been in Jerusalem a considerable time before the death of Stephen? (17) What was the character of Paul's religious and moral life in these days before his conversion to Christianity? See especially Gal. 1:14; Phil. 3:5, 6.

(18) In what spirit did Paul enter into the persecution of believers? (19) On what ground did the Roman procurator probably allow the persecution to go on? (20) What was the success of the persecution in Jerusalem? (21) When does it appear to have died out?

§ 45. **Supplementary Topics for Study and References to Literature.**

1. On the basis of the foregoing paragraphs and of your own study of the New Testament write a chapter on the life of Paul before his conversion. Note especially those points which helped to fit him for his career as a Christian missionary, and include an estimate of his moral character while he was still a Pharisee.

2. On the political status of Jews in the Dispersion read:

Josephus, *Antiquities*, 12.3.1; 14.7.2; 16.6.1; 14.10.13–19; and Schürer, *The Jewish People*, etc., Div. 2, Vol. II, pp. 270–81.

3. On the question of Paul's marriage see:

Gilbert, *Student's Life of Paul*, pp. 20, 21.

4. On rabbinic interpretation see:

Cone, *Paul the Man, the Missionary, and the Teacher*, pp. 7–21.

THE EMPEROR TIBERIUS

CHAPTER VII

THE EARLY CHRISTIAN LIFE OF PAUL

SYNOPSIS

§ 46. **The conversion of Paul.** **Acts 9:1–9; 22:6–16; 26:12–18; Gal. 1:13–17; 1 Cor. 9:1; 15:8; 2 Cor. 4:6**

§ 47. **The three years in Damascus and Arabia.** **Acts 9:19 *b*–22; Gal. 1:16–17.**

§ 48. **The return to Jerusalem and work in Syria and Cilicia.** **Acts 9:23–30; Gal. 1:18–24**

§ 46. **The Conversion of Paul.**—The New Testament says more about the conversion of Paul than is said anywhere in Scripture about the conversion of any other man. And of all the events of the apostolic age probably none was of greater importance for its influence on the subsequent history of Christianity than Paul's abandonment of his Pharisaism to become a Christian. This significant event took place near Damascus, breaking into and ending Saul's career as a persecutor of Christians. It unquestionably involved for him a profound modification of his religious convictions, and led to a total change of his career. From having been a vigorous opponent of the new religion, he became at once a devout disciple of Jesus, and in the years that followed probably the most potent factor of that age in the promotion of Christianity and in the determining of its character. The importance of the event is reflected in the various accounts of it which the New Testament gives. There are three accounts in Acts, two of which purport to be by Paul himself, and in the epistles to the Galatians and Corinthians we have at least three references to it. There is also an indirect but important reference to it in Philippians.

1) *The event according to the epistles.*—According to Galatians, Paul's conversion occurred in or near Damascus, and had been immediately preceded by a career of persecution (1:17; 13–15). He here attributes the change to a revelation of the Son of God in him (1:15, 16). The change is represented as sudden. The work of persecution was instantly abandoned and Paul at once departed into Arabia (Gal. 1:16, 17). This narrative contains no suggestion of an external phenomenon in connection with Paul's conversion. The vital fact in it is a spiritual apprehension of Christ.

The word of Paul in 1 Cor. 9:1, "Have I not seen Jesus our Lord" is to be referred to the same event of which Gal. 1:16 speaks. Paul here derives his apostleship from the fact that he has seen Jesus the Lord; but obviously a beholding of Jesus with the eyes of flesh would have established no claim to apostleship. The passage, therefore, points to that spiritual vision mentioned in Galatians (1:15), which, because it carried conviction of the resurrection of Jesus, sustained a vital relation to Paul's apostleship.

The vision of Jesus mentioned in 1 Cor. 15:8 is to be identified with that of 1 Cor. 9:1 and Gal. 1:16. For the appearance of which Paul here speaks was to him the signal evidence of the resurrection of Jesus; but after the event of Gal. 1:16 he certainly never needed proof of the resurrection. It is to be noticed that the Greek word in 1 Cor. 15:8, which is rendered in English by "appeared," is commonly used of spiritual appearances, and that in Paul's address before Agrippa he speaks of what he saw on the way to Damascus as a heavenly "vision" (ὀπτασία), a word from the same stem as that used in 1 Cor. 15:8.

If the shining into the heart, mentioned in 2 Cor. 4:6, is an autobiographical allusion, it plainly agrees with the conception of Gal. 1:16, but adds also that in the revelation of Jesus as the Son of God, Paul was assured that he obtained also a revelation of the glory of the divine character.

But from the fact that Galatians mentions nothing external in connection with Paul's conversion it can not be at once inferred that there *was* nothing of the sort. We have no right to assume that the passage in Galatians is a complete account of the conversion of Paul. Indeed, the passage 1 Cor. 15:5–8, by associating the appearance of Jesus to Paul with other appearances to large groups of people at once, seems to imply that he ascribed external reality to that which caused his own experience and theirs. The Galatian passage, however, must be taken as specializing what the apostle himself regarded as fundamental in his experience near Damascus.

2) *The event according to Acts.*—Two of the three accounts of Paul's conversion in Acts are ascribed to him, the other is by the author. No two are identical, and the differences between those attributed to the apostle are as notable as the differences between these and that of Luke. The two accounts attributed to Paul have some graphic details that lend support to the view that they did, indeed, originate with him. Thus we are told that it was about *noon* when the event occurred; that the light was *great* above the brightness of the sun; that it shone round about them *all;* that the one who spoke to Paul said: "I am Jesus of *Nazareth;*" that *all* fell to the earth; and that Jesus said to Paul: "It is hard for thee to kick against the goad."

Again, the differences in the accounts which are ascribed to Paul are as easily explained on the theory that they originated with Paul as they are if the accounts are regarded as Luke's own production. We should not expect that Paul, speaking twenty-five years after his conversion, would on different occasions describe the event in the same terms and mention the same incidents.

GENERAL VIEW OF THE CITY OF DAMASCUS

On the other hand, if the accounts had been original with Luke, it is not likely that he would have represented the commission to go to the gentiles as coming to Paul in one case from *Jesus* himself *outside* the city (Acts 26:16–18), and in the other as coming from *Ananias in* the city (Acts 22:14, 15).

Coming now to the points of agreement, two are worthy of especial note: (*a*) The three narratives agree that there was some sort of external phenomenon connected with Paul's conversion. He and his companions beheld a light, and he, at least, heard a sound. (*b*) The narratives agree that Paul met Jesus near Damascus, and since they appear to preclude a physical seeing of him, we must suppose that they desire to represent Paul as having had a spiritual vision. Jesus was thought of as present, yet not in a form that was visible to mortal eyes. He was present in a spiritual body, and in this Paul, whose bodily eyes were blinded, beheld him spiritually. In this point the narrative in Acts agrees with the representation of Paul in the epistles, and this point is fundamental. The fact that Paul does not *mention* any external phenomenon in his letters may simply show that he regarded it as of incidental importance. His silence is not a proof that the narrative in Acts is unhistorical.

3. *Preparation for the event near Damascus.*—There was doubtless something in Paul's inner life that led up to the event by Damascus. He says, indeed, that he received his apostleship directly through Jesus Christ (Gal. 1:1), and also that the hour of his change came when it was the good pleasure of God to reveal his Son in him (Gal. 1:9, 16); but these statements do not imply that the transformation of his belief regarding Jesus came without preparation. To say that he was not the convert of any man, or that he had not received his apostleship from men, is not to say that his conversion had no roots in his previous life.

Paul's language in Galatians precludes the possibility that he had received Christian instruction, and the fact that he was zealously persecuting the church when he went to Damascus seems to indicate that he was not conscious of any leaning toward Christianity. It is of course possible that his heart had been touched by the martyr courage of Christians, but in the absence of any evidence whatever, it is quite idle to speculate.[1] The most valuable hint on the antecedents of the conversion of Paul is furnished by the autobiographical passage in the seventh chapter of Romans. The apostle is here interpreting past experiences in the light of present

[1] The word in Acts 26:14: "It is hard for thee to kick against the goad," may mean simply that Paul's course was vain and brought injury only to himself. It probably does not imply that he doubted the rightness of his course.

TRAVELERS CROSSING THE DESERT

knowledge, and we can not hold that the struggle of the spirit which he describes had been felt by him *at the time* so keenly as he now intimates that it had been. But the passage certainly suggests that he must have felt, at times at least, that his righteousness, though perfect according to the standards of Judaism, was unsatisfactory, if not an utter failure. Observance of the law as it had been interpreted by the scribes, had not been able to do away with a sense of bondage to sin. Here, then, we may see a real preparation for the experience by Damascus. The doubt of which he was sometimes conscious was not a doubt in regard to the claim of Jesus, not a doubt which had been created by the Christian movement in Jerusalem, but a doubt whether the righteousness of works was pleasing to God. The existence of such a doubt is an evidence of the depth and sincerity of Paul's religious nature, and it furnishes a basis for an explanation of his conversion.

4. *The nature of the conversion as a religious experience.*—But of more importance than the preparation for the event is the experience itself. If we then attempt to define from all the evidence what Paul's conversion meant for him as a religious experience, we find that it involved at least three things: (*a*) The new, but firm, conviction that Jesus had risen from the dead (1 Cor. 15:8); (*b*) the no less revolutionary conviction that Jesus was the Christ (Gal. 1:16); and (*c*) the recognition, gained at once or as the early sequel of the initial experience, that the way of righteousness by deeds of law, which he had been pursuing, was a failure (Gal. 2:19; Rom. 7:7–25; 8:3), and that instead, fellowship with God and acceptance by him were to be obtained through believing in Jesus, the Son of God (Phil. 3:7–9), in whose face there shines the light of the knowledge of the glory of God (2 Cor. 4:6).

5. *The commission.*—Inseparable from Paul's conversion, both according to Acts and his own letters, was the conviction that he had a mission from Jesus to the gentiles. He says that this was God's purpose in revealing Christ to him (Gal. 1:16), and he repeatedly connects the mission to the gentiles with his first vision of Jesus (1 Cor. 9:1; 15:8, 9). This conviction of a mission to the gentiles was natural. Paul had lived in the gentile world, and his experience had given him a much broader horizon than the original apostles

had. He knew the gentile world, its elements of power as well as its deep need, and he knew that the gospel had been confined thus far to the Jews. A deeper ground of Paul's conviction that he was divinely

"THE STREET THAT IS CALLED STRAIGHT," DAMASCUS

called to the gentiles may well have been the pure graciousness of God in his own salvation. The vision of Jesus had been granted to him while he was doing his utmost to destroy the disciples of Jesus. Thus, with the acceptance of Jesus as the Messiah there was associated an ineradicable impression of the divine goodness that offers salvation freely to the "chief" of sinners. This salvation, therefore, must be for all men, gentiles no less than Jews. Paul's own deep and sad experience that Jewish legalism is not able to save a man would naturally have intensified his desire to go to his gentile fellow-men with his new message of salvation through Jesus.

§ 47. **The Three Years in Damascus and Arabia.**—The letters of Paul say nothing of what happened in the days immediately succeeding his conversion—his baptism by Ananias, the restoration of his sight, and his preaching in the synagogue. A passage in second Corinthians implies that he preached the gospel in Damascus at some time, but this preaching, according to Gal. 1:7, seems to have followed the sojourn in Arabia (2 Cor. 11:32).

It is probable that Paul was taken to the house in Damascus whither he had expected to go when he left Jerusalem. According to Luke, this was the house of a certain Judas in Straight Street (Acts 9:11). In a short time the Jews of Damascus must have heard something of the strange events connected with Paul's approach to their city, at least they must have heard that he had abandoned his crusade against the disciples of Jesus. Luke tells us that a certain Jewish Christian, by the name of Ananias, heard of Paul's arrival and of his state, and that he came to him in the spirit of Jesus to comfort him (Acts 9:10–17; 22:12–16). There is nothing improbable in the statement that he baptized Paul, for Paul would surely have desired to receive this rite from someone; and why not from Ananias (Acts 9:18; 22:16)? It is easily credible also that Ananias uttered some prophetic words regarding Paul's future. The sudden interruption of his career of persecution and his acceptance of the gospel would have suggested that he might have a remarkable work to do.

That Paul was blinded by the glory of the light which shone upon him by Damascus, and that his sight was restored by Ananias, we learn from Acts alone. There can be no doubt that Luke thought of the restoration of physical sight. A figurative interpretation of the healing, to the effect that Paul came out into the light of faith through Ananias, is excluded by the statements of Paul in the letter to the Galatians.

Immediately after his conversion Paul went away into Arabia, by which term is probably meant the neighboring kingdom of Aretas IV (cf. Schürer, *The Jewish People*, etc., Div. 1, Vol. II, pp. 356 ff.). The purpose of this retirement is nowhere intimated, but we may conjecture that it was for meditation. The changed attitude toward Jesus must have raised many and serious questions, and it would have been natural if Paul desired to get away into solitude to think out his answers to them. The approximate length of this Arabian sojourn can be inferred from a passage in Galatians (1:18). Paul says here that it was three years from his conversion to his return to Jerusalem, and according to Acts his stay in Damascus was comparatively short (Acts 9:19, 23). Hence he appears to have spent the greater part of the three years in Arabia.

Following the suggestion of Paul in Galatians we think of his preaching in Damascus as having been subsequent to the Arabian sojourn. This preaching continued long enough to arouse a bitter opposition to the apostle, with which the governor of the city sympathized (2 Cor. 11:32, 33); long enough also to win certain disciples by whose help Paul's life was saved (Acts 9:25).

§ 48. **The Return to Jerusalem, and the Work in Syria and Cilicia.**—When Paul fled from Damascus he went back to Jerusalem, chiefly, it would appear, for the purpose of becoming acquainted with Peter. He had doubtless already known of him as a prominent leader of the hated sect which he was persecuting as he set out for Damascus three years before, but now he would become acquainted with him as a fellow-disciple of the Christ. In the accomplishment of this purpose he spent fifteen days with Peter. We may believe that in these days and from the lips of Peter he heard in full the story of the ministry of Jesus and stored his mind with a large number of the Master's words. Thus through the experience with Peter he must have gained a picture of the earthly life of Jesus which he needed to associate with his vision of the exalted Christ.

But it is significant that Paul did not spend all his time while in Jerusalem as a hearer of that which Peter could tell him. As in Damascus after his return from Arabia, so here, he had a message to utter, and he seems to have given it with his characteristic vigor, for the Hellenists were soon ready to kill him. It was not this fact, however, that led to his departure from Jerusalem. Indeed, the fact of opposition might very probably have made Paul feel that the Lord had a work for him just then in Jerusalem (see 1 Cor. 16:9). But "the brethren" who knew of the hostility toward him brought him down to Cæsarea to take ship for Tarsus, after he had become convinced that this was the Lord's will.

If he must leave Jerusalem, it was natural that he should turn his steps toward his home in Tarsus; and since he was already filled with the thought that his life was to be devoted to the preaching of the gospel to the gentiles, we may suppose that as he set out for his native province it was with the expectation of entering immediately upon missionary work. How long he spent in Tarsus we do not know. The entire period between his departure from Jerusalem and his going to Antioch as co-laborer with Barnabas (Acts 11:25, 26) may be approximately estimated at ten years. For the fourteen years of Gal. 2:1 cover this period together with the first missionary journey from Antioch, which we may estimate at three years, and also the year spent in Antioch (Acts 11:26).

In his letter to the Galatians Paul does not specify Tarsus, but writes that when he left Jerusalem it was to go into the regions of Syria and Cilicia (Gal. 1:21). If he did missionary work in Tarsus, as we may reasonably suppose that he did, he labored also elsewhere in the province and in the adjoining Syria. For immediately after his statement that he went into the regions of Syria and Cilicia he tells the Galatians that the churches of Judea heard that he was successfully preaching the faith of which he had once made havoc. The necessary inference from these words is that what they heard in Judea concerned his work in Syria and Cilicia. And to the correctness of this conclusion Luke bears indirect witness, for he says that Paul, at the beginning of his second tour from Antioch, went through Syria and Cilicia, confirming the churches (Acts 14:41). Now the fact that Paul visited and confirmed certain churches in these regions leads us to believe that he founded them, for it was his principle not to build on another man's foundation. But if he established these churches, it must have been done during the period immediately after his first visit in Jerusalem.

Acts and Galatians are not wholly in agreement in regard to the events of this paragraph, but the differences are mainly such as might naturally flow from the different aims of the two writers. Paul was showing his independence of those who were apostles before him. This independence did not imply that he isolated himself from *all* believers in Jerusalem. On the contrary, it was consistent with free intercourse with his Christian brethren. The aim of Luke was to give a general sketch of Paul's career, not to show the independence of his apostleship, and having this aim he might naturally dwell on the more public aspect of Paul's visit to Jerusalem. The only statement of Acts which can not be explained in harmony with Galatians is that Paul preached throughout all the country of Judea (26:20). In general, however, Luke's narrative affords a valuable supplement to Paul's brief account of his first visit in Jerusalem after his conversion.

§ 49. **Questions and Suggestions for Study.**—(1) What material have we in regard to the conversion of Paul? (2) What are the main facts of the case according to Galatians? (3) Why is 1 Cor. 9:1 to be referred to the apostle's conversion? (4) Why is 1 Cor. 15:8 to be referred to the same event? (5) Can we assume that the Galatian passage is a complete account of Paul's conversion? (6) What details in the narrative of Paul's conversion in Acts 22 and 26 favor the view that the material came from him? (7) In what main points do the three narratives of Acts agree? (8) Was Paul conscious of any leaning toward Christianity when he went to Damascus? (9) What light does Rom. 7 throw on the conversion of Paul?

(10) Why was it natural for Paul to associate a call to work among the gentiles with his vision of Jesus? (11) Describe the relation of Ananias of Damascus to Paul. (12) How did Luke regard the restoration of Paul's sight? (13) What objection to the figurative interpretation of the language? (14) Where did Paul go immediately after his conversion? (15) What was the probable aim of this retirement? (16) What was the approximate length of the Arabian sojourn? (17) When did Paul preach in Damascus, and how long? (18) Where did Paul go when he fled from Damascus, and for what purpose? (19) Describe his visit to Jerusalem. (20) Where did he go from Jerusalem? (21) How long did he labor in Syria and Cilicia?

§ 50. **Supplementary Topics for Study and References to Literature.**

1. Write a chapter on the early Christian life of Paul. Put the accounts of his conversion in parallel columns, and by the side of these all that bears upon the event which you find in Paul's letters. Describe his conversion, and his earliest missionary work in these places—Damascus, Jerusalem, Syria and Cilicia.

2. On the time of Paul's vision in Jerusalem (Acts 22, 17–21) see:

Ramsay, *St. Paul, the Traveller and the Roman Citizen*, pp. 61–64.

3. On the roads to Damascus and on the history of the city read:
Conybeare and Howson, *Life and Epistles of St. Paul*, 1, 84 ff.

4. For an explanation of the mode of Paul's conversion see:
Bacon, *The Story of St. Paul*, pp. 51–67.

PAUL
(From a Mosaic at Ravenna)

CHAPTER VIII

PETER IN A GENTILE HOME

SYNOPSIS

§ 51. **How Peter came to Cæsarea.** **Acts 9:32–42; 10:9–24*a***
§ 52. **Peter's sermon in the house of Cornelius and its results.** **Acts 10:24*b*–48**
§ 53. **Peter's act recognized in the church at Jerusalem.** **Acts 11:1–18**
§ 54. **The relation of the Cæsarean incident to the gentile mission of Paul.**

§ 51. **How Peter Came to Cæsarea.**—The visit of Peter to Lydda and Joppa is not introduced by Luke for its own sake, though he regarded the two signs wrought in those places as noteworthy; but it is introduced to show by what steps the apostle came to the most extraordinary event of his missionary experience. It came to pass that, as he went throughout all parts, he visited Lydda, and as that town was nigh unto Joppa he was summoned thither in an emergency which had befallen some disciples; and the sojourn in Joppa, in its turn, became in various ways a stepping-stone to the visit in Cæsarea and the occurrence in the house of Cornelius. Thus the narrative of the Cæsarean visit began naturally at Lydda.

It is to be noticed that Peter was not out on an evangelistic tour, strictly speaking, but rather on a tour of pastoral visitation. It was the "saints" at Lydda whom he visited, and it was to comfort certain "disciples" that he went on to Joppa. These two towns, moreover, were almost entirely Jewish, and thus, until the trance in Joppa, there is nothing in the narrative to suggest that Peter was thinking of the relation of the gospel to the gentiles.

Two circumstances of Peter's stay in Joppa, which perhaps are not to be separated from each other, forecast the visit to Cornelius in Cæsarea. Peter lodged with a Jew, presumably a disciple, who was by his trade a tanner, and therefore, according to rabbinical ideas, was levitically unclean. It is to the credit of Peter that he ignored this rabbinical teaching, and accepted the hospitality of Simon. It is possible that he took this step without any inner questioning, acting impulsively according to his nature; but it is also natural to think that during the "many days" which he spent with Simon in Joppa he was constrained sooner or later, perhaps by what some of his friends said of his course, to think seriously of his position and to defend it. In this case we should have an explanation of the particular turn taken by his dream, which was the second of the two circumstances mentioned above. Peter was hungry when he fell into a trance, and accordingly in his vision he beheld abundance of food, but on his appropriation of this food the question which had occupied his waking thoughts had its influence. For the beasts, birds, and creeping things which he saw in the sheet appeared to him unclean, yet he was summoned to kill and eat. Against this summons his Jewish training, which had penetrated, as it were, the subconscious sphere of his life, raised its protest. Then he heard a voice which told him that God had "cleansed" these living creatures in the sheet: they were not, therefore, "common and unclean," as he had supposed. He could kill and eat with impunity. We may see the natural background of this part of the dream-message in a questioning of Peter's mind whether Simon was "unclean" because of his trade, or "clean" because he had been accepted as a disciple of Jesus.

When the trance passed, Peter was perplexed as to its meaning; but the appearance just then of the gentile soldiers with their invitation from Cornelius was a providential hint as to its correct interpretation. In his dream Peter had been summoned to kill and eat what appeared to him to be unclean, and a voice had then told him that God had cleansed it: now, when he was summoned to go and preach to a gentile, one whom he had been brought up to regard as unclean, he could not long have failed to see that the dream-voice had a meaning pertinent to the circumstances. His interpretation was in line with his acceptance of Simon's hospitality, though the lesson of the vision carried him further. In Joppa he had lodged with a Christian *Jew*, who was levitically unclean; now he was called to preach even to a gentile. But the first experience confirmed by the dream made the second step easy.

That Peter realized the gravity of the step which he was about to take, and that he foresaw trouble springing out of it, is suggested by the fact that he took at least six Christian Jews with him to Cæsarea from Joppa (Acts 11:12).

VIEW OF JAFFA FROM "THE HOUSE OF SIMON THE TANNER"

§ 52. **Peter's Sermon in the House of Cornelius and its Results.**— The Roman centurion, Cornelius, though a God-fearing man and acquainted with the Jewish religion (Acts 10:2, 22), was obviously not a proselyte like the Ethiopian treasurer. The outpouring of the Spirit on him and his was a cause of amazement to the companions of Peter, because his household were gentiles (Acts 10:45), and it was for the same reason that the event was considered so significant by the church in Jerusalem (Acts 11:18). The acceptance of the gospel by a pagan who was already a proselyte to Judaism occasioned no particular surprise, as the case of Nicolas, one of the Seven, teaches (Acts 6:5).

Various circumstances suggest that the religion of Cornelius was of a noble and winning character. Thus, e. g., his household agreed with him (vs. 12); even his servants and at least one of his soldiers were in religious sympathy with him (vs. 17). And again, when it was time for Peter to come, Cornelius had his kinsmen and near friends assemble to hear him (Acts 10:24).

The vision of Cornelius which led to his sending for Peter naturally suggests that he had not only heard something about the new movement (see vs. 37), as he may have done when Philip returned to Cæsarea (Acts 8:40), but also that he was thinking about it and desiring to know more.

Luke's brief abstract of Peter's sermon in the house of Cornelius bears witness in its opening sentence to the recent liberalizing of the apostle's view in regard to the gentile world. It must have been plain to Peter that God had communicated with Cornelius, though a gentile, and this fact, following closely upon his strange dream in Joppa, led to a general conclusion regarding all gentiles. This conclusion, since it recognized that the ground of acceptance with God did not consist in the observance of Jewish rites and laws, but rather in a devout mind and in practical righteousness, was adapted to gain the good will of his hearers.

Peter preached to his gentile audience substantially what he had preached to the Jews on the day of Pentecost. He dwelt first on the life of Jesus, which showed that God was with him, then on his death and resurrection, and finally, after claiming that he had been authorized by Jesus to bear witness of him as the judge of men, he pointed out the way of salvation, which was in accord with the prophetic word. This was the way of faith in the name of Jesus, as the one whom God had anointed and ordained to be deliverer and judge.

The result of Peter's sermon in the house of Cornelius was more striking than that which followed his preaching in Jerusalem at Pentecost. Before he had finished his address some of his hearers were moved to ecstatic speech, a proof that the Spirit had been poured out upon them. What had taken place in the upper chamber was repeated here in a pagan home (Acts 11:15), excepting the supernatural prelude to the Pentecostal speaking with tongues. Without any imposition of hands and prior to their baptism these gentiles had received the Spirit. The evidence was so clear that no one could object to their baptism and reception into the company of Christian disciples.

§ 53. **Peter's Act Recognized in the Church at Jerusalem.**—The news of the conversion of gentiles in Cæsarea reached Jerusalem ahead of Peter, who tarried some days with Cornelius and his friends (Acts 10:48). On his return he was called to account by certain Jewish believers (not unbelievers, cf. 11:18), but the narrative of Luke does not make clear why they thus called him to account. According to 11:1, what they heard from Cæsarea was that the gentiles had received the word of God, and in vs. 18 we are told that, after Peter's address, they glorified God, saying: "Then to the gentiles also hath God granted repentance unto life." From these verses it would seem that they had not been favorable to the admission of gentiles into the church, perhaps had not even thought of such a thing, as Peter himself evidently had not before his experiences in Joppa and Cæsarea. With this agrees the defense which Peter made, for he simply told how he had been led to change his view in regard to the admission of the gentiles.

In 11:3 the complaint against Peter is that he had associated with the uncircumcised. This would have been a transgression of the traditional law, which, we know, the Jews observed with painful scrupulosity. To this complaint Peter made no reference in his address, that is, no direct reference. He had, indeed, gone in to men uncircumcised, and there is a strong presumption that he had eaten with them. He was not the man to stop half-way. He could not, then, deny the truth of the complaint, but he sought to quiet the scruples of those who had made it in just the way in which his own scruples had been overcome.

And in this he succeeded. His critics, carried along by the evidence of God's presence with him and God's approval of his course, were constrained to overlook his offense against the ceremonial law.

§ 54. **The Relation of the Cæsarean Incident to the Gentile Mission of Paul.**—The preaching of Peter in the home of the Roman Cornelius did not result, so far as we know, in the establishment of a gentile Christian church; nor is there any indication that Peter afterward labored among the gentiles. The conversion of Cornelius and his household and friends remained the sole instance of its kind in the career of one who was known as an apostle of the circumcision (Gal. 2:7, 8). While, therefore, Peter was the first of the twelve apostles (as might have been expected) to break through the wall which separated gentiles and Jews—a fact that adds much to the glory of his career—we can not bring him into comparison with Paul as a co-founder of the gentile church. We can not even say that he anticipated Paul in preaching to gentiles, for apparently Paul was preaching to gentiles in Syria and Cilicia as early as the time of Peter's visit to Cæsarea (Acts 9:30; Gal. 1:21). Certainly Paul's impulse to go to the gentiles was quite independent of Peter's mission to Cornelius.

However, it is certain that Peter's preaching in Cæsarea was important for the gentile church of the future by way of its influence on the Jewish church at Jerusalem. When Paul came up to the mother-church seeking the recognition of his work among the gentiles (Gal. 2:1–10; Acts 15:1–21), that is, their reception into the Christian body without subjection to the law of Moses, the memory of Peter's experience in Cæsarea must of necessity have been an important factor in the discussion, as Luke declares in Acts 15. It may be doubted whether a friendly understanding would have been reached at that time but for the sporadic work of Peter in the home of Cornelius.

§ 55. **Questions and Suggestions for Study.**—(1) What is Luke's purpose in the account of Peter's visit in Lydda and Joppa? (2) What circumstances of Peter's visit in Joppa prepared for his mission to Cornelius? (3) How is the particular form of Peter's dream to be explained? (4) How was Peter helped to interpret his dream? (5) How many brethren did he take with him from Joppa, and why?

(6) Was Cornelius a proselyte? (7) What was the character of his religion? (8) What does the vision of Cornelius presuppose? (9) How had Peter arrived at the opening thought of his sermon in the house of Cornelius? (10) What was the substance of his sermon? (11) What were the striking features in the conversion of Cornelius and his household?

(12) By whom was Peter called to account on his return to Jerusalem, and why? (13) What law had he violated? (14) What was Peter's defense, and what was its effect?

(15) Why can we not regard Peter as a co-founder with Paul of the gentile church? (16) Is it certain that Peter anticipated Paul in preaching to gentiles? (17) How did his preaching in the home of Cornelius influence the work of Paul in later years? (18) Sum up the whole significance of this incident for the development of early Christianity.

§ 56. **Supplementary Topics for Study and References to Literature.**

1. Write a chapter on Peter's visit to Cornelius, showing how he was led to it step by step, how his mind was prepared for it, how wondrously successful his visit was, and how he defended his act in Jerusalem.

2. Locate Lydda, Joppa, and Cæsarea, describing the roads which connected them with Jerusalem.

See Smith's *Historical Geography of the Holy Land.*

3. On the origin and nature of the traditional law read:

Schürer, *The Jewish People*, etc., Div. 2, Vol. I, pp. 330–39.

4. For the view that Luke is wholly responsible for Acts 11:3 see McGiffert, *The Apostolic Age*, pp. 105, 106.

CHAPTER IX

THE EARLY DAYS OF THE CHURCH IN ANTIOCH AND CONTEMPORARY EVENTS IN JERUSALEM

SYNOPSIS

§ 57. The Beginning of the Gospel in Antioch.

1) *The city.*—The mother-church of the gentiles was founded in Antioch, the royal city of the Syrian kings from the time of Antiochus IV, situated on the Orontes River, at the northeast corner of the Mediterranean Sea, about sixteen miles from the coast and a little more than two hundred miles north from Jerusalem. It was rated by Josephus as the third city in the Empire, Rome and Alexandria probably being the two cities which he put before it (*Jewish War*, 3. 2. 4). Strabo reckoned it as the fourth, placing above it, not only Rome and Alexandria, but also Seleucia on the Tigris. It was a free city, and the residence of the governor of the province. What its population was in the year 44 A. D., when Paul and Barnabas were laboring there, we can only conjecture. According to the book of Maccabees the gentiles of the city raised an army of 125,000 against Demetrius (†150 B. C.), but this was nearly two centuries before the introduction of the gospel. If it ranked next to Rome and Alexandria in the time of Josephus, its population may have numbered a million. There was a large Jewish element in Antioch, who from the ancient days of Seleucus I (†280 B. C.) had possessed the rights of citizenship and had enjoyed special immunities. Their synagogue was second only to that of Alexandria, and had among its ornaments votive gifts of brass which Antiochus Epiphanes (†164 B. C.) had taken from the temple in Jerusalem. Josephus tells us (*Jewish War*, 7. 3. 3) that large numbers of the Greeks in Antioch were always attached to the synagogue as proselytes, a fact important for the beginning of Christian work in the city.

ANTIOCH IN SYRIA

2) *The founding of the church in Antioch.*—There were two stages in the evangelistic work that resulted in the establishment of the mother-church of the gentiles. The first preachers who reached the city spoke the word to the Jews only (Acts 11:19), being themselves, it is not unlikely, Jews of Palestine. A little later there came Hellenists, men of Cyprus and Cyrene, who were of the liberal type of Barnabas and Stephen and Philip; and these men, moved by the Spirit of God, took the historic step of proclaiming the Lord Jesus to the Greeks.[1] This step was doubtless objectionable to some, at least, of the Jewish believers, and it may well have been through these that the new departure was first made known to the church in Jerusalem. In consequence of this report Barnabas was sent to Antioch, where he continued in acceptable and fruitful labor for more than a year (Acts 11:23, 26). During most of this time he was aided by Paul, whom he had sought out and brought from his mission field somewhere in Cilicia or Syria, perhaps from Tarsus (Acts 11:25, 26).

This narrative regarding the foundation and early history of the church in Antioch has been said to be altogether unhistorical (cf., e. g., Weizsäcker, *The Apostolic Age*, Vol. I, pp. 104–10). "No single detail is possible." The account which Paul himself gives of his relation to the church in Jerusalem excludes, we are told, the possibility that he came to Antioch as the helper of Barnabas, who had been sent out from Jerusalem as the official superintendent of the new work. Now if Barnabas had been sent forth as the official director of the work in Antioch, and if he had been recognized and received as such by the church there, then, indeed, the statement of Paul's relation to the establishment of the Antioch church might have occasioned surprise, inasmuch as he declared some years later that he had been quite independent of the original apostles (Gal. 2). We can not, however, assume that Barnabas, a man of like mind with Paul in regard to the right of preaching the gospel directly to the gentiles, was sent out by the church in Jerusalem to guide the Antioch movement in the interest of Jewish Christianity. If that had been the purpose of the church, which Acts does not at all indicate, then their choice of Barnabas certainly defeated their purpose. Moreover, there is no trace whatever that the church in Antioch recognized Barnabas as having any official authority to modify its development in any particular. That church had been founded independently of the apostles, and it had not sent to them for their sanction of what had been done, or to ask for guidance. And Luke does not say that Barnabas *approved* of the work, as

[1] The internal evidence of Acts 11:19–26 seems to prove that the author had Greeks in mind even though he may have used the word "Hellenists," which some MSS. have.

though he was in a sense *over* it; he only says that Barnabas, being full of the Spirit and of faith, was glad of what had been done, and lent himself heartily to the furtherance of the work.

The church in Jerusalem undoubtedly looked with distrust and hesitation upon the free offer of Jesus to the gentiles. This is the teaching both of Paul and of Acts. There had been, prior to the work in Antioch, but one instance of preaching to gentiles, and that seems to have been regarded as exceptional. Even Peter himself had not continued in the field which had been providentially opened to him. In these circumstances the Jerusalem church was naturally solicitous regarding the work in Antioch, and in its solicitude it sent Barnabas thither. The exact purpose of this step is not suggested by Luke, but his narrative does appear to *exclude* the view that the purpose was to control the work in Antioch, to shut the door of the church to the gentiles, or to admit them only by the way of Judaism.

There remains, therefore, no ground for rejecting the statement that Paul came to Antioch at the request of Barnabas and labored with him there for a year, teaching and building up the church. His principle that he would not build on another man's foundation was by no means a declaration that he would not co-operate with others in Christian work, or that he would in no circumstances carry on what another had begun. In Corinth, it is true, he planted and Apollos watered; but in Rome someone else planted and *he* watered. By the very letter in which the words occur (Romans) he was building on a foundation which he had not laid. And we may be sure that the work in Antioch, inaugurated by Hellenists like himself, a work among gentiles like that which he was doing, would have appealed to Paul, and especially as it asked his help by the mouth of his old friend Barnabas.

3) *The name "Christian."*—It is inherently probable that, as Luke says, the name "Christian" arose in Antioch with the first general preaching to the gentiles. He indicates that the name originated outside the church when he says that the disciples *were called* Christians. They called themselves "brethren" and "disciples;" the new name was not of their own coinage. It is likely that it originated with the gentiles, for the Jews did not admit that the disciples of Jesus were followers of the true Messiah or Christ; and so if they had called them Christians they would have appeared to admit what they did not believe.

Since it is natural to call disciples by the name of their master, there is no ground to think that the name "Christian" was given in derision.

§ 58. **Relief Sent from Antioch to the Brethren in Judea.**—While Paul and Barnabas were laboring in Antioch certain "prophets" came down from Jerusalem, one of whom, Agabus by name, signified that there would be a great famine over all the world. This prophecy, which, according to Luke, was fulfilled in the days of Claudius (41–54 A. D.), stirred up the Christians of Antioch to prepare to aid their fellow-believers in Judea, and when the collection was ready, it was given into the hands of Paul and Barnabas to be conveyed to its destination.

Although the proper function of the Christian prophet was not to foretell coming events, there is no reason to doubt that such power was sometimes exercised by them, and there appears to be no good ground to think that Paul would have refused to serve his brethren in the distribution of their gift. Yet both the statement that Paul visited Jerusalem at this time and the other that there was a famine over all the world in the days of Claudius are somewhat difficult. First, regarding the famine. Though Josephus tells of a famine in Judea in the period 44–48 A. D. (*Antiq.*, 20.2.5; 5.2; 3.15.3), and though there is evidence of other local famines during the reign of Claudius (cf. Schürer, *The Jewish People*, etc., Div. 1, Vol. II, pp. 169, 170), there is no evidence of a universal famine, that is, universal in the Roman Empire. Moreover, it is improbable that Agabus, who, as a Christian, was concerned with the kingdom of God and with the world only as it was related to that kingdom, prophesied a universal famine. Had he announced such a famine, the disciples of Antioch must have been concerned to lay up money and food for their own need, of which, however, there is no trace. It is to be held, therefore, that Agabus foretold a famine for Judea, and that the language of Acts shows the influence of the fact that the reign of Claudius was marked by an unusual number of famines in different parts of the Empire.

In regard to Paul's visit in Jerusalem at this time, the narrative seems, indeed, to be at variance with the letter of Paul to the Galatians, for while he there mentions various visits in Jerusalem, he does not mention this. Now Paul is, of course, our final authority on the events of his own life, and if it is plain that he was under obligation to mention all the visits that he made to Jerusalem before the time of the council, then we can not accept the narrative of Luke. But was he under such an obligation to his readers in Galatia? What was the point on which he was insisting in his letter? Nothing else than the independence of his apostleship (see, e. g., Gal. 1:1, 12). He was under obligation to mention all facts which might fairly be said to involve dependence or independence in his relation to the elder apostles. Beyond this his visits to Jerusalem had no bearing on the point in discussion, and hence we have no right to assume that he enumerates *all* his visits in the letter to the Galatians. What the argument requires is that he there mentions all his interviews with the Jerusalem apostles. But plainly he may have gone to Jerusalem in 44 A. D.—that year in which one apostle was beheaded and another, the leader, thrown into prison--and may not have seen any of the twelve, to say nothing of having come into such relation to any of them that he would feel obliged to mention the visit in his letter to the Galatians. Such we consider to have been the case.

§ 59. **The Persecution of Disciples in Jerusalem by Agrippa I.**—Herod Agrippa I was a grandson of Herod the Great, and as he was 54 years old at his death in A. D. 44 (cf. *Antiq.*, 18. 8. 2), he was born 10 B. C. Shortly before the death of Herod the Great, and so about the time of the birth of Jesus, he was sent to Rome to be educated, and there he passed more than two-thirds of his life. Soon after the death of Tiberius (37 A. D.), Agrippa was given the tetrarchies of Philip and Lysanias; in 39 or 40 A. D., the tetrarchy of Antipas was added; and in 41 A. D. Claudius gave him Judea and Samaria. From that time to his death he ruled over the same territory which his grandfather had possessed.

According to Josephus, Agrippa was a man of unbounded generosity, and in consequence was habitually in debt. When he was made king and lived in Palestine, he was scrupulous in his observance of the religious rites and customs of pharisaic Judaism. He was so good a Pharisee—probably from political policy rather than conviction, for among gentiles he lived as a gentile—that he was an enemy of the Christians. But just when he had begun to persecute, sudden death overtook him at Cæsarea. The account which Josephus (*Antiq.*, 19. 8. 2) gives of the manner of Agrippa's death agrees in substance with that of Luke. Both writers regarded his death as a just judgment of heaven because he had not rejected the impious flattery that was paid him by the people.

In the persecution that arose at Stephen's death the leaders escaped, but when Agrippa put forth his hand it was against the apostles themselves. James he killed, and Peter was destined to the same fate. He was put in prison, and was supposed to be securely guarded. When Agrippa was informed of Peter's escape, he examined the guards, apparently the entire sixteen, and commanded that they should be put to death. The natural inference from this procedure is that the king was satisfied that the guards had been criminally remiss in their duty. If we knew what information his examination of the guards elicited, we might perhaps form a better idea of the character of Peter's deliverance. But even if it was shown that one or more of the guards were friendly to Peter and had secured his escape, his deliverance was still an event for which the church did well to thank God.

The details of Luke's narrative in vss. 7–10 must be considered in the light of the significant statement in vs. 11. Here we have the same language that is used to describe Peter's restoration from the trance into which he fell on the house-top in Joppa. It is said that he "came to himself" after he had passed the iron gate. This implies that what had gone before was all as a dream to him. He could not explain it. How his deliverance had actually taken place he apparently did not know. What he knew was that he had been delivered from prison, and he saw in this the good hand of the Lord.

After Peter had reported his deliverance from prison to his brethren who were gathered in the house of Mary, the mother of Mark, he departed, doubtless in the same night, to some place unknown to Luke, unknown also, it may be, to the friends of whom he took leave. The death of Agrippa which occurred soon after this event, and the establishment of a Roman procuratorship, doubtless made it safe for Peter to return to Jerusalem.

§ 60. **Questions and Suggestions for Study.**—(1) What was the mother-church of gentile Christianity? (2) Describe the location of Antioch and its rank in the Roman Empire. (3) What do we know about the Jews and proselytes in Antioch? (4) What was the relation of Barnabas to the work in Antioch? (5) What was Paul's relation to this work? (6) What year did they work together in Antioch? (7) By whom was the name "Christian" given? (8) By what names did Christians call themselves?

(9) What prophet came to Antioch while Paul and Barnabas were laboring there? (10) What was the result of his visit? (11) What reasons are there for thinking that he foretold a famine in Judea alone? (12) Does the mission of Paul to Jerusalem at this time conflict with what Paul says in Galatians?

(13) Who was Herod Agrippa I? (14) Where did he spend the larger part of his life? (15) What territory did he receive from Caligula, and what from Claudius? (16) How long did he rule over all Palestine? (17) What was his attitude toward the Jewish religion? (18) How do the accounts of Josephus and Luke agree in regard to the death of Agrippa? (19) Why did Agrippa put the guards of Peter to death? (20) What is the suggestion of vs. 11 in regard to Peter's own knowledge of his deliverance?

(21) James was killed, Peter escaped and saved his life: does this show that one was under God's protecting care and the other was not? In what sense can we adopt as our own the language of Ps. 91?

§ 61. **Supplementary Topics for Study and References to Literature.**

1. Write out in your own language the story of the founding of the first gentile Christian church. The following outline may be used: The royal city of Syria; the men who first preached Jesus in that city; the work of Paul and Barnabas there.

2. Write a brief account of Herod Agrippa I.

3. On Antioch read:

Conybeare and Howson, *Life and Epistles of St. Paul*, 1:4; Josephus, *Antiq.*, 12.3.1; *Jewish War*, 3.3.4; 7.3.3; and 1 Maccabees 11:41–51.

4. Read and compare Acts 12:21–23 and Josephus, *Antiq.*, 19. 8.2.

CHAPTER X

THE LIFE OF CERTAIN JEWISH-CHRISTIAN CHURCHES IN THE DISPERSION AS REFLECTED IN JAMES AND 1 PETER[1]

SYNOPSIS

§ 62. **Of the origin of James and 1 Peter**
§ 63. **Of the new faith among the readers of James**
§ 64. **Of the new faith among the readers of 1 Peter**

We leave now for a little time the narrative of Acts and the outline of events contained in the letters of Paul, and seek what light the epistles of James and 1 Peter have to throw on the life of the early church. Paul disappears from our sight for the present, as do also the localities with which our history has thus far been associated. We come into a new atmosphere, if not into a wholly new geographical environment. But before searching these letters for information regarding the church of their time we must take a brief survey of the documents themselves, their probable authors, readers, and dates of composition.

§ 62. Of the Origin of James and 1 Peter.

1) *The conflict of present opinions.*—Regarding the authorship, the date of composition, and the fundamental religious character of these two letters, as also in regard to the nationality of their readers, there is still among scholars a wide diversity of views. Thus, e. g., it is said that James was a pre-Christian Jewish writing with a thin Christian veneer (Spitta, Massebieau), or that it was a Christian writing from the early part of the second century, closely related to Clement of Rome and Hermas (Harnack, Jülicher, von Soden); that it was addressed to Jewish-Christians of the Dispersion (Weiss), or that it was addressed to the Christian world at a time when the Jewish element was no longer of any account (von Soden); that it is a true letter (Weiss), or that it is a formless compilation of didactic fragments, prophecies, and words of judgment (Harnack).

In like manner there is a notable disagreement regarding 1 Peter. One regards the letter as dependent on James (Davidson), another makes James

[1] This volume makes use of the letters of the New Testament so far as they contribute to the history of the period. It does not aim to set forth their doctrinal content. Neither does it enter the field of New Testament introduction except in the case of documents regarding which there is no general consensus of scholars.

fifty years later (Harnack); it is said that it was written to Jewish Christians (Weiss), or to gentiles (Holtzmann, H. J.); that it was written by Peter (Bacon), or Silvanus (von Soden), or Barnabas (McGiffert), or perhaps Silas (Holtzmann). It is held that if we leave out the first verse, it would be easier to hold Paul for the author than Peter (Harnack). It is said to have been written in the time of Domitian (von Soden), or possibly twenty-five years earlier (Harnack), or in the year 50 (Weiss).

Of the two writings, the uncertainty of critics regarding the origin of James is greater than it is regarding the origin of 1 Peter, though even 1 Peter is a good deal tossed about as we have just shown.

2) *The author of James.*—No hypothesis regarding the authorship of this letter appears to be so free from objections as that which ascribes it to James, the leader of the Jerusalem church (Acts 12:17; 15:13; Gal. 2:9). This James appears to have been highly esteemed by the Jews (cf. Josephus, *Antiq.*, 20.9.1), for when Ananus, the highpriest, caused him, with others, to be stoned, the indignation of the best citizens was so great that Ananus lost his highpriesthood. This James, by virtue of his position in the mother-church and his relation to Jesus, could speak to the Jewish believers of the Dispersion, even to those who were not Christians, and be sure of a hearing.

It seems to some utterly improbable that this Jew can have been the master of a fine Greek style, such as that of the letter, but even if this be granted, it in no wise precludes his virtual authorship. He doubtless had friends who were masters of Greek, if he was not.

The fact that the letter says so little of Jesus, so little of the fatherhood of God and the kingdom of heaven, can not be regarded as at all conclusive against its authorship by James. For the little that it does say is exactly what we should expect. It conceives of Jesus as the Messiah, the author of the Christian faith, whose word is the law of liberty, and whose future coming is the goal of Christian hope (2:1, 7; 5:7, 8; 1:25). Moreover, it has numerous echoes of the Sermon on the Mount. Its representation of Christianity as the culmination of the Old Testament religion is surely in accord with the view that it was written by the brother of Jesus. The letter thinks of God as the holy Father, unchangeable in goodness, who gives liberally to all who ask, and who looks on a man's life rather than his profession. The kingdom of heaven is for those who are rich in faith. Now these views surely belong to primitive Christianity, and therefore we should not lay too great emphasis on the fact that they are not more prominent in the letter. It is not how often a man says a thing, but rather what he says and the way in which he says it, that enables us to judge of his position.

The worldliness ascribed to the readers of the letter has been regarded as an argument that it can not have been written by James, but must have originated much later. But this argument does not appear to be very conclusive. The worldliness of certain members of the church at Corinth was quite as pronounced as that which James contemplated, yet we know that the letter was written between 50 and 60 A. D. Practical immorality, such as the letter of James deals with, is notoriously a plant of speedy development.

3) *The author of 1 Peter.*—The opposition to the genuineness of this writing is less forcible than that which is urged against the genuineness of James. We will note the chief points. One is that the letter was written in Greek, while Papias (first half of the second century) tells us that Peter had Mark as an interpreter. This is true, but Papias does not say in what language Mark served as an interpreter. It may have been Latin; but even if it had been Greek, that is no reason why the letter should not be Peter's. Were not the sermons which Peter preached through Mark Peter's own sermons? Would the letter be less truly his own, in its thought, if he had help as to its Greek form?

Again, it is said that the author, seeing that he was a genuine Paulinist, can not have been the apostle Peter, for he surely did not go to school to Paul. But is it quite sure that he was a Paulinist? The points of agreement in thought and language between his letter and the letters of Paul[1] appear altogether natural when it is remembered that both Peter and Paul were eminent Christian disciples who were alike competent to interpret and apply the gospel to the needs of men, and when it is also remembered that they lived and worked at the same time. It would be a remarkable phenomenon if their letters to Christian disciples revealed no points of close similarity when dealing with the common themes of faith and life. Paul speaks of the living sacrifice of the bodies of believers as a reasonable or spiritual service. Now when Peter speaks of Christian teaching as reasonable or spiritual milk, and a little later speaks of offering spiritual sacrifice, must we conclude that he was borrowing from Paul?

And it is but fair to remember that while there are points of similarity between 1 Peter and the letters of Paul, there are also fundamental differences. Thus, e. g., Paul's doctrine of Christ is in some points widely unlike that of 1 Peter, and Peter's references to the life, the sufferings, the resurrection, and the future revelation of the Lord are far more conspicuous than Paul's references to the same subjects. This line of argument, therefore, does not appear to be strong enough to endanger the claim of Petrine authorship.

4) *The readers of the letters.*—The address of the letter of James is as broad as the Dispersion, that of 1 Peter is limited to five provinces in what we now call Asia Minor. It is not improbable, however, that the letter of James, though general in its address, took special account of the condition of Jewish believers in Syria and in the provinces which are named in 1 Peter, for it appears to have been in this quarter of the Roman Empire that the gospel first took vigorous root among the Jews. To declare that these addresses are spurious is as arbitrary as to say that their characterization of the readers must be taken figuratively. The address of James, in so far as it points to Jewish readers, is in accord

[1] Holtzmann, *Einleitung*, p. 518, gives the following as the strongest parallels: Rom. 12:1 with 1 Pet. 2:2, 5; 12:2 with 1:14; 12:3–8 with 4:10, 11; 12:13 with 4:9; 12:9 with 4:8; 12:17 with 3:9; 13:5 with 2:19; 13:12 with 2:1; 13:13 with 4:3.

with the letter throughout, which nowhere presupposes that its readers are gentiles. The address of 1 Peter is objected to simply because it contains the name of Peter, not because it is inconsistent with the letter.

The only serious objection to the view that both letters are addressed to Jewish believers outside of Palestine is the fact that we have no certain knowledge of the existence of groups of such believers in the Dispersion. We must, however, remember the exceedingly fragmentary character of our knowledge of the earliest spread of Christianity. If there were Christian Jews in Damascus before the conversion of Paul (Acts 8:10, 13, 14), why may there not have been in Antioch of Syria, or in any of the great cities of Asia Minor, in all of which there were numerous Jews? There is nothing in the account of Paul's work in the cities of Asia Minor which precludes the possibility that there were Jewish Christians in that part of the world.

5) *Dates of composition.*—James, "the righteous," was stoned in Jerusalem in 62 A. D., and Peter, according to very ancient tradition, perished in Rome during the Neronian persecution, 62–64 A. D. If, then, these men wrote the letters in question, we have one limit of the period in which they must have written them. There are, moreover, certain points in the letters which seem to favor a date considerably earlier than 62 A. D. Thus, in James, it is assumed that the Jewish believers addressed still met in the synagogue (2:2), though they had their own organization as a church with elders (5:14). Now, in view of the experience of believers in Jerusalem and the history of Paul's missionary work, this fact regarding a common use of the synagogues by believing and unbelieving Jews favors the period 40–50 A. D., rather than 50–60 A. D., as that in which the letter was written, assuming now, as we surely may (Acts 9, 10), that there were numerous converts among the Jews in the next decade after the resurrection, 30–40 A. D.

Again, the purely ethical character of the letter, the absence of any theological material even in regard to Jesus, favors an early date. This is a feature that allies the letter with the Sermon on the Mount. It furnishes no means of setting an exact date for the composition, but it distinctly favors a relatively early date.

It is doubtful whether the method in which James treats the relation of faith to works can be regarded as helping to settle the date of composition of his letter. The misconception regarding faith which it presupposes is certainly as old as the time of the great prophets of the Old Testament (see, e. g., Is. 1:11–17). The apparent divergence of the thought of James from that of Paul is accounted for by the different aims of the two writers, and does not seem to imply a literary dependence of the former upon the latter.

In conclusion, a relatively early date for James is favored by the allusion to the anointing of the sick with oil and to the accompanying prayer of the elders, or of any fellow-believers (5:14, 16). For, on the one hand, it is plain that the elders are not thought of as an hieratic class, without whom healing was not possible. They are mentioned rather as the natural spiritual leaders of the Christian community, but it is also recognized that any believers can pray one for another, that they may be healed of their sicknesses. On the other hand, this passage points to a relatively early time, because the supernatural healing which was somewhat prominent in the first years of the Jerusalem church rapidly disappears as we leave those years behind. Later cases are sporadic in character. Hence the instruction of James, which is quite general, favors an early date.

In 1 Peter also there are some marks of time, indecisive, it is true, like those of James, and yet, when taken together, having an appreciable value. Thus, in the first place, as the readers are Jewish believers of the Dispersion in Asia Minor, and so, apparently the same, at least in part, as the readers of James, we may infer from the more favorable picture of them in 1 Peter that this letter was later than James, and that the condition of the readers had improved in the interval. It is to be recognized, however, that two men so widely unlike as Peter and James may have taken quite different views of the same people at one and the same time.

Again, the fact that both Silvanus and Mark were with Peter at the time of the composition of his letter may have some bearing on the question of date (1 Pet. 5:12, 13). We know that Silvanus was with Paul on his second missionary journey (49–51 A. D.), and that Mark accompanied him for a time on his first journey (Acts 15:38). Now, in view of the sharp censure which Paul directed against Peter in Antioch shortly after the council in Jerusalem (Gal. 2:11), though this censure may have been received by Peter in good part and may not have alienated him from his brother apostle, it may still be regarded as a little more probable that these fellow-workers of Paul were with Peter before that event in Antioch rather than after it.

Mention is to be made of one other point. Two of the five provinces in which the readers of 1 Peter dwelt belonged in Paul's missionary field, viz., Galatia and Asia. We know that soon after Paul's work in Galatia the question of the gentiles' relation to the law was hotly debated. Now the fact that the letter of Peter makes no allusion to this question appears to favor the view that it was not written while the question was at the front; for though the little circles of believers whom he addressed may have been distinct from the churches of Paul in those regions, they can hardly have continued long without being influenced by that which deeply stirred these churches; and therefore, assuming the genuineness of the letter, this fact points to a composition before Paul wrote to the Galatians.[1]

It is idle to attempt to fix the exact date of the composition of James or of 1 Peter, but the internal evidence appears to favor the early part of the fifth Christian decade for the composition of the former, and to put the latter before the composition of Galatians.

[1] This seems more probable than that the question ceased to be discussed before the death of Peter, so that he could have written even *after* the composition of Galatians without any allusion to it.

§ 63. **Of the New Faith among the Readers of James.**—Like the converts of Paul in Corinth (1 Cor. 1:26–29), the believers whom our letter contemplated were prevailingly "poor as to the world" (2:5), though not exclusively so (1:10). They were exposed to manifold trials (1:2), the chief of which were probably the oppression which they suffered from the rich (2:6; 5:4), their being dragged to the judgment seats (2:7), and the occasional death of one of their number (5:6). As it was their rich countrymen who cited them before the tribunals, and as it seems to have been at such times that they heard the name of Jesus blasphemed, we see plainly that what took place was a repetition of what had occurred in Jerusalem when Paul was ravaging the church (Acts 8:9; 26:11). The tribunals were Jewish, and it was attempted to make believers blaspheme the name of Jesus.

The ethical condition of the readers reveals various defects. There was hastiness of speech (1:19–21), there was a failure to act on the word of truth which they had heard (1:22–27), there were class distinctions (2:1–13), a tendency to sever faith from life (2:14–26), an inordinate ambition to shine as teachers (3:1–18), and, worst of all, a worldly spirit (4:1—5:11). Now these defects, especially the last, were obviously serious, and appropriately called forth serious words of rebuke and warning from James, but it is quite without warrant to represent the state of the readers as one of utter worldliness. The gravest of these defects were found in the Corinthian church, and yet others even worse.

But while there were serious moral defects among the readers of James, these must not be allowed to hide or obscure the virtues which also throve among them. It is not undeserving of notice that, while the letter speaks of the manifold trials of the readers, it does not intimate that any of them fell away from Christ because of these trials. On the contrary, it intimates that some of them endured martyrdom (5:6). Here then we see at least one bright beam of light across the picture. It is also to be noted that the author measured all defects by the ideal standard, and his ideal was so high that he declared a man's religion altogether vain who did not bridle his tongue and whose life did not accord with his profession. In view of these facts we may probably conclude that the readers of James were about the average Christians of their day, and not greatly unlike the average among us today.

The new faith appears in James as an ethical force rather than an elaborate doctrine. It furnished an ideal of moral perfection, which was thought of as the *consummation of the old law*, and it furnished a great motive in the future coming of the Lord. The fatherhood of God and the messiahship of Jesus are in the background of the letter, but they are there as fundamental facts. The fatherhood is universal as in the gospel, and Jesus is thought of as the one who has taught us to believe in God. Christian faith is called the faith of our Lord Jesus Christ, and this word, like Heb. 12:2, we understand to mean that the faith which Jesus exercised was the type of true Christian faith. Thus on these fundamental points, it is assumed that the position of the readers was that of primitive Christianity.

§ 64. **Of the New Faith among the Readers of 1 Peter.**—The message of 1 Peter, like that of James, is pre-eminently a message for those who suffer. The source of persecution was now no longer the Jewish fellow-countrymen of the readers, but it was the gentiles (2:12; 4:3; 4:16). The ground or grounds of gentile hostility at the time when Peter wrote are indicated by him only in the most general manner. It was charged against his readers that they were "evil-doers," and this broad accusation is somewhat illuminated by two passages. The first suggests that the special form of evil-doing of which Christians were said to be guilty was disregard for rulers (2:13–17), and the second has the somewhat different suggestion that they were hated and spoken evil of because they refused to walk in "lasciviousness, lusts, wine-bibbings, revelings, carousings, and abominable idolatries." This ground, if the last item be excepted, points to a social separation of the believers from former companions. The *animus* of the charge in this case was that the Christians by this separation of themselves from the practices and customs of others thereby tacitly condemned those practices and customs as evil. If by the "abominable idolatries" be meant an idolatrous regard for any earthly ruler, such as the worship of the images of the emperors on the coins, then this passage has to some extent a political color.

It is also thought possible by the author (4:14, 16) that some of the readers may be reproached for the name of Christ, that is, simply because they bear this name, whether a charge of evil-doing is brought against them or not. From this passage it has been inferred by some writers that the letter can not have been written in the time of Nero, and by others that it was written in the time of Domitian. But it seems plain that as soon as the name "Christian" was coined (44 A. D.), believers may have been persecuted as Christians. The mere use of that name does not define the origin and nature of a particular persecution. Furthermore, there is no suggestion in 1 Peter that the trials to which the readers were exposed were due to the policy of the reigning emperor, and we have no right to make such an assumption.

Now in their trials the readers were variously aided by the new faith. They were to consider that the very call to be Christians involved a call to suffering (2:21; cf. Matt. 10:16–39), and also that the endurance of suffering for righteousness' sake put them into the same class with Jesus (3:17, 18), made them partakers of his sufferings (4:13), and so made them heirs of the spirit of glory and of God (4:14). Special stress is laid on the significance of fellowship with Christ's sufferings. His example in all his sufferings is an example to be followed by his disciples, and following that example out of regard for Jesus and in his spirit one is delivered from sin.

Peter also encouraged his readers, as did James, with the thought that the end was at hand (4:7). After suffering a "little while," they would be perfected (5:10). Therefore they were to set their hope on the grace that was to be brought to them at the revelation of Jesus Christ (2:13).

Although the specific occasion of our letter was the trials to which the readers were exposed, we see into their life as Christians at another point which is worthy of notice. The letter assumes that there were "elders" among the readers in various places throughout the five provinces (5:1), though it does not refer to a church. These elders are described as the spiritual guides of the flock, who are to serve in love, having that authority which comes from a holy and attractive example. Bishops and deacons are not mentioned, neither is there allusion to meetings for worship. Peter assumes among his readers a knowledge of the life and death, the resurrection, and future coming of Jesus. He makes no allusion to any other source of this knowledge than the messengers who had brought to them the good tidings (1:12, 25). He also assumes, as does James, that his readers are familiar with the Old Testament.

§ 65. **Questions and Suggestions for Study.**—(1) How widely divergent are the current views regarding the origin of James and 1 Peter? (2) To what James are we to ascribe the letter of that name? (3) What is to be said of the objection that James can not have written elegant Greek? (4) What of the fact that the letter says little of Jesus, of the fatherhood of God, and of the kingdom of heaven? (5) Does the worldliness of the readers prove that the letter was written after the time of James? (6) Does the fact that Peter is said to have had an interpreter, while our 1 Peter was written in good Greek, prove that he was not the author of this letter? (7) What is to be said of the similarities between 1 Peter and the letters of Paul in their bearing on the authorship?

(8) To whom are James and 1 Peter respectively addressed? (9) What is the most serious objection to the view that both letters were written to Jewish believers of the Dispersion? (10) How is the objection to be met?

(11) When did James and Peter die? (12) What is there in the letter of James that points to a relatively early date? (13) What marks of time are found in 1 Peter?

(14) To what social class did the readers of James belong? Of what nationality were they? (15) To what trials were they exposed? (16) Who persecuted them? (17) What were the moral defects of the readers? (18) What virtues did they show? (19) What type of Christian doctrine is suggested by the scanty doctrinal references in the letter?

(20) Whence did persecution arise to the readers of 1 Peter? (21) Does the use of the name "Christian" indicate the source of the persecution? (22) With what considerations did the author seek to sustain the readers in their trials? (23) What conception of elders is found in the letter?

(24) To what extent are the teachings of James appropriate to Christians of the present day? Name specific examples.

(25) What teachings of 1 Peter impress you as of special value for men of today? (26) What impression do you gain from these two letters as to the character of the Christians and the Christian life in the early apostolic age? (27) What does the reading of them suggest as to (*a*) the rate at which the Christian church is advancing from age to age; (*b*) our duty at this hour in reference to the progress of the church?

§ 66. **Supplementary Topics and References to Literature.**

1. On the basis of a study of James write a short chapter on the life of the readers—their nationality, social position, trials, and Christian faith.

2. On the basis of a study of 1 Peter write a similar short chapter on the life of its readers.

3. Collect all the New Testament references to James the brother of Jesus, and add Josephus, *Antiq.*, 20. 9. 1.

4. On the use of Greek in Palestine in the first century see:

Schürer, *The Jewish People*, etc., Div. 2, Vol. I, p. 48.

PART III

THE PAULINE MISSION IN ASIA MINOR, MACEDONIA, AND GREECE

CHAPTER XI

PAUL'S FIRST MISSIONARY JOURNEY

SYNOPSIS

§ 67. **Barnabas and Paul Sent Forth from Antioch.**—When Barnabas and Paul returned from their mission to Jerusalem, whither they had gone with the offering from Antioch, they took with them John Mark (Acts 12:25), and in this fact we have a suggestion that they were already contemplating such missionary labor as that on which they soon entered. The work in Antioch had been thoroughly established, and it was natural that the thought of Paul should be turning to new fields. He felt that he was called to preach to the gentile world (Rom. 1:5), not merely to one city or one province.

The separation of Paul unto missionary work implies that, among the Christians in Antioch, no claim to apostleship had thus far been made by him. Had his fellow-laborers known that he considered himself an apostle and divinely ordained to work among the gentiles, it is hardly probable that they would have ventured to dedicate him to such work. Hence we must suppose that he had put forth no apostolic claim; doubtless there had been no occasion for it. The consciousness of apostleship was a secret of his own bosom, and we might never have heard about it from his own lips if his authority had not been attacked. There is no reason whatever to think that his dedication to missionary work had anything to do either with his claim to apostleship or with the bestowal of the title upon him.

Barnabas and Paul were set apart not by the church in Antioch, but by other prophets, viz., Symeon, Lucius, and Manæn. While these five men were fasting on a certain occasion, and perhaps contemplating their relation to the wide field, it was borne in upon Symeon, Lucius, and Manæn, by the Spirit, that Barnabas and Paul should be separated unto the work to which they had been "called," that is, as appears from what follows, evangelistic work in gentile lands.

There was a good preparation for such a spiritual communication in the successful work which these two had already done in Antioch, which was largely a work among gentiles. The fitness they had shown for this work may well have convinced their brethren, that God would have them especially dedicated to it. And therefore, inasmuch as Barnabas and Paul were ready to go, these brethren laid their hands upon them after fasting and prayer, and so sent them forth.

The dedication was solemn, as the work before them must have been recognized as one of great magnitude and responsibility, but it was in no sense an ecclesiastical ordination (see Hort, *Judaistic Christianity*, p. 63). It established no official relationship between Paul and the church in Antioch. He was not supported or directed by it. He was as independent in his future work as he had been before he came to Antioch to assist Barnabas. But since the church in Antioch was in part his own creation, since also it was centrally located and of great importance, it was natural that he returned thither again and again during the years of his missionary labor.

§ 68. **The Work in Cyprus.**—Barnabas was a native of Cyprus (Acts 4:37), and this fact may very likely have decided the missionaries to go first to that island, especially as in going thither they would be moving toward the great center of the Roman Empire. The gospel had already been preached in Cyprus to some extent (Acts 11:19), but how widely and with what success we do not know. Again, some of the men who had labored in Antioch before the arrival of Barnabas and Paul, and who had perhaps also labored with them, were Cypriote Jews, and hence there may have been among the Christians in Antioch a special acquaintance with the needs of Cyprus, which had something to do in determining the route of Barnabas and Paul.

The missionaries probably walked from Antioch to its harbor Seleucia, sixteen miles distant, and there they took a boat for Salamis, the eastern port of Cyprus, which lay about 140 miles to the southwest. John Mark whom they took with them as an assistant in some

PAPHOS

capacity which is not defined, was a cousin of Barnabas (Col. 4:10).

Beginning their work in Salamis, Barnabas and Paul went through the whole island to Paphos, a distance of about 100 miles. This was the chief city of the island, and the residence of the proconsul. Luke says that they preached in synagogues, but makes no reference to any contact with gentiles. This suggests what is confirmed also by other evidence, that though Paul recognized himself as a missionary to the gentiles, he yet judged it wise always to begin work with the Jews, at least in every city where there was a Jewish community. We hear a note out of his missionary experience when he says of the gospel that it is God's power unto salvation to everyone who believes, to the Jew *first* and also to the Greek.

The single incident of the entire tour which Luke preserves is the meeting of the missionaries with the Roman proconsul Sergius Paulus, who summoned them to his presence. They appear to have met Bar-Jesus the sorcerer, who was with the proconsul, before they had audience with Sergius Paulus himself (Acts 13:6), and it is possible that the proconsul heard of the missionaries through him. However that may be, when they sought to present their message to Sergius Paulus, the sorcerer, fearing that the newcomers might supplant him in the favor of the proconsul, withstood them. This aroused the spirit of Paul, who denounced Elymas, and who, according to the narrative, spoke words of judgment that were straightway fulfilled in the temporary blindness of the sorcerer. When the proconsul saw what was done, "he believed, being astonished at the teaching of the Lord."

His belief involuntarily reminds us of Simon the Samaritan. If the sorcerer was smitten with blindness at the word of Paul, the heathen procurator would naturally look upon Paul as a more powerful sorcerer. It seems probable, however, that the actual events have been somewhat obscured in transmission, perhaps were so obscured before Luke incorporated the story in his narrative. Smiting an opponent with physical blindness would have been an act without parallel either in Paul's experience or in that of any other apostle, though Peter had had even greater reason to call down judgment on Simon the Samaritan. The fate of Ananias and Sapphira was of quite a different order, as has been shown elsewhere. Moreover, it seems to be altogether contrary to the genius of the gospel to call in supernatural power for the overthrow of an antagonist. Jesus did not act in this wise, nor did he intimate that such a dangerous weapon might be wielded by his followers. He taught that when they should stand before governors and kings, they would have heavenly wisdom in utterance, not a power for destruction. Therefore it seems probable that the story of what took place in the presence of Sergius Paulus underwent modification as it was transmitted.

Luke changes the name of his hero at this point in his narrative. Before this he had called him *Saul* exclusively, and after this he calls him *Paul* exclusively. The reason of the change is not known. It is not unlikely that Paul had both names from childhood, in accord with a practice common among the Hellenists and not unknown among the Jews of Palestine (e. g., Acts 12:25), and that Luke introduced the Roman name at this point because Paul had now for the first time preached to a Roman official and had won him to discipleship. The work in Cyprus does not seem to have been attended with great success, for though Luke is in the habit of recording results, he is silent here.

§ 69. **In Pisidian Antioch.**—We do not know what determined the route which the missionaries pursued from Cyprus. Perhaps, for the first stage of their journey, it was nothing more than the presence of a ship bound for the coast of Pamphylia. The voyage from Paphos to Perga is one of about 175 miles. At Perga no work seems to have been done, but it was here that Mark turned back. The reasons which led to this step were regarded by Paul as showing a decided unfitness for further missionary service (Acts 15: 37–41).

The new stage in the journey of the missionaries was to Antioch in the highlands of Asia Minor, a distance of some 90 miles in a straight line from Perga, but much further than that by any traveled route. Antioch (modern Jalowadj), which Strabo describes as *near* Pisidia, was a Roman colony planted by Augustus, and consisted of veterans of the fifth Gallic legion. As a Roman colony it was not under the control of the governor of the province, but had its own senate and popular assembly.

Of the details of the work in Antioch we know little,[1] though the outcome of it is clear. The address attributed to Paul is obviously

[1] If the church in Antioch be regarded as one of the "Galatian" churches (Gal. 1:1), then we have a few details regarding the work there in the letter to the Galatians.

too short to be a verbatim report of what he said, and further, as a literary production, it points to Luke rather than to Paul. It is not, however, necessary to conclude that it is a free composition by Luke. The analogy of other addresses attributed to Paul is distinctly against this view. Since the thought of the address bears the stamp of Paul, we may hold that Luke worked with materials derived from a trustworthy source.

After the second Sabbath in Antioch, on which a great concourse of people was addressed, the majority of the Jews, moved by jealousy of this new faith which claimed to get on without the aid of Judaism, contradicted the missionaries and railed against them. This event was recognized by the missionaries as a signal that they should turn to the gentiles, which, accordingly, they did, laboring among them with such success that the word was spread abroad throughout the regions. The degree of their success may be inferred from the bitterness of the hostility of the Jews, who did not rest until they had driven the missionaries out of their borders. In this act they secured the co-operation of the chief men of the city, that is to say, the Roman officials; but on what ground the officials aided them we can only conjecture. The circumstance that there were prominent female proselytes engaged in the movement against Barnabas and Paul shows that, though the proselytes generally furnished a receptive soil for the gospel, they were not by any means all carried away from Judaism by the new faith.

§ 70. **In Iconium.**—What determined the course which the missionaries took when driven from Antioch is quite unknown. They went southeast about 80 miles to Iconium, which, according to the Roman organization, was in Lycaonia, but which Luke, by implication (Acts 14:6), seems not to have regarded as Lycaonian, but probably as a city of Phrygia. Iconium was an important city; and as it was created a Roman colony in the reign of Claudius, it may have enjoyed this distinction when Paul and Barnabas preached the gospel in its synagogue.

Luke's narrative makes the impression that the work in this city was even more successful than that in Antioch had been. Many Jews as well as Greeks believed, and this may explain why the missionaries were not driven out of the synagogue, and why for a long time they were able to speak boldly. It also shows how they may easily have become aware of the plan to stone them, and so were able to escape the wrath of their foes.

§ 71. **The Work in Lystra and Derbe, and the Return to Antioch in Syria.**—About eighteen miles southwest of Iconium, near the modern village of Khatyn Serai, recent investigators have located the ruins of Lystra (J. R. Sterrett, *Papers of the American School of Classical Studies in Athens*, Vol. III, p. 142; Ramsay, *The Church in the Roman Empire*, pp. 47–54), and sixteen miles to the southeast from Lystra, in the ruins of Bosola and Losta (Sterrett) or at Güdelissin (Ramsay), they have discovered, as they believe, the site of ancient Derbe.

There is no reference to a synagogue in Lystra or Derbe. The multitudes in Lystra, who were stirred up against Paul, were persuaded by Jews from Antioch and Iconium. This would indicate that the Jewish element in these towns was slight, if, indeed, there was any at all.

The first cure attributed to Paul in Acts is that of a cripple in Lystra, which appears to have been recorded by Luke because of its consequences. When the people saw what had been done, they concluded that Paul and Barnabas were gods, as the people of Melita argued, when Paul took no harm from the bite of the viper (Acts, 28:6). This was the pagan inference from a miracle, while the Jewish inference was that the one who wrought the miracle was a prophet (e. g., John 9:17). The Lycaonians identified Barnabas with Zeus, perhaps because the worship of Zeus was especially cultivated among them (Acts 14:13), and naturally identified Paul with Hermes, the interpreter and spokesman of Zeus. The cure of the cripple, inasmuch as it convinced the people that Paul and Barnabas were supernatural beings, was productive of evil rather than good, so far as the people themselves were concerned.

A strong light is thrown on the passionate opposition to Paul on the part of the Jews of Antioch and Iconium by the fact that they followed him to Lystra, and there, as they supposed, killed him. They stoned him and dragged him out of the city. How Barnabas escaped their fury we are not told. Though Paul had been stoned, he had received no mortal blow: he had only been stunned and after a time, his enemies having apparently departed, he recovered consciousness, and was able to go forth the next day to Derbe. Here the missionaries labored for a considerable time, and made many disciples. No reference is made to the presence of Jews or to any opposition to the preaching of the gospel. From Derbe and Lystra came two converts whom we find associated with Paul in later years—Gaius, from Derbe, and Timothy, from Lystra (Acts 16:1; 20:4).

Derbe was the only one of the four Asiatic cities in which Barnabas and Paul had labored from which they departed in peace. What led them to face the peril of a return through the cities where they had been persecuted, instead of going on homeward through the pass of the Taurus Mountains, we can not tell. The only suggestion of the text is that they had heard of trials to which their young converts were exposed (Acts 14:22), and that they hoped by visiting them to confirm their souls and to promote their growth. To this end they appointed two or more elders in each church. When they reached Perga on their return journey, they stopped for a time and preached, with what results Luke does not say. From Attalia, the port of Perga, they sailed direct to Antioch. Why they went back, instead of continuing at once their labors further west, whether it was to encourage the home church by the report of what had been accomplished among the gentiles, or to get rest, or because some rumor of the danger which threatened the church in Antioch had reached them, we do not know.

This journey of Barnabas and Paul was full of physical hardship, of mental and spiritual labor. It was a long journey for those days, covering perhaps 1,400 miles of land and water. It had occupied, on a conservative estimate, three years. The tangible results were at least four churches in important centers, and the evangelization of large adjacent regions. These churches, though having a Jewish element, were predominantly gentile, and, with the church at Antioch in Syria, measured the advance which Christianity had thus far made into the pagan world.

§ 72. **Questions and Suggestions for Study.**—(1) What suggests that Paul and Barnabas were contemplating a missionary tour when they returned from Jerusalem? (2) What indicates that Paul had made no claim to apostleship during his work in Antioch? (3) By whom and how were Paul and Barnabas set apart to the missionary work? (4) What was the nature of this dedication, and what sort of relation, if any, was established between the missionaries and the church in Antioch? (5) What circumstances may have led Barnabas and Paul to go to Cyprus? (6) Among whom, Jews or gentiles, did the missionaries labor in Salamis? (7) On what principle did Paul apparently proceed in approaching the gentiles? (8) What do you think of the wisdom of this principle? (9) Can you state it in general terms applicable today also? (10) Describe the journey from Antioch to Paphos. (11) Describe how the proconsul was led to believe. (12) What reasons are there for thinking that the actual events may have been obscured in transmission? (13) Why may Luke have changed the name of his hero after the event in Paphos?

(14) Locate Perga and give its distance from Paphos. (15) What did Paul think of Mark's return to Jerusalem? (16) Describe the journey from Paphos to Pisidian Antioch. (17) What was the political status of Antioch? (18) Why did the Jews of Antioch oppose Paul? (19) What was the result of the labors of Barnabas and Paul in Antioch?

(20) Locate and describe Iconium. (21) In what respect did the work differ from that in Antioch? (22) Where were Lystra and Derbe? (23) What and where was the first cure attributed to Paul in Acts? (24) What consequences did it have? (25) How was the persecution at length stirred up against Paul, and how did it result? (26) Describe the work in Derbe? (27) What may have led the missionaries to go back to the cities where they had been persecuted? (28) Why may they have returned to the Syrian Antioch? (29) Give a summary statement regarding the entire journey. (30) What characteristic did the missionaries manifest in their work on this tour?

§ 73. **Supplementary Topics for Study and References to Literature.**

1. Write a chapter on Paul's first missionary journey, having, perhaps, the following outline: Consecration to the work, companions, trials, and results, with a diagram showing the cities visited.

(2) On the practice of sorcery read:

Josephus, *Antiq.*, 8.2.5, and Ramsay, *St. Paul the Traveller and the Roman Citizen*, p. 78.

3. For the view that the churches of Galatia were in south Galatia see:

Weizsäcker, *The Apostolic Age*, Vol. I, pp. 270 ff.; for other views, Gilbert, *Student's Life of Paul,* Appendix III.

THE EMPEROR CLAUDIUS

CHAPTER XII

PAUL'S SECOND SOJOURN IN ANTIOCH AND THE CONFERENCE IN JERUSALEM

SYNOPSIS

§ 74.	**The "false brethren" or judaizers.**	**Acts 15:1; Gal. 2:3–5**
§ 75.	**The conference at Jerusalem.**	**Acts 15:2–29; Gal. 2:1–10**
§ 76.	**Report of the compromise to the church in Antioch.**	**Acts 15:30–35**
§ 77.	**Peter's visit to Antioch.**	**Gal. 2:11–21**

§ 74. **The "False Brethren" or Judaizers.**—When Paul and Barnabas, after an absence of some three years, returned to Antioch, they found [1] the church agitated over the question of the relation of gentile believers to the law of Moses. This agitation had been brought on by certain legalists from Jerusalem, who, when they had spied out the liberty which gentiles had in Christ Jesus, declared that the observance of the law was necessary to salvation. There were undoubtedly some facts to which they as followers of Jesus could appeal with a show of reason. Thus they could say that he had never abrogated the law for his disciples, but, on the contrary, had spoken words that seemed to involve its perpetual observance. They could also point to his performance of various ceremonies and to the uniform practice of his apostles and of the mother-church in Jerusalem. All this appeared to favor the view that the gentile converts could not ignore the Jewish law. If anyone had cited the case of Cornelius and his friends, whom Peter had received without subjecting them to the yoke of the law, the judaizers might have replied that this was an exception, and only justified by the supernatural vision.

[1] The imperfect ἐδίδασκον, *taught*, in Acts 15:1 may be regarded as contemporary with the imperfect in 14:28, in which case the judaizers may not have anticipated Paul and Barnabas in reaching Antioch. It seems better, however, to define it by reference to the return of the missionaries, and to understand that they were engaged in such teaching, when Paul and Barnabas arrived; for if they had been on the ground with their story of God's wonderful work among the gentiles, it is doubtful whether the judaizers could have made any deep impression on the church.

These men from Jerusalem must have presented their view with great ability, else they could not have gained a favorable hearing from gentile Christians who had been nurtured in the freedom of Christ. It was inevitable that Paul and Barnabas should at once oppose this doctrine of servitude to the law, and natural that the church thought of a conference with the apostles and elders regarding the matter. The appointment of Barnabas and Paul as leaders of the committee to visit Jerusalem indicates how the majority of the church looked at the proposition of the judaizers.

§ 75. **The Conference at Jerusalem.**—The word "council," often applied to the gathering in Jerusalem, is objectionable in so far as it suggests an ecclesiastical body with power to legislate. The gathering was simply a friendly conference of a younger church with an elder one. And the younger church acted on its own initiative: it was not *summoned* to appear at Jerusalem, by delegates, for the settlement of the question in dispute. It did not assume that the church in Jerusalem had any other authority than such as belonged to the wisdom and the experience of its individual members.

The real question at issue was whether the statutes of the Old Testament law were of permanent and universal authority, a part of the will of God for all men and all time, and so a vital part of Christianity. The precise question in which this great problem took form at the moment was whether gentile Christians must be circumcised.

The conference in Jerusalem was important for the immediate future. Paul himself recognized this for he said that he laid his gospel before the leaders in Jerusalem, "lest by any means I should be running or had run in vain" (Gal. 2:2). These words indicate that he deeply desired the approval of the leaders of the Jerusalem church, fearing that their opposition might hinder the accomplishment of that which he had in view. At the same time he emphatically declared that those leaders "imparted nothing to him," that is, gave him no new authority or in any wise altered his relation to the gentile mission.

We have two accounts that treat of the conference in whole or in part, viz., Acts 15 and Gal. 2:1-10. In his letter to the Galatians Paul speaks of a private meeting with the leaders of the church, and of no other. At this conference his work was recognized as no less divinely appointed than that of Peter, and he received the right hand of fellowship from James and the two foremost apostles. Paul tells us that his work was recognized by these men because they saw that it had manifestly been owned of God—the same argument that prevailed when Peter's course in Cæsarea was called in question. As an illustration of his gentile mission, he had taken Titus along with him to Jerusalem, somewhat as Peter, at an earlier day, had taken his friends from Joppa, who could testify that the Spirit had been poured out upon the Gentiles who heard the gospel in the house of Cornelius. As God had manifestly accepted Titus, though uncircumcised, Paul could maintain that he should not now be circumcised to gratify the advocates of the law.

In Acts, we hear nothing of a private meeting or of Titus, but only of a public gathering at which, after the Pharisaic believers had been heard and Peter had spoken, Barnabas and Paul rehearsed what signs and wonders God had wrought through them, and James brought the discussion to a close with a proposition acceptable to the whole church. That the matter was brought before the church as a whole, and not merely before the leaders in a private manner, and that the opponents of gentile freedom had an opportunity to speak, is surely probable, nor does such a meeting conflict with Galatians. A private conference with the apostles and elders may well have preceded the general gathering. The words ascribed to Peter and James at this gathering accord with all that we know about the men. Peter was the first to speak, and he appealed to his experience in the home of the gentile Cornelius. James, whom Paul mentions as the first of the three "pillars" of the mother-church, appropriately closed the discussion. The proposition attributed to him in Acts suits what we know of his religious position. It included three or four of the seven so-called Noachian prohibitions, whose observance by gentiles was a condition of intercourse between them and Jews (Schürer, *The Jewish People*, etc., Div. 2, Vol. II, p. 318). These prohibitions are (1) to abstain from pollutions of idols, such as eating sacrificial meat; (2) to abstain from fornication, that is, probably from the intermarriage of near relatives; (3) to abstain from that which has been strangled; and (4) to abstain from blood.

The decision of the council was against the necessity of circumcision for the gentile Christians, and thus in effect in favor of Paul's contention that the law was not to be imposed upon gentile Christians. The prescriptions which gentile Christians were requested to observe were simply a basis of social intercourse with their fellow-believers of Jewish descent. Without some such regulations the new Christian faith would have been offensive in the eyes of the Jews. But they did not in any wise affect, nor were they claimed to affect, their standing before God. If these observances had been regarded as a stigma on gentile believers, it would hardly have been said in Acts that the church in Antioch "rejoiced for the consolation" (Acts 15:31). And it is plainly impossible to suppose that James, who, according to Galatians, had already endorsed Paul's work, went before the church and proposed a measure that put any dishonor upon the gentile believers.

Luke calls the terms of the document which was sent back to Antioch "decrees" (δόγματα) (Acts 16:4), but this must not be misunderstood. The prohibitions which James proposed were *necessary* if there was to be free fellowship between the gentile and the Jewish believers. Their observance by the gentiles was the price they must pay for this Christian fellowship. The measure, therefore, was a compromise. It is plain that it belonged in the sphere of the unessential, and that the liberty of the gentile believers in regard to the law of Moses was not lessened. The aim of the judaizers was completely repudiated by the mother-church. The "decrees" did not touch the specific question which the church in Antioch had brought to Jerusalem. That question was answered in the right hand of fellowship which the leaders gave to Barnabas and Paul. The decrees were simply in the interest of fellowship.

§ 76. **Report of the Conference to the Church of Antioch.**—The proposition of James was embodied in a letter and sent to Antioch by the hand of Judas and Silas with Barnabas and Paul. The church in Antioch, presumably Jews as well as gentiles, "rejoiced for the consolation." They were glad that their position was approved by the elder church. There is no indication that the gentiles considered it a hardship to comply with the terms of the letter regarding fellowship.

According to Luke, this letter was intended for gentile Christians in Syria and Cilicia as well as for those in Antioch, and he says that when Paul and Silas went through those parts on the second missionary journey, they delivered it to the churches (Acts 15:23; 16:4). It is to be observed, however, that Paul never referred to it in any letter, and never gave his gentile converts instructions similar to those of the decree. On the contrary, he told the Corinthians that they might eat meat that had been offered to idols, unless such an act were liable to cause a brother to stumble. Probably he took the same attitude toward the other prohibitions, which were all ceremonial in character. The fact that Paul never refers to the decrees in his letters may indicate that they did not prove to be of practical value. There was certainly nothing in them, however, which was not also involved in Paul's principle to become a Jew to the Jews.

§ 77. **Peter's Visit to Antioch.**—Having returned from Jerusalem to Antioch, Paul continued there for a time, perhaps to counteract the impression made by the judaizers and to promote the peaceful co-operation of gentiles and Jews with the church. During this time Peter visited Antioch, an indication that the gentile mission was a matter of great interest to Christians in Jerusalem. Peter found Jewish believers eating with gentile believers; and he did the same. This point had not been discussed at Jerusalem so far as our records inform us, and from the compromise adopted there it was possible to draw contrary inferences in regard to Jewish believers sitting at table with gentile disciples. One might, on the one hand, infer that the gentile's freedom from circumcision carried with it freedom from *all* the statutes of the law, and thus that a Jewish Christian was at liberty to eat at a gentile's table. But, on the other hand, one might insist that the letter of the compromise at Jerusalem was not to be transcended, at least not by Jews, that the gentile's release from the necessity of circumcision did not mean at the same time the Jew's release from his own ceremonial law.

It is plain from Peter's embarrassment and subsequent action that the decree had not been interpreted in Jerusalem to mean that the Jewish believers might *eat* with gentile Christians, that is, that all ceremonial distinction between them was done away. It is also plain that Paul had so interpreted it, for the Jews of the Antioch church were eating with the gentiles (Gal. 2:13). Peter, then, was placed in a difficult position by the arrival of believers from Jerusalem who held with James. If he continued eating with the gentiles, he would separate himself from his brethren in Jerusalem; if he withdrew from this form of fellowship, he would surely alienate some of his brethren in Antioch, though perhaps he did not anticipate the sharp reproof of Paul. In this situation Peter yielded to the pressure from Jerusalem, the pressure of all his past life, and retreated from the high position which his Christian feeling had led him to take. His example prevailed with the Jewish element of the church, and even Barnabas was moved to take the same stand. The unity of the Jewish-Christian body, which had been threatened by their recent liberal action, now weighed more in their estimation than the matter of perfect fellowship with the gentile believers.

Paul looked upon this step of Peter as a failure to walk according to the truth of the gospel, that is, as a serious moral fault; to him it meant in effect an attempt to compel the gentiles to live as did the Jews, and that justification by works of the law would take the place of justification by faith in Christ. In other words, Paul treated Peter's act as belonging to the sphere of fundamental principles. Peter, of course, had not considered it in this light. He probably had no desire to compel the gentiles to live as did the Jews, conforming to the law. Nor had he any thought of seeking justification save through faith in Christ. It was to him, doubtless, a question of Christian expediency, and nothing more.

What effect Paul's words had on Peter we do not know. There is no proof that they embittered him. Barnabas was in the same position as Peter, and he was not alienated from Paul by what he had said. But there can be no doubt that from this time the issue between gentile and Jewish Christianity was more sharply drawn. Paul had made his position clear, that no Christian believer, Jew or gentile, is under the law. If any one claimed that the decree of Jerusalem implied this, then it is plain that Paul must have rejected that decree. To him the question at issue was nothing less than that of the ultimate basis of religion. Is it physical or moral and spiritual? If Paul regarded the action of Peter and the view of those who came down from James as giving the authoritative interpretation which the apostles and elder brethren put upon the decree, it is certain that he did not deliver it to the churches which he had founded (Acts 16:4).

§ 78. **Questions and Suggestions for Study.**—(1) Who were the "false brethren"? (2) What show of reason had they for their position? (3) How did the church seek to settle the question? (4) What was the nature of the conference in Jerusalem? (5) Did Paul regard it as important? (6) What accounts have we of the conference? (7) What was the character of the meeting according to Galatians? What argument prevailed and what was the outcome? (8) What was the character of the meeting according to Acts, and who were the speakers? (9) What argument did Peter advance? (10) What was the proposition of James? (11) In what sense was it "necessary"? (12) Did it concern the fundamental question that had agitated the church of Antioch? (13) Where and how was that question answered?

(14) How was the letter of the Jerusalem conference received at Antioch? (15) When Peter came down to Antioch, what relation did he find subsisting between Jewish and gentile believers? (16) What did he do? (17) Was this consistent with the Jerusalem interpretation of the decree? (18) How is the act of Peter to be explained? (19) What effect did his example have? (20) In what light did Peter's step appear to Paul? (21) What effect did Paul's words have on Peter? (22) What was the nature of the real underlying issue in all this controversy? (23) Who saw most clearly what was involved in it? (24) Which side do you judge was really in the right? (25) How do you account for the difference between Peter and Paul on this point? Did they disagree fundamentally, or did one see more clearly than the other what was really involved in the discussion? (26) Paul stands forth in the narratives clearly defending the freedom of Christians from the statutes of the law and a purely spiritual idea of religion. Did Peter really disagree with this view, or only hold to it less consistently through lack of clear perception of what it involved? (27) Who were the real opponents of Paul's view?

§ 79. **Supplementary Topics for Study and References to Literature.**

1. Write a chapter on the trouble that arose in the church of Antioch in reference to the observance of the Jewish law, and how it was settled.

2. On the general subject of Paul's conflict with the judaizers read:

McGiffert, *The Apostolic Age*, pp. 192–234.

3. On the relation of Acts 11:27–30 and Acts 15 to Gal. 2 see:

Gilbert, *Student's Life of Paul*, pp. 86–94.

CHAPTER XIII

PAUL'S SECOND MISSIONARY JOURNEY

SYNOPSIS

§ 80. **The Discussion between Paul and Barnabas.**—When John Mark left Paul and Barnabas at Perga in Pamphylia, he returned to Jerusalem (Acts 13:13), but later, as appears from Acts 15:37, came to Antioch. What motive had brought him thither we do not know. It is possible that, when Barnabas was in Jerusalem at the conference, he suggested to Mark that he should hold himself in readiness for another missionary journey. At any rate, Mark was in the Syrian capital when Barnabas summoned Paul to revisit the churches which they had founded. Barnabas wished to take Mark, but Paul refused on account of his conduct on the former trip. The contention was so sharp that the old friends and co-laborers separated. Barnabas went to Cyprus, taking Mark; and Paul chose Silas as his companion, one of the two delegates from the Jerusalem church to the brethren in Antioch. But this alienation of Paul and Barnabas was not permanent, neither was Paul's feeling of antipathy toward Mark. In his letter to the church at Colossæ, he sent a salutation from Mark (Col. 4:10), and commended him by saying that he was a cousin of Barnabas. Thus the Colossians were assumed to be acquainted with Barnabas, which fact in turn suggests that Barnabas may have worked there, or in the immediate neighborhood. But in that case he was probably on friendly terms with Paul, for it was Paul who introduced the gospel into the province of Asia, in which Colossæ was located. Again the manner in which Paul refers to Barnabas in the first letter to the Corinthians (1 Cor. 9:6) is hardly consistent with the view that the disagreement over Mark led to permanent alienation.

§ 81. **The Churches in Southern Asia Minor Revisited.**—It is to be noted that when Paul left Antioch on what proved to be the second great missionary tour, there was no plan to enter new fields. His proposition to Barnabas was that they should visit the brethren in every city in which they had proclaimed the word of the Lord. In going through Syria and Cilicia he was on the ground where he had labored before he went to the help of Barnabas in Antioch in the year 44 A. D. (Gal. 2:21). Then, having crossed the Taurus Mountains, he came to Lystra and Derbe, probably also to Iconium and Antioch of Pisidia, though Luke does not mention these cities by name. If Paul delivered the "decrees" of the Jerusalem conference to the various churches which he visited in southern Asia Minor, as Luke reports, two things are certain: first, it is certain, in view of what had happened in Antioch on the occasion of Peter's visit, that he interpreted the decrees as placing no obstacle in the way of the Jewish and gentile believers eating together; and second, that he reported the more important part of the Jerusalem conference, viz., that the leaders of the mother-church had fully recognized his mission to the gentiles.

§ 82. **The Vision in Troas.**—When Paul had completed his tour of the churches, naturally at Antioch, he thought of going right on west into the Roman province of Asia, whose capital, Ephesus, was about 200 miles distant. But as he meditated on this course, he became convinced that it was not God's will that he should preach in Asia at that time. On what ground this conviction was based we have no means of determining. Then Paul and his two fellow-laborers—for he had taken Timothy from Lystra as he passed through that place (Acts 16:1–3)—turned to the northwest, and passed through some part of Phrygia and Galatia. Luke does not indicate that they made any stop in these regions. If the view be correct that the churches of Galatia (Gal. 1:2) were in the territory which was so-called because of its Gallic population, then it must have been on this trip that Paul founded them (Gal. 4:12–4). It is somewhat surprising that Luke, if he had knowledge of this work, did not mention it, and yet after all it is in keeping with the character of his narrative. For it is certain that he gives us only fragments and outlines. He does not mention the Arabian sojourn or the long work in Syria and Cilicia. The work in Galatia may have occupied but a few weeks, and Luke may have omitted any reference to it—assuming now that he knew of it—because it did not mark a forward step in the progress of the gospel toward the metropolis of the world.

From the letter to the Galatians it appears that Paul had not planned to preach in Galatia,[1] but was led to do so by an infirmity which detained him (Gal. 4:13), a statement which it is hard to harmonize with the view that the churches of Galatia were those of Antioch, Iconium, Lystra, and Derbe, for Luke's narrative of the founding of these not only makes no allusion to any sickness of Paul, but seems to exclude the possibility of any serious illness, and it also makes the impression that the tour was planned, at least in a general way. The Epistle to the Galatians informs us further that Paul had been received by the readers as an "angel of God, even as Christ Jesus," and it is a little difficult to see how he could have used such strong language in regard to his reception in Antioch, Iconium, Lystra, and Derbe. But we will not pursue the question further. Some references to the literature of the subject are given at the close of the chapter.

According to Luke, the second field which Paul sought to enter was Bithynia, a Roman province lying on the Black Sea. But again it was made plain to him that he was moving contrary to the divine will, and so he turned to the west. As Mysia, into which he now came, was a part of the province of Asia in which he had already been forbidden to preach, he passed by it, that is to say, he did not stop to labor there, but kept on to Troas. It appears, then, that at this time as he entered Mysia, if not before, Paul must have had

[1] At this period the term Galatia was used to designate either (*a*) a district in the center of the peninsula of Asia Minor, in which certain tribes of Gallic blood had long since settled and become the dominant element of the population, or (*b*) the Roman province of Galatia, which included the district above named and much additional territory on the south and southwest in which were cities visited by Paul on his first missionary tour. The question in which sense Paul uses the word Galatia is one on which scholars of repute are divided.

Europe in mind, for he knew that when he had once crossed Mysia he would arrive at the sea.

The vision which Paul had in Troas was unlike the supernatural intimations regarding his course which had recently come to him, for those had been negative in character but this was positive. What preparation there had been for the vision the narrative does not suggest. Paul may have become acquainted with a Macedonian in Troas, possibly with Luke himself,[1] who told him of the need in his country and of the wide opportunity for the gospel.

83. **The Work in Philippi.**—Paul's mind was thoroughly determined by the vision, and he lost no time in setting out for Macedonia, in particular for its chief city Philippi. He took ship to Neapolis, a distance of about 140 miles, which was reached the second day (cf. Acts 20:6), and then a walk of ten miles brought him to Philippi, the first Macedonian city as they went inland from Neapolis, and, according to Luke, the most important city of the province. It had been made a Roman colony by Augustus, 42 B. C.

The Jewish population in Philippi seems to have been small, as the narrative does not mention a synagogue, and as those who were gathered in the "place of prayer,"[2] to whom Paul spoke the word, were entirely women.

The first European convert was not a Macedonian, but a woman from Thyatira in the province of Asia. She appears to have been a person of some means, for she had a house or lodgings in which she entertained Paul and his three companions. How many others besides Lydia were led to faith in Jesus the narrative does not indicate. Paul's work continued for many days without interruption, and the converts, whether many or few, became the nucleus of a church of which Paul said a few years later that it was his joy and crown (Phil. 4:1). The mission of Paul was at length interrupted by gentiles whose business was thereby injured.

[1] The student will notice that with the tenth verse the narrative begins to use the first person. Thus we come here to the beginning of the diary which is ascribed to Luke.

[2] The term here used, προσευχή, might denote a building for worship (Josephus, *Vita*, 54), perhaps not different from a synagogue (Schürer, *The Jewish People*, etc., Div. 2, Vol. II, p. 69), but here it probably denotes a place in the open air.

A certain maid with a spirit of divination, who appears[1] to have been a slave, or, at any rate, to have sold her services, was much impressed by the missionaries and testified in public that they were servants of the most high God. She followed them, apparently to the place of prayer, and continued to do this for some days. We must assume that her motive in this procedure was friendly, and we can not suppose that what she said was in itself offensive to Paul. Only he was troubled that this testimony should come from one who was possessed by a spirit. The case was somewhat parallel to that of the demoniacs in the gospels who recognized the messiahship of Jesus. Paul treated it in the same way that Jesus treated the demoniacs, and summoned the spirit to come forth. His word was effectual, for the maid ceased from soothsaying. Judging from her previous attitude toward Paul and his message, it is not too much to suppose that she became a disciple.

When the owners of the maid were convinced that she had lost her power, they haled Paul and Silas before the magistrates (prætors) on the double charge that they were a disturbing element in the city and that they set forth customs unlawful for a Roman to observe—an appeal to the pride of the citizens of Philippi in those rights that belonged to them as citizens of a Roman "colony." The accusers did not fail to say that the missionaries were Jews, thus appealing to a widespread popular hatred. Their reference to customs unlawful for Romans was probably based on a misunderstanding of what Paul had said of Jesus as messiah and king.

As a mob had gathered and were clamoring against Paul and Silas, the magistrates, without waiting for any examination, commanded that they should be beaten with rods, and then cast them into prison. Perhaps this would have been prevented if Paul and Silas had declared their Roman citizenship (cf. Acts 22:25), but for some reason they did not do this.

The night spent in prison was full of remarkable incidents. The most significant of these for the history of Christianity was that the missionaries sang hymns of praise to God at midnight. The joy of

[1] Luke says that the spirit in her was a "python," a Greek designation of a ventriloquist. She had also the gift of soothsaying (μαντευομένη), hence was doubly endowed.

the new faith, the joy of serving Jesus and helping to build up his kingdom, made them unmindful of their cruel sufferings and found expression in loud hymns of praise. The occurrence of an earthquake in consequence of which the prison doors were opened and the bonds loosed which had been fastened in the walls, was regarded at that time as supernatural. At present, while we do not hesitate to say that the Lord delivered them out of prison, we may not think of the mode of deliverance as Luke and his generation did. The dramatic incident of the jailer's rescue from suicide and subsequent conversion illustrate both the quickness of Paul and the effectiveness of his preaching of the gospel.

It was probably an expression of the sober second thought of the magistrates that they sent in the morning to have the prisoners released. They knew that their hasty course had been unlawful, and when the pressure of the mob had been removed, they decided to set the prisoners at liberty. But the sergeants brought back word that the men were Roman citizens and that they insisted on being released by the magistrates in person. This was accordingly done, and the magistrates asked them to go away from the city. After a farewell meeting with the brethren in the house of Lydia they complied with this request.

Thus the work in the first European field, which had begun quietly in a little company of devout women, ended with violence and suffering, as had been the case in three out of the four Asiatic cities in which Paul had labored on his first missionary journey.

§ 84. **In Thessalonica.**—The narrative of Paul's movements as he left Philippi is continued in the third person, and therefore it may be held that the one who had joined him in Troas, who was the author of the "we-passages,"[1] remained in Philippi. Perhaps this was his home.

From Philippi the missionaries followed the Egnatian road a distance of 33 miles to Amphipolis, the capital of one of the four parts into which the Romans divided Macedonia. This was southwest of Philippi on the Strymon River about three miles from the Ægean Sea. A two days' walk from Amphipolis westward along the same

[1] A name applied to those parts of Acts in which the narrative is told in the first person.

GENERAL VIEW OF THE MODERN CITY OF THESSALONICA

great Roman highway brought them to Thessalonica. Why they passed through the centrally located and important city of Amphipolis and the town of Apollonia without preaching the gospel we are not told. It is possible that there was no Jewish colony in either city, and Paul, though he was the apostle of the gentiles, made it his rule to work outward from the synagogue through the proselytes.

Thessalonica, situated on the northeast side of the Thermaic Gulf, was at first the capital of the second division of Macedonia, and since the year 44 A. D. had been the seat of government of the entire province. It bore the title of metropolis, and was independent in its administration. Here there was a Jewish synagogue, a considerable Jewish population, and many proselytes from the better class of citizens. Hence it offered to the missionaries a favorable opening for their work. Luke says that they continued three weeks in the synagogue; and if we had no other references to the visit we should conclude that the riot which occasioned their departure came at the end of these three weeks. There are, however, certain facts that indicate a stay in Thessalonica of considerably more than three weeks. Thus we learn that Paul was there long enough for his condition to be reported in Philippi and for aid to be sent from that church on two separate occasions (Phil. 4:16). Again, in his first letter to the Thessalonians, he spoke of having worked day and night while among them, that is, worked for his own support that he might not burden them. But if he twice received aid from Philippi, it seems hardly probable that it would have been necessary for him to labor day and night unless he stayed more than three weeks in the place.

The result of Paul's labors in Thessalonica was, according to Acts, the conversion of some Jews and a "great multitude" of devout Greeks. The overwhelming predominance of the gentile element may have made it natural that, in his letters to the Thessalonians, Paul should address them as former gentiles, making no special reference to a Jewish element (1 Thess. 1:9).

It is not necessary to see any serious divergence between Acts and the first Thessalonian letter in regard to the persecution which the missionaries suffered in Thessalonica. The letter does not allude to the Jews as having had part in this persecution, while according to Acts they were ring-leaders. This latter statement appears altogether probable from what we know concerning the attitude of the Jews toward Paul elsewhere. At the same time, Luke's account allows us to think that the great majority of those who assaulted the house of Jason were Greeks, and therefore it is not at variance with the letter.

At the time of the assault on the house of Jason, who, to judge from his name, was a Macedonian, Paul and his fellow-laborers

THE SO-CALLED "ARCH OF CONSTANTINE" IN THESSALONICA
(Erected in the First or Second Century A. D., torn down in 1876)

were his guests, though fortunately not in the house. Therefore Jason and certain other disciples were taken before the rulers, and were obliged to give "security," that is, put down a money deposit as a pledge that the missionaries would cause no further disturbance. Possibly they promised the rulers that Paul should depart from the city. At any rate that is what Paul immediately did in company with Silas. Timothy remained for a time, and then followed Paul to Berœa (Acts 17:14).

Though Paul's work in Thessalonica was broken off by persecution, he had been the means of creating a vigorous Christian community, which soon became an example to all believers in Macedonia and Achaia (1 Thess. 1:7, 8; 4:10). Two members of this church accompanied Paul on his last visit to Jerusalem, and of these one

INSCRIPTION ON THE INSIDE OF THE "ARCH OF CONSTANTINE"
Containing the names of the six rulers, "Politarchs," of Thessalonica

took the long voyage with the apostle when he was sent a prisoner to Rome (Acts 20:4, 27:2).

§ 85. **In Berœa.**—The third and last Macedonian town which Paul visited was Berœa, about 47 miles from Thessalonica by the shortest route, and 20 miles from the sea. There was a synagogue in the city, and its members received Paul's message with all readiness of mind. Many believed, and those who did not kept silence, allowing the missionaries to continue their work. Some of the leading Greeks of the city accepted the gospel. The work was finally interrupted by Jews from Thessalonica, who, having come to Berœa, stirred up the multitudes, probably by such political charges as had been effectual in their own city. There is no indication that any of the Jews of Berœa joined them. Before the opposition had resulted in violence, Paul left the city. Silas and Timothy remained.

The length of Paul's sojourn in Berœa can only be conjectured. As it was long enough for his work to be reported in Thessalonica and for Jews to come thence to Berœa and to work up an opposition to the missionaries among the multitudes, it can hardly have been less than two weeks, and may have been twice that time. Of the church which Paul established in Berœa we have no further knowledge from New Testament sources than that one of the men who went with Paul to Jerusalem to take the contribution of the churches was a Berœan by the name of Sopater (Acts 20:4).

With his departure from Berœa Paul's work in Macedonia ended. He had preached and gathered a circle of believers in three cities, and had been driven from each by persecution. The gospel seems to have been carried out from these centers with great rapidity and success. As early as Paul's letter to the Thessalonians he spoke of brethren in *all* Macedonia (1 Thess. 4:10), and said that the word of the Lord had sounded forth through Macedonia and Achaia.

§ 86. **In Athens.**—If Paul made bitter enemies, he also made devoted friends. When his short stay in Berœa came to an abrupt end, there were some of his converts who accompanied him to the sea-coast, perhaps at Dium in the extreme southeast of Macedonia, and thence by water to Athens, a distance of about 200 miles.

We have but a single allusion from Paul himself to a visit in Athens. He says in his first letter to the Thessalonians that he had sent Timothy back from Athens to Thessalonica to establish and comfort the church (1 Thess. 3:1, 2). When Timothy returned to him from this mission, he was already at work in Corinth. He himself says nothing of any activity in Athens.

According to the narrative in Acts, when Paul reached Athens he sent back word to Berœa that Silas and Timothy should come to him with all speed (Acts 17:15), but no reason is there suggested for this step. Light is thrown upon it, however, by the first letter to the Thessalonians, for we learn from this of Paul's earnest desire to return to Thessalonica (1 Thess. 2:18; 3:11), and also that he sent Timothy from Athens to Thessalonica. It is natural then to con-

Propylaea Parthenon Lycabettus

THE ACROPOLIS OF ATHENS

clude that he summoned Timothy and Silas from Berœa because he wished to send a message to Thessalonica. Possibly, indeed probably, he sent Silas to Philippi when he sent Timothy to Thessalonica. For (*a*) he would probably have the same reasons for desiring news from Philippi as from Thessalonica; and (*b*) from 2 Cor. 11:8 compared with Phil. 4:15 we learn that the Philippians probably sent him money while he was in Corinth, when the "brethren" came from Macedonia. Now since we know that Silas was with Paul when he wrote 1 Thess. (1 Thess. 1:1) and that Timothy had just arrived from Macedonia (1 Thess. 3:6), it is highly probable that with Timothy had come also Silas—this, indeed, Acts 18:5 *says*—the former from Thessalonica, the latter from Philippi.

Luke's narrative, no less than the first letter to the Thessalonians, makes the impression that Paul's stay in Athens was short. It was an interval in which he "waited" for Silas and Timothy (Acts 17:16), and his preaching was due to an external cause, viz., the idolatry of the city, rather than to a plan of his own. There was a synagogue in Athens, and in this Paul reasoned with Jews and proselytes. We are not told whether this activity bore any fruit. He also spoke in the market-place to the gentiles, where he was singularly misunderstood and won but few converts (vs. 34). He was not regarded as a philosopher with an independent message, but rather as one who had borrowed his wisdom from others. He spoke of Jesus and the resurrection, and the hearers thought these were two new demons whose worship Paul would introduce. As anything new interested the Athenians for a little time, the notion that Paul was acquainted with new demons occasioned the Areopagus address. What is meant by "Areopagus," whether the Hill of Mars itself or a council which had its name from that hill, because it had originally met there, is disputed. But however that word is taken, it is plain that the hearing of Paul was not a judicial trial. He was thought to be a setter-forth of strange demons; but, in a city where there was the greatest liberality toward all cults, this could not have been regarded as a ground for procedure against him. There is also no suggestion in our narrative of a formal trial. No charge was brought, no defense made, and when Paul was interrupted in his address he went forth unhindered.

The Areopagus address is marked by the same liberality of thought in regard to the gentiles that we have in the Lycaonian address (Acts 14:15–17), and in the epistle to the Romans (2:12–16). Paul admits that the Athenians worship God, but declares that their worship is in ignorance. He says that all nations have one origin and one destiny, and recognizes that Greek poets teach some truth about God and man. The call to repentance in view of approaching

THE AREOPAGUS

judgment, this judgment to be through Jesus, may not be as characteristic of Paul as is the doctrine of justification by faith; but the situation may account for the emphasis which he appears to have laid on the former thought and for his entire omission of the latter. The address is said to contain no message of salvation through Christ, which is true; but this fact is hardly to be considered as valid evidence against its genuineness. What it does contain is Pauline, and that is of more weight than the argument from silence.

§ 87. **In Corinth.**—When Paul set out from Macedonia on the long sea-voyage to the south, it is not unlikely that he had Corinth prominently in view. This was the capital of the province of Achaia, a Roman colony founded by Julius Cæsar, upon nearly the site of the older Corinth destroyed just a century before, a large city which, because of its central location between the East and the West, had a far-reaching influence.

It appears from the first letter to the Thessalonians (1 Thess. 3:11), written from Corinth, as was also 2 Thess., that Paul did not expect to remain long in Corinth at that time; but in the ordering of Providence it came about that he labored there longer than in any other city except Ephesus. At the outset of his stay in Corinth he formed one of the most fruitful friendships of his life, that with Aquila, a Pontian Jew, and with his wife Priscilla. With them he made his home, and possibly was in their employ. In any case it is natural to suppose that Aquila, as he was acquainted with the city, took the product of Paul's work and disposed of it with his own. Both earned their living by weaving cloth from goats' hair.

At first Paul's preaching in Corinth was somewhat lacking in power because of his solicitude for his Thessalonian converts, but when Timothy brought a good report from this church (Acts 18:5; 1 Thess. 3:6), he was able to throw himself wholly into his work. A speedy result of this greater earnestness on his part was such an opposition of the Jews that he was forced out of the synagogue. After this he preached in the house of Titus Justus, a proselyte and probably a Christian as well. Here he continued his work for somewhat more than a year and a half. The number of converts among the Jews appears not to have been large, but it included at least one prominent man, Crispus, a ruler of the synagogue. But of the Greeks many were won to the new faith. This is not only affirmed by Luke, but it is also implied in the letters to the Corinthians, which were written four or five years after the church was founded (e. g., 1 Cor. 1:12; 12:1–11; 16:3).

It appears from 1 Cor. 1:26, 28 that the Greek converts were chiefly from the lower class. Erastus, who was treasurer of the city (Rom 16:23), Gaius who entertained Paul and the whole church (Rom. 16:23), and Chloe and Stephanas were exceptions to this rule.

THE ACROCORINTHUS, AND THE SITE OF CORINTH AS IT WAS PREVIOUS TO THE RECENT EXCAVATIONS

Paul tells us that while he was in Corinth he was unusually oppressed with a sense of weakness and fear (1 Cor. 2:3), with which agrees the statement in Acts that the Lord spoke to Paul in a vision and encouraged him (Acts 18:9, 10). This state of mind may have been due to the almost hopeless moral condition of Corinth and to the recent discouraging experiences in Athens. It is perhaps also significant that Paul speaks of this weakness in connection with his resolution to speak the gospel in simple words, without any of the arts of wisdom and eloquence which the Greeks loved. He knew that his message would be foolishness to most of his hearers (1 Cor. 1:23).

That Paul was not driven from Corinth by Jewish persecution was due not to any lack of the persecuting spirit, but to the temper of the proconsul. When his enemies brought him before the judgment seat, and charged that he persuaded men to worship contrary to the law, Gallio the judge, a brother of the Stoic philosopher Seneca, refused to entertain the charge. Since all modes of worship were lawful, he concluded that their accusation had force only from the standpoint of their own Jewish law. As the Jews were driven away from the judgment seat, Sosthenes the ruler of the synagogue was beaten without protest from Gallio, though the proceeding was obviously riotous and unlawful.[1]

Why Paul at length departed from Corinth our sources do not say. In Cenchreæ, the eastern harbor of Corinth, about eight miles from the city, Paul, when about to take ship, had his hair cut short in token of the fulfilment of some vow. What this was we do not know, possibly a vow made in the early days of the Corinthian work when Paul had felt himself weak and oppressed with fear.

§ 88. **The Return to Antioch.**—When Paul sailed from Cenchreæ, his destination was Syria, and in particular, without doubt, the city of Antioch, but his ship touched at Ephesus, probably for a very short time, and he became somewhat acquainted with the synagogue there. He was asked to remain, but did not consent, though he promised to come back if the Lord was willing.

[1] This attack on Sosthenes must have been made by the Greeks, as there is no motive apparent why the Jews should have fallen upon their own leader at this time. The popular gentile hatred of the Jews is sufficient explanation of the unprovoked assault.

According to Acts 18:22 Paul sailed from Ephesus to Cæsarea, whence he went up and saluted the church, and then at length returned to Antioch. But there are serious difficulties involved in this verse. It seems altogether improbable, in the first place, that Luke would have referred to a visit of Paul to Jerusalem in the indefinite words, "he went up and saluted the church;" Jerusalem is not even named, nor any motive for the visit suggested. Again, when Paul went to Jerusalem with the contribution three years later, he went in great trepidation, being in doubt whether he should be delivered from the disobedient in Judea. But if he went in fear at that time, though having a large offering for the

RUINS OF TEMPLE AT CORINTH
(Seen also in previous picture)

church, it is singular that he should have gone quietly on his return from Corinth, empty-handed and without any special motive. There is, however, no doubt that he went to Antioch and told of his work in the west.

He had been absent, on a conservative estimate, two and a half years. He had traveled some 2,500 miles, and had established the gospel in the two important provinces of Macedonia and Achaia. He might well believe that the story of this work would be blessed of God to the upbuilding of the church in Antioch.

§ 89. **Questions and Suggestions for Study.**—(1) Where had Mark gone when he left Paul and Barnabas at Perga? (2) What may have brought him to Antioch? (3) Why was Paul opposed to taking him again? (4) What evidence is there that the dissension between Paul and Barnabas did not lead to permanent alienation? (5) With what plan did Paul leave Antioch at this time? Whom did he take with him? (6) Whither did Barnabas go? (7) What new field did Paul first think of entering after he had visited his churches? (8) What direction did he finally take? (9) What churches may he have established at this time?

(10) What was the second new field which Paul sought to enter? (11) Whither did he then go? (12) What may have prepared the way for the vision in Troas? (13) Describe the journey from Troas to Philippi. (14) Describe Philippi. (15) Where did Paul preach and to whom? Who was the first convert? (16) How was the work of Paul finally broken off? (17) On what charges were Paul and Silas brought before the magistrates? (18) Describe the events of the night spent in prison. (19) What use did Paul and Silas make of their Roman citizenship?

(20) Describe the journey from Philippi to Thessalonica. (21) Why may the missionaries have passed through Amphipolis and Apollonia without preaching? (22) Describe the location of Thessalonica. (23) How long did Paul labor there? (24) What circumstances led to his departure? (25) Of what element was the church in Thessalonica chiefly composed? (26) Describe Paul's work in Thessalonica as he himself characterizes it in 1 Thess. chap. 2.

(27) Locate Berœa and tell how Paul was received there. (28) How long did he labor in Berœa? (29) How was he driven away? (30) Give a brief summary of Paul's work in Macedonia.

(31) Describe the journey from Berœa to Athens. (32) Why did Paul summon Timothy to come from Berœa? (33) How long did Paul remain in Athens? (34) What led to his activity there? (35) How was he regarded by the Athenians? (36) Describe the Areopagus address. Where was it delivered? (37) What was the result of the work in Athens? (38) Locate Corinth. (39) How long did Paul labor there? (40) What important friendship did he form at the beginning of his stay? (41) What was the character of Paul's first work in Corinth, and what brought about a change? (42) What two letters still extant did Paul write while he was in Corinth? What do these letters show as to Paul's state of mind while in Corinth?

(43) What attempt did the Jews make to drive Paul away from Corinth and why did it fail? (44) What was Cenchreæ and what did Paul do there before sailing for Syria?

(45) Describe the course of Paul's return trip to Antioch. (46) What are the reasons for thinking that he did not go to Jerusalem? (47) Give a brief summary of the second missionary journey.

§ 90. **Supplemental Topics for Study and References to Literature.**

1. Write a chapter on Paul's second missionary journey. This may describe, first, his companions; second, the geography of the tour; third, its trials; and finally, its results.

2. On the great Roman road, *via Egnatiana* see:

Smith's *Classical Dictionary.*

3. On the historical character of Luke's narrative of the work in Athens see:

McGiffert, *The Apostolic Age*, pp. 526–62.

4. On Paul's vow in Cenchreæ see:

Knowling in *The Expositor's Greek Testament*, Vol. II.

5. On the location of the "churches of Galatia" read:

Lightfoot, *Commentary on Galatians;* Chase, *Expositor*, Vol. XIII; Weizsäcker, *The Apostolic Age*, Vol. I, pp. 270 ff.; Ramsay, *The Church in the Roman Empire*, and *Historical Commentary on Galatians.*

CHAPTER XIV

THE LIFE OF A MACEDONIAN CHURCH AS REFLECTED IN PAUL'S LETTERS TO THE THESSALONIANS

SYNOPSIS

§ 91. **Paul's own story of his work in Thessalonica.**
§ 92. **Organization of the Thessalonian church.**
§ 93. **Conspicuous doctrinal feature.**
§ 94. **Practical Christian life of the Thessalonians.**

§ 91. **Paul's Own Story of His Work in Thessalonica.**—From the allusions which Paul makes to his work in Thessalonica in his two letters to the Thessalonians we can form a somewhat vivid picture of his manner of life and of preaching while there. Probably the first thing to which he attended on reaching the city, after he had found a lodging, was some means of self-support. There was no missionary society behind him to look out for his expenses. He might have asked support from those to whom he preached, but he chose to be independent, even though that obliged him to work nights (1 Thess. 2:9; 2 Thess. 3:8). It is probable that he did some evangelistic work every day, telling his story as he could find opportunity and laboring here and there with individuals who had accepted his message (1 Thess. 4:11); but it is also probable that the work by which he supported himself was not all done in the night. It is plain, however, that he had a hard struggle to earn his daily bread, pay for his lodging, and do all that his heart moved him to do in making known the Christian faith. We do not know certainly what kind of work Paul did in Thessalonica. We know what his special trade was (see Acts 18:3), but whether there was opportunity to follow it in Thessalonica one can not say. He may have had to turn his hand to some other kind of labor.

It is possible to learn from the Thessalonian letters some of the special topics on which Paul spoke while in Thessalonica. Of course, in general, the message which he brought was the gospel, *his* gospel (1 Thess. 1:4), the gospel of *God* (1 Thess. 2:2, 8), or of *Christ*

(1 Thess. 3:2), but we can also notice some of the points on which he dwelt with particular emphasis. Thus, e. g., he had taught the Thessalonians that the end of the gospel message was, with reference to God, twofold, viz., that they should have faith in him (1 Thess. 1:8), and that they should walk worthily of him (1 Thess. 2:12). He had told them of the sufferings and death of Jesus (e. g., 1 Thess. 1:6; 2:15; 4:14), his resurrection from the dead (1 Thess. 4:14; 5:10), his coming and the glory which he would then bestow upon his followers (1 Thess. 1:10; 2 Thess. 2:14). He had told them in detail what kind of outward life is pleasing to God, dwelling on purity and industry (1 Thess. 4:1, 3; 2 Thess. 3:10).

We have said that the time spent in Thessalonica was a time of struggle for Paul. It was also a time of quick and remarkable response to his message, as we shall see in the course of the present chapter. A deep attachment sprang up between him and the Thessalonian believers, and when he had gone away and thought of them at a distance, they stood before his inner eye as his glory and joy (1 Thess. 2:20).

§ 92. **Organization of the Thessalonian Church.**—The apostle addressed the Thessalonian believers as a "church" (1 Thess. 1:1; 2 Thess. 1:1), he also compared them with the churches in Judea (1 Thess. 2:14), and yet it seems plain that they had no formal organization. Paul knew of certain persons in Thessalonica who were conspicuous for their labors in behalf of the church, and he recognized these as being in a sense *over* the rest (1 Thess. 5:12). He asked that these persons might be esteemed highly for their works' sake. But there is no suggestion of any claim which they might have made by virtue of an office with which the church had clothed them. Moreover, all the brethren of the church are exhorted to admonish the disorderly, even as those who are said to be over the church admonish them; and in other respects also, all members are exhorted to do pastoral work, and it is assumed that they are actually doing it (1 Thess. 5:11). This fact indicates that those who were over the church were not officers formally chosen by the brotherhood or by Paul, but rather those who, by their leadership in service, had gained a certain pre-eminence and certain moral right to leadership in government and worship.

Thus at the time when the letters to the Thessalonians were written, we see "a church without a bishop," and, indeed, without any formal ecclesiastical organization. There were a number of persons who were beginning to constitute what Dobschütz calls an "educational staff" (cf. *Christian Life in the Primitive Church*, p. 88), and there can be little doubt that from their number bishops were duly chosen in the near future; but there was vigorous life—that is the point to be noticed—while as yet the Christians were an outwardly unorganized body.

§ 93. **Conspicuous Doctrinal Feature.**—The thought and life of the Thessalonian church, at the time when Paul wrote his letters to them, were largely colored by the doctrine of the second coming of Christ. Other doctrines were not ignored, especially the teaching of the apostle in regard to patience and brotherly love and purity; but of doctrines not directly concerned with ethics no one had an influence at all comparable with that of the *parousia*, or second coming of the Lord.

How near this coming was thought to be, and how essential even to the believer's continued existence, is seen from the impression created by the death of some members of the Thessalonian church. This event had caused great sorrow. Evidently it had been hoped and believed that the Lord would come before any one of their number died. And it is plain from the words of Paul that the Thessalonian believers seriously doubted whether their dead members would share in the heavenly kingdom at all (1 Thess. 4:13—5:11). It is obvious from this that Paul had presented the second coming of Christ simply with relation to the living. He had not considered the possibility that any would die before the day of the Lord's return. In other words, he had not treated the doctrine in a systematic and exhaustive manner, but only in its practical bearing upon those who heard him speak. He had probably used it chiefly as a motive to godly living (cf. 1 Thess. 3:13; 2 Thess. 2:14).

It may be supposed that what Paul said in his first letter with regard to those believers who had died comforted the church. He did not refer to the point in his second letter. But on the subject of the nearness of the day of the Lord's coming his first letter only reiterated the general teaching which he had given them in person. It said that the day was near (1 Thess. 1:10; 4:15), that it would come as a thief in the night (1 Thess. 5:2), and that they should therefore watch and be sober (1 Thess. 5:6).

Now this doctrine of the nearness of the Lord's coming, entirely apart from its relation to those who had died, was already exciting and confusing the church when the first letter was written. Some persons were neglecting their business, and thereby becoming dependent on others, for the Thessalonian Christians were very poor (2 Cor. 8:2). This idleness made a bad impression, Paul thought, on those outside the church. It did not commend the gospel. Some report of the harmful influence of the doctrine reached the apostle, and occasioned the second letter to the Thessalonians. In this he besought them not to be troubled by the thought that the second coming of the Lord was immediately at hand, for it was not. He then told of certain things which must precede, and said that he had already given them this information while he was with them (2 Thess. 2:5). They were not to stop their ordinary work, and give themselves up to religious excitement (2 Thess. 3:12). Any who did this were to be avoided by the rest (2 Thess. 3:6, 14).

It appears, then, that the life of the Thessalonian Christians, or of many among them, was disturbed and injured by their understanding of the doctrine of the Lord's second coming. But Paul did not make any essential change in his teaching. He only sought to enlighten the ignorance of the Thessalonians in regard to their dead friends, and to emphasize what he had said personally concerning the signs which were to precede the Lord's coming.

§ 94. **Practical Christian Life of the Thessalonians.**—By the side of the unfortunate doctrinal excitement on the part of some members of the church in Thessalonica there was also, in the earliest days, that is, before and at the time of the composition of the letters of Paul to the church, an extraordinary manifestation of the Christian spirit. In the glow of his generous affection for his converts, the language of Paul regarding their estate was doubtless somewhat exaggerated, but nevertheless the facts must have been remarkable.

When he wrote his first letter, from two to six months after his work in Thessalonica, he said that the faith of the Thessalonian Christians had become known throughout Macedonia and Achaia (1 Thess. 1:8); and when he wrote the second letter he had received such evidence of Christian life from Thessalonica that he spoke of the exceeding *growth* of their faith (2 Thess, 1:3). He also asked the Thessalonian Christians to pray that the word of the Lord might run and be glorified in Corinth even as in Thessalonica—language which he certainly could not have used had he not been in a high degree satisfied with the activity of his young converts.

But this faith toward God, which was proved by their activity and their patient endurance of persecution, was equaled or even excelled by their love one toward another. It was not needful, Paul said, to write to them on this subject, for they were obviously taught of God (1 Thess. 4:9). And when he wrote his second letter, he spoke again of the abounding love which his readers had for each other (2 Thess. 1:3). It was doubtless this fact of mutual love which made it possible for the church to be at peace and to thrive, though having at the most a very rudimentary and unofficial organization.

But the church was not altogether of this sort. There were instances of falling back into gentile immoralities (1 Thess. 4:3–8); there were apparently some who made light of the second coming of the Lord (1 Thess. 5:6, 8), as there were other extremists who could speak of nothing else than that coming; and then there were also some quarrelsome, some faint-hearted, and some weak (1 Thess. 5:13, 14). Yet when it is considered that the recipients of these letters had been out of heathenism less than half a year, the way in which the gospel had laid hold upon them, and transformed them, is a fact of the utmost significance.

§ 95. **Questions and Suggestions for Study.**—(1) What do the Thessalonian letters say in regard to the manner of Paul's life while in Thessalonica? (2) On what point of teaching regarding God and Christ and the Christian life do they indicate that Paul laid stress? (3) What do the Thessalonian letters indicate in regard to the organization of the church in Thessalonica? (4) What doctrine was especially prominent among the Thessalonian believers? (5) What fear was entertained regarding those who had died? (6) How did Paul comfort his readers in this matter (see 1 Thess. 4:14)? (7) What other harm came from a misunderstanding of the same doctrine? (8) What were the prominent features of the Christian life of the Thessalonians? (9) What defects in their life are manifest?

§ 96. **Supplementary Topics for Study and References to Literature.**

(1) On the basis of a careful study of the letters to the Thessalonians write a short chapter on Paul's presentation of the gospel to the Thessalonians and the early days of the Thessalonian church.

(2) With reference to a change in Paul's view of the nearness of the Lord's coming study, in addition to the passages in Thessalonians, 1 Cor. 15:51, 52; Rom. 13:12; Col. 3:4; Phil. 4:5; 1 Tim. 6:14; 2 Tim. 4:1, 6.

(3) On the genuineness of 2 Thessalonians see:

Bacon, *Introduction to the New Testament*, and Weizsäcker, *The Apostolic Age*, Vol. I, pp. 295–98.

(4) What other letters did Paul authenticate as he did 2 Thessalonians? Why did he do this?

CHAPTER XV

PAUL IN EPHESUS ON HIS THIRD MISSIONARY JOURNEY

SYNOPSIS

§ 97. **Christian forerunners of Paul in Ephesus.** Acts 18:19*a*, 24–28
§ 98. **Paul's work in Ephesus according to Acts.** Acts, chap. 19
§ 99. **Significant events of the Ephesian period witnessed to by Paul's letters.**

§ 97. **Christian Forerunners of Paul in Ephesus.**—When Paul sailed from Cenchreæ for Syria, his friends Priscilla and Aquila were with him, and it seems not unlikely that he had asked them to go, with the thought of work in Ephesus. It appears that he no longer felt toward work in Asia as he had at an earlier day (Acts 16:6), for when his ship touched at Ephesus, he went into the synagogue and reasoned with the Jews, and though he did not think it best to remain, he intimated that he would come back. If, then, he was already considering Ephesus as a field of labor when he left Corinth, it was natural that he should desire to have these congenial and gifted fellow-laborers with him.

About the time when Aquila and his wife settled in Ephesus, Apollos also came to the city and began to speak boldly in the synagogue concerning Jesus, that is to say, he preached that Jesus was the Messiah. Luke's language that he taught "accurately the things concerning Jesus" implies that he was acquainted with the leading facts of his life and teaching, and with his resurrection. As Apollos was an Alexandrian by race, and so presumably had been instructed in the way of the Lord in that city, we have indirect evidence that the gospel was preached in Egypt before Paul worked in Ephesus. The word used by Luke when he says that Apollos had been instructed in the way of the Lord (κατηχούμενος) suggests that he had received his instruction orally rather than from writings (cf. the use of the word in Luke 1:4; Acts 21:21, 24; 1 Cor. 14:19; Gal. 6:6).

Apollos was a Christian, but was unacquainted with Christian baptism. The same position was occupied by the twelve disciples whom Paul found in Ephesus (Acts 19:1–7). They knew only the baptism of John. Apparently they had not heard of Pentecost, and the doctrine of the presence of the Spirit of God. Aquila and Priscilla had a conference with Apollos, and, according to Luke, "expounded unto him the way of God more accurately." He appears to have received their instruction, for when, later, he was disposed to go over to Achaia to preach, the brethren commended him, and his work in Achaia was profitable to believers. Doubtless he was

GENERAL VIEW OF EPHESUS AS IT WAS IN 1830

baptized, perhaps by Aquila, as the other disciples who shared his position received baptism from Paul.

The narrative of Luke does not connect the group of believers whom Paul found in Ephesus with Apollos. If they had been his disciples, it would be strange that he did not take to them the fuller knowledge which he had received from Aquila and Priscilla; strange, too, that Aquila and Priscilla themselves did not meet them. In view of these considerations one is inclined to think that they may have come out of the same Alexandrian circle from which Apollos had come, and that Apollos had gone from Ephesus before they arrived.

§ 98. **Paul's Work in Ephesus According to Acts.**—When Paul set out on his second missionary journey, he visited the churches of Syria and Cilicia as well as those of Pisidia and Lycaonia (Acts 15:41; 16:1–5). But when he next left Antioch, he went, according to Luke, into the region of Galatia and Phrygia (Acts. 18:23). After a period whose length is not at all indicated, he reached Ephesus.

Ephesus, situated near the Cayster River on the coast of Lydia,

EPHESUS: RUINS OF THE TEMPLE OF DIANA

had long been the chief of the cities of Asia Minor when Paul came thither with the gospel. It had been the capital of the Roman province of Asia for nearly two centuries (since 133 B. C.). It had a large Jewish population, many of whom were Roman citizens (*Antiq.*, 14. 10. 16, 19), and all of whom were citizens of Ephesus (Schürer, *The Jewish People*, etc., Div. 2, Vol. II, p. 279). The city was as important religiously as it was politically, for it was the seat of the worship of Diana. Her temple, which was more than three hundred years old when Paul visited Ephesus, was regarded as one of the wonders of the world. The field, therefore, promised to be especially difficult as well as especially important.

Paul labored longer in Ephesus without interruption than in any other city. In the synagogue he spoke boldly three months, and in the school of Tyrannus he labored more than two years. He refers to his sojourn in Ephesus as having lasted three years (Acts 20:31). During this time he taught daily, both in public and from house to house (Acts 20:20). The depth and extent of his influence are variously illustrated. Thus, in his first letter to the Corinthians, Paul sends salutations from the "churches" in Asia (1 Cor. 16:19); but as he himself had planted the gospel in this province, these churches were all, directly or indirectly, his creation. Again, Luke says that while Paul was in Ephesus, all who dwelt in Asia—a region approximately the size of New England and thickly populated—heard the word of the Lord, both Jews and Greeks. This language is obviously hyperbolical, but it can hardly be supposed that it would have been used had not the influence of Paul's work in Ephesus been known to be widely pervasive. Multitudes who came to Ephesus on business or to worship must have seen and heard him. When any of these were converted, they, of course, bore the seeds of the gospel to their own homes. And doubtless there were Ephesian converts who went forth as evangelists into the surrounding region.

Another illustration of Paul's influence in Ephesus is the story of the collapse of magic, which need not be wholly discredited simply because it can not be regarded as wholly historical. We may well believe that Jewish exorcists conjured with the potent names of Jesus and Paul. This would not indicate that they had faith in Jesus or respect for Paul, but only that they were keeping abreast of the times. If they used these names, it was, of course, for material gain.

Luke tells how two Jews, sons of a chief priest, when seeking to exorcise a demon by means of the names of Jesus and Paul, were attacked by the demoniac and put to flight. He said that he knew Jesus and Paul, and this word became widely circulated and was regarded as a veritable recognition of Jesus and Paul by the powers of evil. One consequence was that many magicians, feeling that demoniac power would succumb to no exorcism save that of Jesus and Paul, voluntarily burned their books on magic. Of course it does not follow that these men became Christians. The act of burning their books may have been quite as superstitious as anything they had hitherto done. The value of the incident, if historical, is that it witnesses to the power of Paul's personality and to the deep impression made by his gospel.

It may have been the fact of Paul's great success in Ephesus which gave rise to the story that extraordinary miracles had been wrought by his hands. Luke says that sick persons and demoniacs were healed by the application of handkerchiefs and aprons which

EPHESUS: SITE OF THE THEATER

had touched the body of Paul. Now if Paul authorized this practice, he must have known that the persons in need had faith to be healed in this way, and accordingly made a concession to the superstition of Ephesus. But this seems extremely improbable. The "signs" of an apostle were indeed wrought by Paul (2 Cor. 12:12; Rom. 15:18, 19), but they were altogether unlike the acts of which Luke makes mention at this point.

The work of Paul in Ephesus was at length interrupted by gentiles who had suffered pecuniary loss from his preaching. A prominent industry of the city was the manufacture of shrines of the goddess. In this industry a certain Demetrius was engaged, who appears to have been a large employer of skilled labor. He gathered the craftsmen together, and wrought up their passions by telling them that they were losing their means of support through Paul's preaching, and that even their goddess was in danger of being deposed. Their excitement communicated itself to others as they rushed through the city to the great theater, dragging with them two companions of Paul, Gaius and Aristarchus. The gathering in the theater was without intelligent control. The greater part of those present knew not why they were there. A Jew by the name of Alexander attempted to speak, but in vain. He only increased the excitement, for he was recognized as a Jew, and it was of course known that Paul belonged to this hated race. The circumstance that this Alexander was put forward by the Jews may indicate that voices had been heard in the theater charging the trouble to the Jews, and that they wished to defend themselves.

When the multitude had exhausted themselves with shouting, the town-clerk, who also may have been one of the highpriests friendly to Paul (vs. 31), but who was in any case clothed with high authority, persuaded the crowd to disperse. He declared that Diana's position was perfectly secure. No one could deny that her heaven-descended image was in the temple. He said also that no valid complaint had been lodged against the Christians; that Demetrius and the craftsmen had ample legal provisions by which to secure their rights; and finally that such a riotous meeting might bring serious accusations against the city. Thus Demetrius failed to get any official support for his opposition to the Christians, and also failed to excite such popular feeling that it resulted in assaults on Paul and other leaders.

But though Paul was at liberty to continue preaching in Ephesus, he at once voluntarily left the city, perhaps fearing that his presence would aggravate the situation and interfere with the progress of the gospel.

§ 99. **Significant Events of the Ephesian Period Witnessed to by Paul's Letters.**—The years spent in Ephesus, even according to Luke's narrative, were crowded with labors and dramatic incidents.

If to this narrative we add certain hints found in Paul's letters, we get a greatly heightened impression of the apostle's capacity for work and of his ability to direct a great religious movement.

If the Ephesian period was remarkable for its successes, so was it also for its perils. It was here that Paul fought with beasts (1 Cor. 15:32). Whether we understand this language literally or figuratively, it implies extraordinary danger. Even if the "beasts" were

A THEATER OF THE FIRST CENTURY (POMPEII)

men, as we are probably to hold, the very term of the comparison and the fact that fighting with beasts seems to be regarded as a stronger expression than the preceding words, "I die daily," require us to think of some peculiarly savage attack on Paul.

It was also probably[1] in Ephesus that an affliction befell the apostle out of which his deliverance seemed to him as a resurrection from the dead—so manifestly divine was it (2 Cor. 1:8–11). The

[1] 2 Cor. 1:8 specifies the scene of this event as "in Asia," i.e. in the province of which Ephesus was the capital. But we do not know of work by Paul in the province outside of Ephesus.

nature of this event is not indicated; the readers are assumed to be acquainted with it, at least in a general way. The "marks of Jesus," which Paul tells the Galatians that he bore branded on his body, may have recorded some of his extreme sufferings while in Ephesus.

But these physical perils and afflictions were perhaps of less concern to Paul than the trials to which some of his newly founded churches subjected him. Thus it was probably while he was at Ephesus that he heard of the alarming turn of affairs among his Galatian converts. How profoundly he was moved by this report is shown by every page of his letter to them. No less deeply was he stirred during this time by events which were taking place in the Corinthian church. To this church he wrote a letter which has not been preserved (1 Cor. 5:9), and to this also, in the judgment of many scholars, he made a visit from Ephesus of which Acts has no record. The clearest indication of such a visit is 2 Cor. 2:1.[1] If Paul visited the Corinthian church during the Ephesian period, the visit was painful because of the bold opposition of his adversaries (2 Cor. 2:1; 1 Cor. 4:18).

Thus we see the anxiety for churches at a distance, where the very existence of Paul's work was in jeopardy, mingled with the immediate toils and perils of the Ephesian ministry. But he bore the toils, escaped the perils, and by his letters to the Galatians and Corinthians successfully asserted his spiritual authority among them.

§ 100. **Questions and Suggestions for Study.**—(1) Whom did Paul take with him when he left Corinth, and for what purpose? (2) Who was Apollos, and what was lacking in his Christian instruction? (3) What evidence is there that he accepted the instruction of Aquila and Priscilla? (4) Are the men in Ephesus who held the same view as Apollos to be regarded as his disciples? (5) By what route did Paul go from Antioch to Ephesus? (6) Locate and describe Ephesus. (7) Why was it an important and difficult field? (8) How long did Paul labor in Ephesus? (9) Illustrate the depth and extent of his influence.

(10) What light do the letters of Paul throw on his perils and sufferings while in Ephesus? (11) What other great trials befell him

[1] Other passages which may be held to imply this visit are 2 Cor. 12:14; 13:1, 2.

at this time? (12) What journey is it possible that he made of which Acts has no record?

§ 101. **Supplementary Topics for Study and References to Literature.**

1. Write a chapter on the work in Ephesus, especially as illustrating Paul's capacity for work and the sufferings which befell him.

2. On Apollos as a disciple of John the Baptist see:

McGiffert, *The Apostolic Age*, pp. 290–92.

3. Regarding a third visit in Corinth not mentioned in Acts see:

Weizsäcker, *The Apostolic Age*, Vol. I, pp. 343–49.

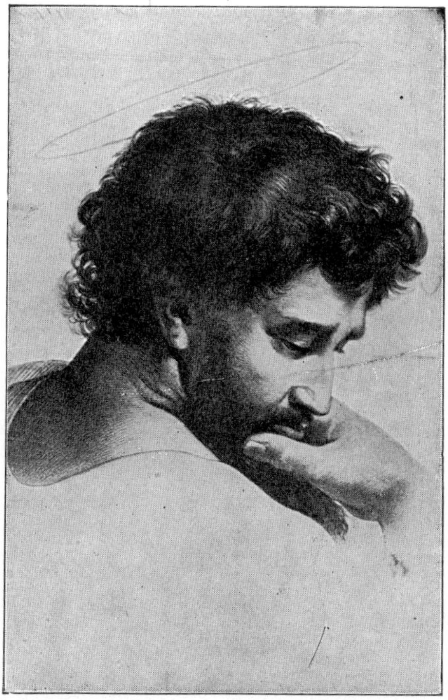

RAPHAEL'S HEAD OF PAUL

CHAPTER XVI

THE LIFE OF THE GALATIAN CHURCHES AS SEEN THROUGH PAUL'S LETTER TO THE GALATIANS

SYNOPSIS

§ 102. **The Christian Estate of the Galatians before Their Apostasy.**—It was pointed out in the last chapter that among the heavy burdens which Paul had to bear while in Ephesus was the sudden and extreme peril confronting his Galatian converts. We are now to consider, so far as Paul's letter makes it possible to do so, the nature and extent of this peril. Incidental to the aim of the letter to the Galatians are certain remarks which enable us to form some idea of their estate before they were troubled by the "false brethren" (Gal. 4:14). Thus we learn that they had welcomed Paul as an angel, or even as though he had been Christ Jesus himself, which was of course due to the message which he brought. When it is said that they would have plucked out their eyes and have given them to Paul (Gal. 4:14, 15), we see in that language how keenly they appreciated his gospel. They had come to know God and had received the Spirit (Gal. 3:2; 4:9). The impression made upon them by Paul's preaching had been deep and abiding. They had run well the Christian race (Gal. 5:7). They had been called to suffer much (Gal. 3:4), that is, on account of their faith, and it is implied that they had endured their sufferings as Christians should. That their general condition had been eminently satisfactory to the apostle is apparent from the surprise and deep emotion with which he heard of their turning aside (see, e. g., 1:6; 3:1). The news was as lightning out of a clear sky.

The letter contains indications that, while the general spiritual condition of the Galatians had been worthy of high praise, there had been some defects in their life, notably, sensual sins, sorcery, and factiousness (Gal. 5:19, 20). These had characterized them before they accepted the gospel, and Paul had warned them that they could not practice such things and yet hope to inherit the kingdom of God. The fact that he repeats this warning shows that it was still needed.

§ 103. **The Judaizers or "False Brethren."**—The churches of Galatia had become unsettled by Jewish Christians who, visiting the Galatians in Paul's absence, insisted upon the observance of the law. Paul gives these men no specific name, but clearly characterizes their position. Men who held the same views at Antioch, and whose agitation led to the conference in Jerusalem, were called "false brethren;" and Paul's words of rebuke to Peter in Antioch shortly after the conference suggest the name "judaizers" for the same class of people (Gal. 2:14).

One would not gather from Paul's letter that he regarded these men as Christians, and it is clear that they, in turn, can have had but scant respect for his Christianity. He declares that they would pervert the gospel (1:7); that their motive, or one of their motives, was to avoid persecution (6:12); and he virtually pronounces an anathema upon them (1:8, 9). They have no profit from Christ because they are under the law (5:4). Such, briefly, was Paul's estimate of the judaizers. When we turn to the other side, we see that they thought poorly of him. They evidently had said that he was no apostle, or at best had only a second-hand apostleship, for Paul takes great pains to show that his apostleship "was authorized by God himself, vouchsafed to him through the vision of Christ, exercised in independent missionary work, recognized by the authorities in Jerusalem, and maintained against them" (Dobschütz). They said also that Paul was seeking to please men, that is, in preaching a gospel of freedom from the law (1:10), and that he was inconsistent, for sometimes he himself preached circumcision (5:11). Then they declared that he was really the enemy of the Galatians (4:16). Whether they anathematized him, as he anathematized them, we do not know. Certainly the difference between them was fundamental, and each thought the other hopelessly wrong.

Whence these false brethren came to the churches of Galatia the letter does not directly suggest. It is conceivable that they arose in that very field, for among the Jews of Galatia who accepted the gospel there might have been some who from the first had resented the free admission of the gentiles, and who after Paul's departure instituted a vigorous propaganda in support of the Jewish law. We know that the Hellenistic Jews could be as fanatically devoted to the customs of the fathers as those who had spent their lives in the shadow of the temple. But while such an origin of the judaizers of Galatia may be conceivable, it appears quite improbable. The fact that men of this type had come down from Jerusalem to Antioch, and the implication that they had also gone throughout Syria and Cilicia (Acts 15:23, 24) suggest that the agitation in Galatia is to be traced to the same source. There is also a passage in the letter to the Galatians, which, if it does not directly suggest this view, at least favors it. That is the allegory of Sarah and Hagar. Hagar answers to the "Jerusalem that now is," whose children are in bondage, Sarah to the Jerusalem which is above, whose children are free. This passage is most forcible if the judaizers were from Jerusalem, the mother-church, and if they claimed that, on this account, they had superior authority. Holtzmann suggests that one of their watchwords was this, "Jerusalem is our mother."

It is unfortunate that we have no description of the views of the judaizers by one of themselves. For though their aim is clear from Paul's letters, and we can have no doubt on which side essential truth lay, yet we could judge of the men better if we knew just how the great question of the gentiles' relation to the law looked to them, and with what arguments they supported their position. That the arguments seemed to them absolutely conclusive there can be no doubt. And there is no more reason to question their sincerity than there is to question the sincerity of their great adversary. Their apprehension of the gospel was obviously defective in the extreme, but this does not imply that their motives were impure.

The position of the judaizers as seen through Paul's letters can be briefly stated. They taught that the law was in force, and that salvation for gentile as for Jew was by works of the law. The messianic deliverance was for the sons of Abraham, and gentiles who would share in that deliverance must first become sons of Abraham by coming under the law. Perfection was not to be had by faith, as Paul taught, but by works (3:3). It is possible that they did not at once insist upon the observance of the entire ceremonial law. This is suggested by the fact that while some in the church had already adopted Jewish feast days (4:10), they seemed to be wavering in regard to circumcision (5:2). But this hesitation on the part of the Galatian believers to accept circumcision is to be attributed to their own doubt as to its necessity rather than to any willingness of the judaizers to exempt the gentiles from this fundamental part of the ceremonial law. They may have sought to bring the Galatians under the yoke by easy stages, leading them first to keep the Jewish feast days, but there is no reason to suppose that they offered them a compromise.

What the judaizers said about Jesus, and what it was that constituted their "gospel" (1:6), the letter does not clearly indicate. They, of course, accepted Jesus as the Messiah and believed in his resurrection, but they held that his life and work had left Judaism intact.

§ 104. **Why and How Far the Galatians Were Carried Away by the Judaizers.**—It is plain from the intense feeling of the letter to the Galatians that the false brethren had already taken a firm hold on the churches of that region. Their "different gospel" had to some considerable extent carried the day. Some of the Galatians, apparently many of them, had accepted the principle of salvation by works of the law. They were already keeping the Jewish feasts, one of these doubtless being the observance of the Jewish weekly Sabbath. That many had been circumcised seems improbable (5:2), though there may have been some instances in which this step had been taken (6:12). Evidently the report of affairs in the Galatian churches was to the effect that the believers were *at the very point* of accepting circumcision. Paul may have felt that it was quite possible that this step had been taken even while the report was on the way.

The judaizers had not carried the entire membership of the Galatian churches with them. Paul can still speak of some who are "spiritual" (6:2), though the evil leaven threatened to leaven the whole lump (5:9). Such an expression of confidence as that in 5:10 indicates that some persons were known to him who still stood fast in their Christian freedom. If the sharp contentions among the Galatians were occasioned by the judaizers (5:13–15), that also would indicate that there was a party who remained loyal to Paul.

The apostle marveled that the Galatians were so quickly removing from the faith (1:6), but it is not altogether strange that they were captivated by the Jewish view of salvation. In the first place, a religion of works was nearer to their old religion and far more intelligible than Paul's spiritual conception of the Christian life. If Paul's conception is still too high, too mystical, for many people, after centuries of Christian experience, it is easy to believe that for people just taken out of nature-worship it was difficult to grasp, and that the Jewish doctrine was a positive relief. Then, again, the doctrine of the judaizers seemed to be powerfully commended by the fact that it was plainly loyal to the Scriptures, on which Paul also claimed to stand, and because it accorded with the practice of Jesus and of his apostles. These facts could not be gainsaid, and must have weighed heavily for the position of the judaizers. Finally, in addition to these things, it is altogether probable that the Jewish members of the Galatian churches, who were, of course, far more familiar with the Scripture argument than the gentiles could be, were the first to withdraw from Paul's position, and their example could not fail to influence their gentile brethren. The success of the judaizers, therefore, is not inexplicable.

What effect Paul's letter had in the Galatian churches we can not tell. His reference to a collection in those churches, made at his direction (1 Cor. 16:1), indicates that there were some, at least, who recognized his authority, but it does not necessarily imply that the judaizing element was brought back by the letter. If the Galatian churches were the churches of Pisidia and Lycaonia, then the fact that Gaius of Derbe (Acts 20:4) appears among the delegates of the churches to Jerusalem suggests, though of course it does not prove, that the influence of the letter was salutary.

§ 105. **Questions and Suggestions for Study.**—(1) Where was the Roman province of Galatia? (2) What are the opinions in regard to the part of that province in which the Galatian churches were situated? (3) Who founded these churches? (4) Name the main characteristics of the gospel which was preached to them. (5) To what disturbing influence were these churches subjected in Paul's absence from them? (6) What names can be derived from Galatians, chap. 2, to describe the men who troubled the churches? (7) What was Paul's estimate of these men? (8) What was their estimate of Paul? (9) What reasons are there for thinking that the judaizers came from Jerusalem? (10) Whence do we get our knowledge of these men? (11) What was the belief of the judaizers?

(12) By what argument did they endeavor to convince the Galatians? (13) How far had the Galatian churches been carried away by the judaizers? (14) Explain why the position of the judaizers had so great influence with the Galatians? (15) What effect did Paul's letter have?

§ 106. **Supplementary Topics for Study and References to Literature.**

1. Write a chapter on the crisis in the churches of Galatia. In describing the judaizers, make use of Acts 15, 2 Cor. 10–13, and Rom. 16:17–20, as well as the letter to the Galatians.

2. On the date and place of composition of the letter to the Galatians see:

Weiss, *Introduction to the New Testament*, Vol. I, pp. 234 ff., who thinks it was written from Ephesus about 56 A. D.; Bacon, *New Testament Introduction*, pp. 57, 58, who thinks it was written from Corinth in the year 50 A. D.; and McGiffert, *The Apostolic Age*, pp. 226 ff., who thinks it was written from Antioch before the second missionary journey.

CHAPTER XVII

THE LIFE OF THE CHURCH AT CORINTH AS SEEN THROUGH PAUL'S LETTERS TO THE CORINTHIANS

SYNOPSIS

§ 107. **Constituency and organization of the church.**
§ 108. **The parties in the church.**
§ 109. **The survival of gentile immorality.**
§ 110. **Marriage versus celibacy.**
§ 111. **The use of sacrificial meat.**
§ 112. **Women in public worship.**
§ 113. **Spiritual gifts; prophecy and speaking with tongues.**
§ 114. **Denial of the resurrection.**
§ 115. **Sacred ordinances.**

§ 107. Constituency and Organization of the Church.

a) *Constituency of the church.*—The Corinthian church, like all the other churches founded by Paul, was predominantly gentile, but the Jewish element seems to have been of considerable size. We are told that Crispus the ruler of the synagogue was converted with all his house (Acts 18:8; 1 Cor. 1:14), and it is probable that the "Cephas" party had its nucleus in the Jewish contingent. Of the gentiles in the Corinthian church it is likely that the great majority were Greek, but as Corinth was one of the most cosmopolitan of cities[1] the converts of Paul may well have included a considerable variety of races. His host (Gaius) on both occasions when he spent any length of time in Corinth appears to have been a Roman (Acts 18:7; 1 Cor. 1:14), also his amanuensis (Tertius) when he composed the letter to the Romans, and two of those who sent greetings in that letter (Lucius and Quartus).

In regard to the social, educational, and financial standing of the Corinthian believers, the indications are that a large majority of them belonged to the lower class. Paul reminded them that not many wise, not many mighty, not many noble had been called (1 Cor. 1:26). Yet the poverty and ignorance of the Corinthian member-

[1] Mommsen, *Provinces of the Roman Empire*, Vol. I, p. 304, says that Corinth was the least Greek town in Hellas.

ship must not be too strongly emphasized. Families like those of Chloe and Stephanas, who could undertake long journeys at their own charges and who ministered to the saints, evidently had means. Crispus and Gaius and Erastus were probably men of education and property. Again, believers who went to law (1 Cor. 6) were certainly not of the poorest, and Paul never intimates that a collection for the saints in Jerusalem would be any special hardship to the Corinthian Christians, as it was to those of Macedonia. The fact that Paul labored with his own hands while founding the church in Corinth (Acts 18:3), and was not a burden to the converts (2 Cor. 11:7; 12:13), was for reasons independent of their worldly estate (2 Cor. 12:9–12).

Of the size of the Corinthian church at the time when the letters were written we have no very definite knowledge. It is assumed that they all met together for worship, apparently in a private house, which suggests that the number was comparatively small, perhaps one to three hundred.

b) *The organization of the church in Corinth.*—In the church at Corinth, which was five or six years old when the letters were written, there appears to have been no formal organization. The house of Stephanas "set themselves to minister to the saints" (1 Cor. 16:15), and the language of Paul implies that there were some others who had done the same. Paul "besought" the brethren to be in subjection to such leaders, but plainly their position was quite unofficial. The entire absence of any ordained spiritual leaders appears from the account of the public worship (1 Cor. 14:26–40). Directing and governing were as yet only functions variously exercised, and not fixed in regularly appointed officers (1 Cor. 12:29).

The Corinthian church, however, may not have been exceptional in this matter of organization. We do not know that Paul ever repeated the course that he adopted with the churches of Pisidia and Lycaonia. There were bishops and deacons at Philippi when Paul wrote to that church, but it is not known that Paul had anything to do with their appointment. In any case, he thought it best to leave the Corinthians to work out an organization when it should please them to do so. He may have been the more inclined to this course because of the strongly developed individualism of the Corinthians. Whether the disorders of the Corinthian church would have been less, had there been bishops and deacons, we have no means of determining.

§ 108. **The Parties in the Church.**—Four parties sprang up in the Corinthian church within the two years following Paul's departure, whose watchwords were Paul, Apollos, Cephas, and Christ

(1 Cor. 1:12). The work of Apollos in Corinth, who had come over from Ephesus with the approval of Aquila and Priscilla and other brethren, probably gave the first impulse to the formation of a party. It was doubtless after the departure of Apollos that some members of the church openly professed their allegiance to him in preference to Paul, and this profession led others to declare that Paul was their standard. Paul and Apollos had preached the same gospel, as the language of Paul plainly implies when he says that he had planted and Apollos had watered (1 Cor. 3:6). It is implied also in the fact that, even after the division had arisen in the church, Paul urged Apollos to go again to Corinth (1 Cor. 16:12). The basis, therefore, of the unfortunate division in the church must have been the manner rather than the matter of the teaching of Paul and Apollos. The teaching of Paul had not been in persuasive words of wisdom, it had not carried men along by its studied eloquence, but had been a plain and direct appeal to the reason and heart. Apollos, on the other hand, was a man of decided emotional temperament, a speaker of exceptional brilliancy and force (Acts 18:24, 25, 28). Since he was an Alexandrian, he may well have come under the powerful influence of Philo's philosophy, in which case his teaching would have been the more likely to find enthusiastic adherents among the Greeks of Corinth.

We may suppose that, at the time when First Corinthians was written, these two parties, that of Apollos and that of Paul, were more conspicuous than the other two. The Cephas party and the Christ party are barely named, and there seem to be very few allusions to them in the first letter. As to the former of these parties, we can only conjecture what their distinctive position was. Peter had not been in Corinth, and there is no evidence that he had purposely sought to have influence there. But his name and work may easily have become known to members of the synagogue, and it was probably among these that his type of teaching was held as being in some respect superior to that of Paul or that of Apollos. We may not err if we suppose that this party was mildly legalistic, their teaching being a half-way station between the gospel of Paul and the doctrine of the Christ party (cf. Pfleiderer, *The Influence of the Apostle Paul on Christianity*, Hibbert Lectures, 1885).

But the Christ party, since their leaders seem to be the people against whom Paul directs his argument in the last four chapters of second Corinthians, are well known. The originators of this faction were the same sort of people as those who unsettled the churches of Galatia, that is, they were judaizers, advocates of circumcision and of salvation by works of the law. The fact that when Paul wrote our first letter to the Corinthians he barely mentioned this party indicates that the messengers from Chloe had said little about it. It is not unlikely that the most influential judaizers had not yet arrived in Corinth, and that the party was still in its infancy. But in the interval between our first and second letters, the party, whether through a powerful reinforcement from abroad or by a rapid internal development, became the most serious menace to the church. The leaders claimed to be apostles and evidently laid much stress on the character of their appointment (2 Cor. 12:11). They of course did not claim to have been appointed by Christ; but they probably represented themselves as apostles of the mother-church at Jerusalem. The letters of commendation with which they seem to have been furnished (2 Cor. 3:1) doubtless purported to be from the authorities of that church. Why they called themselves by the name of Christ,[1] whether because they claimed to have seen him in the flesh, or only because they claimed to represent his teaching in its purity, we can not tell.

The work of these men in the Corinthian church abounded in personalities. They called in question Paul's apostleship (1 Cor. 9:1; 2 Cor. 12:12, etc.); they denied that he had ever received revelations from the Lord (see 2 Cor. 12:1–11); they spoke disparagingly of his presence and speech, as lacking the authority which belongs to the apostolic consciousness (2 Cor. 10:10); they apparently put the same interpretation on the fact that Paul had not taken support from the Corinthian believers while he labored among them (2 Cor. 11:7; 12:16–18); and they declared that he walked according to the flesh (2 Cor. 10:2), and lacked the signs of an apostle (2 Cor. 12:12). These personalities Paul answered with other personalities,

[1] The view that the words "I of Christ" in 1 Cor. 1:12 give Paul's own position, and are not the watchword of a separate party in Corinth, is not only contrary to the next verse, but is also excluded by 2 Cor. 10:7.

but also with a crushing weight of argument. We are not told what influence his letter had on this particular party, but it is plain that the church as a whole remained faithful to him (see, e. g., Rom. 16:21–23; Acts 20:3). The party spirit which had developed with such amazing vigor, fed chiefly by the intellectual pride of the Corinthians, did not wreck the church.

§ 109. **The Survival of Gentile Immorality.**—The common standard of immorality was probably lower in Corinth than in any other city in which Paul labored, unless Antioch be excepted (cf. Mommsen, *Provinces of the Roman Empire*, Vol. II, pp. 145 ff.). To live as a Corinthian had become a proverb. Licentiousness was part of the recognized service of that goddess whose temple was the most conspicuous in Corinth. It was not strange, therefore, that among the converts to Christianity there was now and then a recrudescence of gentile immorality. Two immoral tendencies had become especially prominent before the writing of the first letter, viz., a tendency to unchastity and a tendency to quarrelsomeness. Fornication seems not to have been infrequent (1 Cor. 6:12:20; 7:2; 10:8). Even after the first letter had been received in Corinth, and perhaps also after Paul had again visited Corinth and had written another letter which is no longer extant, we learn that many had not repented of their uncleanness and fornication and lasciviousness (2 Cor. 12:21). The culminating sin of this sort was that a member of the church lived in an unlawful relation with his father's wife, who herself, since Paul addresses no word to her, may be regarded as an unbeliever. The sin was aggravated, if possible, by the fact that the father was still living (2 Cor. 7:12),[1] and was apparently a member of the church.

The most significant feature of this case was that the church, or at least a large number of the members, were puffed up regarding it (1 Cor. 5:2), yea, actually gloried in it (1 Cor. 5:6). This seems at first incredible, for the sin, as Paul says, was condemned even by the gentiles (for instances see Findlay on First Corinthians in *The Expositor's Greek Testament*). But what the church gloried in was not the bare sin itself. Such an assumption would be pre-

[1] It is open to question whether the offender of 1 Cor. 5 and that of 2 Cor. 7:8–12 are the same person. That appears to me, on the whole, the most probable view.

posterous. Their standard of life had not become lower since they accepted the gospel, but vastly higher. They were puffed up regarding the act, and for a time defended the perpetrator of it, simply because it illustrated the principle of liberty, which they held with passionate fervor but with a total lack of moral discrimination. The man who had married his father's wife was regarded as a sort of hero in the church because his act gave the boldest illustration of the new doctrine of individual emancipation. This was the reason why Paul had such hard work to carry the church with him and secure the punishment of the wrong-doer. They felt that a principle was at stake, which they were unwilling to see narrowed in the least.

It seems most probable that the obscure passage in 2 Corinthians 2:5–11 refers to the case of incest, and not to some unknown insult offered to the apostle on that visit in Corinth which fell between our two letters (Weizsäcker, *The Apostolic Age*, Vol. I, pp. 349–53). A certain punishment was, accordingly, inflicted on the wrong-doer, but not by the entire church; there was a minority who still held out against Paul's injunction (2 Cor. 2:6). Moreover, if we put a visit of Paul to Corinth between our first and second letters (2 Cor. 2:1, 12:14; 13:1), and if we refer 2 Cor. 2:4 to a lost letter, both the visit and the letter seem to have been concerned with this sin of incest, and we have thus yet more evidence of the struggle which it cost the apostle to teach the Corinthians that Christian liberty is not license. And even then many seem to have remained untaught (2 Cor. 12:21).

The other outcropping of gentile immorality in the Corinthian church was litigiousness. Brother went to law with brother, and that before unbelievers. The root of this trouble seems to have been a spirit of covetousness. There was fraud and overreaching in the business relations of Christians. Those who brought lawsuits against their brothers rather than be defrauded were themselves open to prosecution for their wrong-doing. It is plain that in all such cases business life did not yet feel the force of the gospel which had been formally accepted.

§ 110. **Marriage versus Celibacy.**—Under the influence of the new religious views, there soon arose in the Corinthian church a decided tendency toward an ascetic treatment of marriage. A strong revulsion of feeling from the former lax conceptions of the relations of the sexes carried some of the church far toward the other extreme of celibacy for the unmarried and a discontinuance of marital relaions between husbands and wives. The question was also discussed whether an unbelieving wife or husband ought not to be divorced. On these points, as on some others, they wrote to Paul for counsel. Whether this was by vote of the whole company of believers or was the act of a part only, we have no means of determining.

This questioning in the Corinthian church is an evidence that some men were seeking in a serious manner to make application of the principles of the gospel, and is also evidence that their glorying in the act of incest was, as we sought to show in the last paragraph, not an indication of sympathy with the relation itself but of their hysterical devotion to what they imagined was Christian liberty.

It is not in accord with the plan of this work to go into a detailed study of Paul's teaching on the subject of marriage, but we shall simply consider it with a view to learning the thought and spirit of the Corinthian believers. Paul begins with the declaration that it is *good*, morally becoming and right, to live in celibacy. The form of the statement seems to imply that the Corinthians had put the question regarding the advisability of celibacy as though expecting an affirmative answer. But though Paul admits that celibacy is good, he thinks it it not wise for his Corinthian converts as a whole (1 Cor. 7:2). And he indicates plainly why he regards it as good, viz., because of the present distress (vs. 26; 2 Thess. 2:2). The work of the Lord was considered to be urgent because the end of the age was thought to be near, and for this reason it seemed advisable for the unmarried to remain as they were, provided that they had the gift of continency. Paul did not lay down a general principle that celibacy is morally becoming, still less that it is preferable to the married state, or even necessary to the attainment of holiness.

To those who were married to unbelievers Paul applied the principle, recognized by Jesus, that the marriage bond is indissoluble. If the unbelieving husband or wife chose to depart, it was to be allowed, but evidently Paul inclined to the view that the believing member of the household should seek to hold the unbelieving member rather than to promote his departure by cold treatment. There was hope that the unbelieving member would be won over to the gospel. And this exhortation to those who had unbelieving wives or husbands, that they should continue in their present state, was addressed also to those who were questioning in regard to circumcision and the duty of Christian slaves. The presence or absence of circumcision, Paul wrote, was not a matter to be discussed as though it pertained to godliness, and the Christian slave, seeing that he was the Lord's freeman, was not to be troubled by his servitude to an earthly master.[1]

[1] The translation of 1 Cor. 7:21*b* is uncertain. Vss. 20 and 24 favor the view that Paul would have the Christian slave remain with his master even though he had an opportunity to become free.

§ 111. **The Use of Sacrificial Meat.**—In regard to the use of sacrificial meat there were two views among the Corinthian believers. It is plain that the majority had, or thought they had, "knowledge" regarding idols, and did not scruple to eat the sacrificial meat. The question, therefore, was not raised by these on their own account, but on account of certain persons who hesitated to use such meat. These are referred to by Paul as those who had not knowledge, or as those whose consciences were weak, or simply as the weak. The question may have come from this minority orginally, but it is obvious that they who wrote the letter to Paul were not of the "weak." Their view of the matter can be seen through Paul's reply. They felt that an idol was naught, and therefore the meat which had been sacrificed remained just the same as it had been before. One could eat it without hesitation; and evidently this is what they did. And they were inclined to look upon those who shrank from using the sacrificial meat as being rather stupid. Paul agreed with them that an idol is naught, but said it was not enough to recognize this fact; that there was something yet more important in its bearing on their conduct, and that was their brother's good. In itself it was not wrong to sit at meat in an idol's house, but it was wrong if thereby a brother's conscience was wounded.

Believers were not required to ask about meat when they went to the markets to buy (1 Cor. 10:23—11:1). That would be an unnecessary concession to the weak brother. But when they were eating in another's house, the house of an unbeliever, and it was told them that the meat was sacrificial, they should refrain from eating on account of the other's conscience. The word employed here to designate the meat (*ἱερόθυτον*, not *εἰδωλόθυτον*) indicates that the information regarding it was assumed to come from an unbeliever, either from the host himself, or, more probably, from a guest. What the motive could be in such a case is not altogether clear, but Paul appears to suggest that it might be the unbeliever's conscience, and that for this reason he counseled abstinence.

§ 112. **Women in Public Worship.**—We have no means of ascertaining what proportion of the Corinthian church were women, but it is plain that the women of that church, whether more or less in number, were conspicuous in the meetings for worship. The doctrine of liberty was illustrated by the fact that women participated freely with the men in public prayer and prophecy, which was in harmony, indeed, with Paul's teaching that in Christ Jesus there can be neither Jew nor Greek, neither bond nor free, neither male nor female. The apostle never laid any restriction on woman's participation in worship, either in Corinth or elsewhere. For when he enjoined on the Corinthian women to keep silence in the churches (1 Cor. 14:34, 35; cf. 1 Tim. 2:11, 12), the context shows that the speaking which was prohibited was not praying or prophesying, that is, not participating in public worship, but speaking to "learn." This may have been a forward asking of questions.[1] It certainly was not participation in worship.

There was, however, one point in the participation of Corinthian women in public worship of which Paul decidedly disapproved, that is, their praying and prophesying with unveiled heads. This was allowed by the Greeks in their worship (see Meyer's *Commentary* on First Corinthians 11:5), and hence it was perfectly natural that the Greek converts retained the custom. But it was contrary to the practice of the synagogue, in which women were veiled, though they did not take part in the service. Paul may have been prejudiced against the custom of the Greek women because of his training in the synagogue. But his arguments against it were general in character. He claimed that it showed a lack of subordination to man and also that it was contrary to nature, for nature by giving women long hair indicates that her head should be covered. One can not blame the Corinthian women if they failed to be convinced by these arguments. But here, as in so many other cases, we do not know what effect Paul's directions had.

§ 113. **Spiritual Gifts, especially Prophecy and Speaking with Tongues** (Glossolaly).—No feature of the religious life of the Corinthians stirred Paul more deeply than that of their spiritual gifts (*charisms*). There appears to have been among them a singular wealth of manifestations which they attributed to the Holy Spirit. This was seen in the gatherings for public worship, where one contributed an original psalm, another some teaching, a third a revela-

[1] For other explanations see Findlay in *The Expositor's Greek Testament*, Vol. II, p. 914.

tion, yet another spoke in a tongue, and another had the gift of interpreting tongues. Nor does this list exhaust the spiritual manifestations in the Corinthian church. One man was distinguished for his remarkable faith, another had the gift of healing, a third wrought miracles, a fourth prophesied, and another could discern spirits. It is not strange that in this wealth of spiritual activities there was sometimes doubt whence they came. In their letter to Paul, the Corinthians asked how they could recognize the Spirit, and he in his reply gave them a very general practical test (1 Cor. 12:3).

It is plain that the "spiritual" gifts of the Corinthian believers were not altogether for their spiritual good. They promoted pride and an unspiritual comparing of gift with gift, as though there were many Holy Spirits, one working in this manner and another in that. They also rendered the public gatherings for worship disorderly, for one was apt to assume that his special communication was of more importance than his brother's, and hence he did not hesitate to interrupt his brother.

The lack of a sane and spiritual estimate of the gifts was particularly shown in the fact that few cared to prophesy (i. e., teach), but many desired to speak with tongues. Now this speaking with tongues was an inarticulate utterance of emotion, wholly meaningless without an interpreter. The speaker was beside himself; his understanding was unfruitful. To outsiders he appeared like a mad man. Paul considered it childish that the Corinthians were so eager to have this gift, the most spectacular of all, but also the one of least practical value. He wished them rather to cultivate the gift of prophecy, or better still, to cultivate love (cf. Gal. 5:22, 23), for Paul did not think of the Spirit as specially manifest in strange or supernatural works, but rather as the Spirit of the new life throughout (cf. Wood, *The Spirit of God in Biblical Literature*, pp. 203–6).

§ 114. **Denial of the Resurrection.**—The most important doctrinal feature of the Corinthian church was a denial of the resurrection. How general this was we can not learn from Paul's letter. He simply says there were "some" (*τινές*) among his readers who held this view. It is most unfortunate that we do not know more fully what these skeptical Christians thought on the subject of the resurrection. Did they deny the immortality of the soul? Did they say that the gospel was good only for this life? Or did they simply deny a resurrection of the material body, but hold the immortality of the soul? Were they influenced by the philosophy of the Stoics, who believed in the soul but denied its conscious existence after death, or by the philosophy of the Epicureans who denied the existence of the soul altogether, or by the philosophy of Plato who taught that the soul is immortal?

They evidently admitted the resurrection of Jesus (1 Cor. 15:12), and presumably in the form in which Paul had taught it. It would seem, therefore, as though they must have admitted that man, or at least a good man, may have a conscious life after death. But, on the other hand, Paul speaks as though their doctrine were dangerous to good morals (1 Cor. 15:33), and as though it lessened one's interest in the work of the Lord (1 Cor. 15:58), which statements seem to imply that their denial of the resurrection was understood by Paul to involve a denial also of immortality. And Paul himself, moreover, did not believe in the resurrection of the material body. What is raised, he says, is not flesh and blood; it is not material, but spiritual. If, then, the skeptical Corinthians merely denied a physical resurrection, they might still have been in substantial agreement with Paul; but his language does not encourage us to believe that this was the case.

On the whole, therefore, it seems probable that those among the Corinthian believers who said that there is no resurrection were at least skeptical on the subject of immortality, if they did not positively affirm that death ends all. They were virtually of the same mind with the people of the neighboring city of Athens who mocked at the thought of a resurrection (Acts 17:32). On what grounds the Corinthian believers set aside the doctrine of resurrection we do not know. It is suggested by 1 Cor. 15:35 that they considered it irrational, but this may have been affirmed by them of physical resurrection only. It is highly suggestive that they accepted the proof which Paul gave of the resurrection of Jesus. Their position would have been immeasurably strengthened could they have shown good reason for rejecting that proof. But there is no evidence that it was even questioned by them. Paul's entire argument rests on the assumption that his readers agree with him in regard to the resurrection of Jesus.

§ 115. **Sacred Ordinances.**—We complete our survey of the inner life of the Corinthian church with some reference to their observance of baptism and the Lord's supper.

Paul had treated baptism as a matter of secondary importance while laboring in Corinth, as he did elsewhere. He was not sent to baptize, but to preach the gospel (1 Cor. 1:17). He had indeed, baptized Crispus and Gaius, also the household of Stephanas, but the baptism of the rest of his converts had been left to other hands.

After Paul went away, the Corinthians came to attach greater significance to baptism. This is evident from the custom of being baptized for the dead, to which we have incidental allusion. It appears that certain Corinthian believers received the rite of baptism on behalf of their departed friends, who of course had not been baptized, who, indeed, may have died before Paul came to Corinth. Since there were no officers in the Corinthian church, no elder or deacon, we must suppose that the rite was administered either by the head of the family or by some prominent member of the church like Stephanas. Now this practice obviously involved peculiar and utterly un-Pauline conceptions of baptism. It would not have occurred to people to be baptized for their dead friends if they had not believed that the rite was in itself efficacious, a saving ordinance. The power or virtue of it was also thought of as transferable from one person to another, and even from the living to the dead. Thus we see that the rite had come to be thought of in a most unspiritual manner, as being little more than a superior sort of magic. The incidental way in which Paul alludes to the practice may indicate that it was as yet only an exceptional phenomenon in Corinth.

The method of observing the Lord's Supper in Corinth affords a startling proof of the crass immaturity and unspirituality of the church. In the first place, the common meal with which the Supper was associated appears to have been the important thing, and little thought was given to the Supper itself. But even this common meal was kept in an utterly unbrotherly and un-Christian manner. It was not eaten in common, with any regard for its symbolic character, its illustration of the truth of Christian fellowship, but it was like any other meal of the day, an eating and drinking to satisfy the cravings of appetite. Each had regard to his own hunger and thirst. Some of the more prosperous members drank to excess, and some of the poor went away from the gathering hungry. In what manner these people afterward partook of the Lord's Supper we are not told. As they ate in separate groups, and at different times, we may suppose that they partook of the symbolical bread and wine in the same fashion. From the fact that Paul gave them again in his letter an account of the institution of the Supper, it may be inferred with much probability that their observance was seriously defective. This is also evident from the circumstance that Paul thought of the cases of sickness and death in the Corinthian church as a divine judgment caused by their profanation of the Supper. We must, therefore, suppose not only that the common meal was kept in an unbecoming way, but also that the memorial celebration of the Lord's death was practically emptied of its meaning.

As to the time when the members of the church in Corinth met for the Lord's Supper we get no certain information from the letter. When speaking of the collection for the saints in Jerusalem, Paul assumed that the church met on the first day of the week (1 Cor. 16:2), and it is probable that the Supper was a part of the service at this meeting. It was perhaps in the evening, as was the meeting in Troas at which the Supper was celebrated (Acts 20:7), the time when the members were naturally most free from business cares. The language of Paul indicates that the Supper was observed at each meeting (1 Cor. 11:20).

§ 116. **Questions and Suggestions for Study.**—(1) Name some prominent Jews and Romans in the Corinthian church. (2) What inference regarding the constituency of the church may be drawn from the character of the city? (3) What was the social and financial standing of the membership of the church. (4) What indications have we of the size of the Corinthian church? (5) What was the condition with regard to organization?

(6) How many parties were there in the Corinthian church, and what were their watchwords? (7) Describe the origin of the parties of Paul and Apollos. (8) What was probably the character of the

Cephas party? (9) Where do we find the leaders of the Christ party described? (10) Why is there so little about them in the first letter? (11) What did the leaders claim for themselves? (12) How did they work against Paul? (13) What effect did Paul's letters have on the party spirit in Corinth?

(14) What was the moral condition of Corinth? (15) What particular form of gentile immorality soon appeared in the church? (16) How did the church regard the case of incest? (17) How is their attitude toward it to be explained? (18) What evidence is there that Paul had a hard struggle to carry his point in this matter? (19) What was the root of litigiousness among the Corinthian believers?

(20) What tendency of thought regarding marriage did Christianity produce in Corinth? (21) What questions regarding it had the Corinthian believers sent to Paul? (22) What did he say on the general principle? How did he justify his view? (23) What did he say regarding cases where either husband or wife was an unbeliever?

(24) What two views were held at Corinth regarding sacrificial meat? (25) How did the majority feel in regard to its use? (26) What fundamental principle did Paul lay down to guide his converts? (27) Describe the case of a Christian at dinner with an unbeliever. (28) What was the place of women in public worship in Corinth? (29) Did Paul seek to narrow this liberty? (30) What did he object to in the matter of woman's dress in public worship, and why?

(31) What spiritual gifts were found in the Corinthian church? (32) How did the wealth of gifts work injury? (33) What gift was most sought? (34) Describe this gift. (35) How did the Corinthians expect the Spirit to manifest itself?

(36) What was Paul's view on this point? (37) What important doctrinal error was there in the Corinthian church? (38) How widely was it held? (39) What reasons are there for thinking that those who denied the resurrection did not believe in immortality? (40) How did they regard the resurrection of Jesus?

(41) How did Paul regard baptism in comparison with preaching the gospel? (42) What practice arose in the church of Corinth in reference to the dead? (43) What conception of baptism did this

practice imply? (44) How was the common meal observed in the Corinthian church? (45) How did they observe the Lord's Supper? (46) What proofs are there that the Supper had been emptied of its meaning? (47) What is probable regarding the time of the observance of the Lord's Supper? (48) Is there any party spirit in the church of today like that which we see in Corinth? (49) Is Paul's method of dealing with the party spirit of value now? (50) Has the church outgrown gentile immoralities? (51) Is the position of woman in modern church work in line with Paul's principles? (52) What was there in a meeting of Corinthian believers for worship that you think would appeal to you?

§ 117. **Supplementary Topics for Study and References to Literature.**

1. Write a chapter on the life of the Corinthian church, having an outline somewhat as follows: General survey of the church as to size, organization, and character; conspicuous defects of the church; prominent questions under discussion; description of a meeting for worship.

2. On the general subject of organization see:

Hatch, *The Organization of the Early Christian Churches*, and Thatcher, *A Sketch of the History of the Apostolic Church*, pp. 288–300.

3. On the parties in the church at Corinth see:

Weizsäcker, *The Apostolic Age*, Vol. I, pp. 325–33.

4. On the position and dress of women in Greece read:

Becker, *Charicles*, pp. 413–44, 462–98.

CHAPTER XVIII

CHRISTIANITY IN ROME AS REFLECTED IN PAUL'S LETTER TO THE ROMANS

SYNOPSIS

§ 118. **Paul in Macedonia and Achaia.**—Before the riot of Demetrius occurred, Paul had purposed to leave Ephesus in the near future. Luke tells us that he proposed to visit Macedonia and Achaia, thence go to Jerusalem, and after that to Rome and Spain (Acts 19:21). And this statement is supported by what Paul says in the letter to the Romans, written within a few months after he left Ephesus, namely, that he had longed to come to Rome for many years (Rom. 1:13). Thus it appears that, in spite of his exhausting labors in Ephesus with their many perils and sufferings, he was contemplating longer journeys and greater undertakings in the interest of the gospel.

Prior to the interruption of his work in Ephesus, Paul had sent Timothy and Erastus into Macedonia, probably in the interest of the collection which he was making for the mother-church in Jerusalem. This had been in progress in Achaia for about a year (2 Cor. 9:2), and was also being made in Galatia (1 Cor. 16:1). Paul's proposed visit to Jerusalem was to convey this collection. At the private conference in Jerusalem, Paul had been urged by the leaders of the church to remember the poor, that is, the poor of the Jewish-Christian church, and the collection which he was about to complete as he left Ephesus was the first response to that request of which we know.[1] Paul felt that it was quite right that the gentiles,

[1] Gal. 2:10 may possibly suggest that Paul had been mindful of the poor in Jerusalem even *before* the conference, but this interpretation on the whole does not seem probable.

even though poor, should make this offering because it was from the Jewish believers that they had received the gospel (Rom. 15:27). He doubtless hoped also that this practical manifestation of a Christian spirit on the part of the gentile believers would help to bind more closely together the two great divisions of the church.

As Timothy and Erastus seem to have been sent into Macedonia to work for the collection, so Titus with two unnamed persons had charge of the business in Corinth (2 Cor. 8:6, 18, 22). Paul speaks of having given orders to the churches of Galatia (1 Cor. 16:1), either when he was last there before coming to Ephesus, or, perhaps, by letter from Ephesus, and this order may have covered the appointment of delegates to take charge of the funds. Paul did not receive any of this money into his own hands, nor did he make personal solicitation for it except by letter. From various circumstances we infer that this contribution for the mother-church was large. This is suggested, in the first place, by the fact that it was general, coming from the churches of Galatia, Macedonia, and Achaia, also from the province of Asia, if we regard Tychicus and Trophimus as delegates (Acts 21:29; 20:4). It was being gathered through a period of about two years, and was conveyed to Jerusalem by a company of at least seven men besides Paul. And, finally, Paul tells us that some of the churches which contributed gave far beyond their power (2 Cor. 8:3). All these facts suggest a large offering.

The course of Paul when he left Ephesus was determined not only by the collection but also by anxiety for the church at Corinth. Disquieting reports had reached him in Ephesus which had occasioned two letters to the Corinthian church, one of which is no longer extant (1 Cor. 5:9), while the other is our first letter to the Corinthians. This had been sent by Titus, and when Paul had come into Macedonia he waited until Titus came to him, reporting the condition of affairs in Corinth. He had expected to meet Titus in Troas (2 Cor. 2:12), but failing in this expectation he came on into Macedonia (2 Cor. 2:13). Here at length he met him, received an encouraging report about the Corinthian church, and thereupon wrote to it another letter. His tour among the Macedonian churches of which Luke speaks (Acts 20:2) doubtless followed the return of Titus, for before that time he was in no condition to visit and exhort them (2 Cor. 2:13; 7:5–16).

From Macedonia Paul went into Achaia where he spent three months (Acts 20:3). He was entertained by Gaius, in whose house he probably wrote the letter to the Romans (Rom. 16:23). We are not told how Paul spent these three months, but considering the state of the church in the recent past, it is most likely that he devoted himself to its establishment in the faith. From the fact that the Jews conspired to kill him we may infer that he made his influence felt in the city (Acts 20:3).

§ 119. **Early History of the Roman Church.**—The fragmentariness of our records of the apostolic age is nowhere more strikingly illustrated than in the fact that we know nothing of the fortunes of Christianity in the metropolis of the world until nearly a generation after the resurrection. We are told that both Jews and proselytes from Rome heard the preaching of Peter in Jerusalem at Pentecost (Acts 2:10), and it is altogether probable that within six months of that time some of those Jews and proselytes who had been converted and baptized were back in Rome. During the 26 years that elapsed before Paul wrote to the Roman believers, there were doubtless many Christians from the East who visited Rome, both in the way of business and as evangelists. But if the seed of the gospel was not planted in Rome by some who had been in Jerusalem at Pentecost, it is almost necessary to think that it was planted there soon after the martyrdom of Stephen, when messengers went forth in all directions and a gentile church was established in Antioch. If men of Cyrene in North Africa were drawn to Antioch, so doubtless were others drawn to Rome. There was easy and constant intercourse between Rome and her provinces, and no people were more given to travel than the Jews, who also were the most widely scattered of all the peoples (cf. Sanday and Headlam, *Commentary on Romans*, p. 418).

We must suppose, then, that there had been disciples of Jesus in Rome for a period of twelve or fifteen years before Paul's letter, if not for a much longer time. But who first told the story of Jesus in the capital of the world and gathered the first little circle of believers, whether it was a Jew or a proselyte, a native of Rome or a traveling evangelist, no one can tell. This, however, appears to be clear, that the Roman believers at the time when Paul wrote to them were Christians of his type,[1] and not of the conservative legalistic sort (see e. g., Rom. 1:8, 11, 12; 15:14).

§ 120. **Constituency and Organization.**—The Christian community in Rome was mainly composed of gentiles. If its original nucleus had been Jews, as was perhaps the case, the time had long since passed when they were in the majority. Paul repeatedly assumes that his readers are gentiles (see 1:13; 10:1; 11:13, 28; 15:16), not exclusively but predominantly. When he said: "I speak to men who know the law," and again: "Ye were made dead to the law through the body of Christ" (7:1, 4), he doubtless had in mind the Jewish element among his readers. This element is represented in the list of greetings by Aquila and Herodion, probably also by Priscilla; and the members of the household of Aristobulus who are saluted were doubtless Jews, if this Aristobulus was the grandson of Herod the Great, as is supposed. Mary, too, may have been a Jewess, and of course it is possible that some of the persons who bore Greek and Roman names were nevertheless Jews. Jesus who was surnamed Justus, who sent greetings in the letter to the Colossians, is more likely to have been a member of the Roman congregation whom Paul found in Rome than a convert whom he himself made there. As far, then, as we may judge of the entire company of believers in Rome by the list of names in chapter 16, we may rate the Jewish element at about one-seventh of the whole.

The Roman believers at the time of Paul's letter to them appear to have had no formal organization whatever. Paul does not address them as a church. There is no trace of a bishop or a deacon. This was found to be the case in respect to the church at Corinth also, but it is more remarkable in Rome because the gospel had been planted there many years. There seem to have been at least three companies of Roman believers, viz., those who met in the home of Aquila and Priscilla, those who were associated with the five brethren, Asyncritus, Phlegon, Hermes, Patrobas, and Hermas, and, finally, the group of whom Paul mentions Philologus, Julia, Nereus and his sister, and Olympas. The fact that there were three Christian circles in Rome suggests that there was a relatively large number of believers there, more than could meet conveniently in one home or in two. In each of these three groups there was probably one person and perhaps more than one, who had preponderating influence and who were looked

[1] This suggests what indeed is probable on other grounds, that in the Roman congregation there were converts of Paul from the cities of Greece and Asia Minor.

up to as leaders. Aquila and Priscilla were probably the leaders in their home-church, Asyncritus may have been the most prominent in the second group, Philologus and Julia in the third. But these people, if they were the leaders of the three Roman congregations, were such solely by virtue of their services and gifts, not by formal appointment.

Those of the Roman fellowship whose labor for the gospel in Rome is especially mentioned by the apostle were all women, with the exception of Aquila. Of two of these women—Mary and Persis—Paul speaks as though their labor belonged chiefly to the past, and we may think of them as having retired from active work on account of age or some other infirmity; the remaining three—Priscilla, Tryphena, and Tryphosa—were still in active service. But there is no suggestion that these women were clothed with any official power by the Roman believers. They were simply persons whose zeal and ability had given them an honorable prominence among the brethren.

§ 121. **The "Strong" and the "Weak."**—When Paul speaks of the "strong" and the "weak" in his letter to the Romans we are constrained to see local coloring in his words, and not merely an echo of past experiences. For, so far as we know from earlier letters, he had met no Christians who, for conscience' sake, were vegetarians, as were the weak in Rome. There were divisions in the Corinthian church on the matter of eating sacrificial meat, but we hear of no one who was opposed to eating *any* meat whatsoever. Since then we find a new phenomenon in the Roman letter, and since the language of Paul is just such as we should expect if he had had actual facts of the Roman church in mind, we ought not to say that he is generalizing.

The party of the weak in Rome were a minority (14:1). They ate herbs and abstained from the use of wine (14:2, 21). They also esteemed one day above another (14:5). They judged those who ate flesh and drank wine and esteemed all days alike (14:3). Now as the Jews were not forbidden to eat flesh or to drink wine, we are probably not to regard the weak as Jewish Christians. They were gentiles who took up an ascetic position with reference to meat and wine, as certain Corinthians had done with reference to marriage. The reasons which they gave for their view are scarcely indicated.

They appear to have regarded meat as unclean in itself (14:14), but we are not told why. The reason of their opposition to wine is not at all suggested. Their esteeming one day above another was hardly the same as the Jewish regard for feast days, which we find among the Galatians (Gal. 4:10). This was simply a detail of the observance of the law, and did not imply that the particular day was in itself different from other days. But the Roman believers

THE INTERIOR OF AN ITALIAN HOUSE OF THE FIRST CENTURY (POMPEII)

who are styled "weak" appear to have held precisely this notion. The "strong" esteemed all days alike (14:5). That, of course, does not mean that they did not meet for worship on the first day of the week. There was no company of gentile Christians, so far as we know, who did not keep this day holy, as Jewish Christians kept the Sabbath. Therefore the statement that the "strong" in Rome esteemed all days alike means that they attached no peculiar sacredness to one day in comparison with others. Accordingly, the position of the "weak" was, by contrast, that peculiar sacredness does attach to a certain day. We are not told what particular day or days the "weak" esteemed; it is not improbable that the regular day of worship was included.

§ 122. **Those Who Caused Divisions.**—The people who were causing divisions in the Roman church when Paul wrote are described in general terms, no one of which makes it plain who they were. They claimed to be Christians; they used smooth and fair speech; their doctrine was evil; and Paul seems to refer to their overthrow when he says that God shall bruise "Satan" under the feet of the faithful shortly (16:17–20). All these characteristics fit the judaizers, though it can not be said that they necessarily require us to think of these opponents of Paul. Perhaps the most illuminating term in the description is "Satan." This appears to point to the judaizers because, in the first place, it was against the judaizers that Paul used the strongest language of condemnation (e. g., Gal. 1:8, 9; 5:12; 6:12, 13), and second, he called the Corinthian judaizers "messengers" of Satan.

In the letter to the Philippians which was written from Rome, Paul speaks of some persons who were preaching Christ of envy and strife, thinking thereby to raise up affliction for him (Phil. 1:15, 17). This language also points to judaizers, for there were no other people who, professing to be Christians, preached in opposition to Paul. This Philippian passage, therefore, is an argument for understanding Rom. 16:17–20 as referring to judaizers.

Finally, the doctrinal portion of the letter to the Romans seems to imply that there was a Jewish propaganda in the Roman church. Had not Paul known that there were judaizing influences at work there, it is difficult to believe that he would have admitted so large a controversial element into his letter. He would hardly have done this to provide for a possible *future* peril.

It is not necessary to dwell on this controversial element. It lies on the surface in many places. Why, e. g., should Paul prove that the Jews were in need of salvation by faith (chap. 2) unless there were those in Rome who were insisting upon the necessity of works of the law? Why should he argue that his doctrine of salvation by faith "established" the law unless there were those who said that it made the law of none effect (3:31)? Why, in a letter to the Romans, should he insist upon his love for the Jewish people unless there were those in Rome who said that he was a renegade and no true Jew (9:1, 2; 10: 1)? It will at least be admitted that such passages as these have added point and significance if Paul was dealing with concrete facts and not indulging in abstract generalities. Moreover, all other letters of Paul deal with local conditions, with certain definite questions and persons, and hence there is a presumption that this was the case with the letter to Romans. We are to hold, then, that those who were causing divisions in Rome were none other than Paul's old enemies the judaizers.

§ 123. **Questions and Suggestions for Study.**—(1) When did people from Rome first hear the gospel? (2) What reasons are there for thinking that the Roman church must have been founded as early at least as 44 A. D.? (3) State the evidence for regarding that church as essentially gentile. (4) How large a Jewish element might we infer from the list of greetings? (5) How many centers does the Christian community in Rome appear to have had? (6) Whom may we regard as the leaders of these circles? (7) Who are greeted by Paul as prominent in Christian service in Rome?

(8) Why are we to regard the passage on the "strong" and the "weak" as reflecting actual conditions in the Roman church? (9) Describe the weak. (10) Why can we not hold them to have been Jews? (11) How did their esteem for days differ from that of the Galatian Christians?

(12) Describe the people who caused divisions in the Roman church? (13) What reasons are there for considering them judaizers? (14) What is the bearing of the letter to the Philippians on this point? (15) What bearing upon it has the general character of the letter to the Romans?

§ 124. **Supplementary Topics for Study and References to Literature.**

1. Write a chapter on the origin and life of the Church at Rome as it is reflected in the letter to the Romans.

2. On the local color to be found in the letter to the Romans read:

Weizsäcker, *The Apostolic Age*, Vol. II, pp. 104; also Sanday and Headlam in the *International Critical Commentary on Romans, Introduction*, pp. xxxix–xliv.

3. Look up the names and locations of all individuals mentioned by Paul who had a church in their house.

PART IV

THE LAST YEARS OF THE APOSTLE PAUL

CHAPTER XIX

PAUL'S LAST VISIT TO JERUSALEM

SYNOPSIS

§ 125.	**The journey from Corinth to Jerusalem.**	**Acts 20:4–21:16**
§ 126.	**Paul's reception by the church in Jerusalem.**	**Acts 21:17–26**
§ 127.	**Paul's arrest in Jerusalem.**	**Acts 21:27–36**
§ 128.	**The address from the castle stairs.**	**Acts 21:37—22:29**
§ 129.	**Paul before the Sanhedrin.**	**Acts 22:30—23:11**
§ 130.	**Paul's removal to Cæsarea.**	**Acts 23:12–35**

§ 125. **The Journey from Corinth to Jerusalem.**—The discovery of the plot of the Jews changed Paul's plan of travel. He decided to go back through Macedonia instead of taking ship for Jerusalem from Corinth. According to Luke there were at least seven men who accompanied him from Corinth (Acts 20:4), whom we are to regard as delegates of the churches to carry the collection to Jerusalem (1 Cor. 16:3, 4; Acts 21:29). It appears then that these men had gathered in Corinth, expecting to take ship there for Syria. If this was indeed the case, it suggests that the fact which occasioned the change of plan was of exceeding gravity, for that change meant that all the seven were to retrace their steps, some of whom had journeyed several hundred miles to reach Corinth. One important consequence of Paul's change of plan was that Luke was added to the company. This addition is inferred from the "we" of Acts 20:6. The narrative which has been in the third person since the account of Paul's work in Philippi now continues in the first person. Whether Luke went as a delegate from the Philippian church does not appear.

From Philippi Paul and Luke seem to have journeyed alone to Troas, the others having gone on ahead for some unknown reason. In Troas, where Paul had desired to stop for a time when he left Ephesus (2 Cor. 2:12), and where there was now a company of believers, he and his fellow-travelers tarried a week. The narrative of this visit is especially interesting because of its reference to the observance of the Lord's Supper. The Christians of Troas and their guests met for this on Sunday evening. Paul gave an address which lasted until midnight, and then after the Supper he continued his discourse until break of day. This observance of the Supper, like the first, took place in an upper chamber of a private house, and in the night. The incident of Eutychus, who went to sleep under Paul's preaching and fell out of the window, we would gladly have done without if Luke had told us in its place the particular manner in which they observed the Supper, or what Paul said as they took the bread and wine.

From Troas Paul went on foot, and apparently alone, about twenty miles, to Assos, while Luke and the others went around the Lectum Promontory by ship. Paul met the ship at Assos, and then all proceeded together to Miletus, the metropolis of Ionia, about thirty-five miles from Ephesus, at the mouth of the Mæander River. Here they stopped long enough to have a meeting with the elders of the Ephesian church whom Paul summoned on his arrival. From his address on this occasion it appears that the apprehension which he had felt when writing from Corinth to Rome (Rom. 15:30, 31) had become deeper. He now felt that bonds and afflictions awaited him. To what this deepening of apprehension was due we do not know. It may have come simply from the fact that he was drawing nearer and nearer to Jerusalem.

From Miletus they continued their journey by way of the islands of Cos and Rhodes to Patara of Lycia, where they left their first ship and took one bound for the Phoenician coast. Having reached Tyre, they went ashore and spent a week with the Christian community of that city. When or by whom this Tyrian church was founded we do not know, possibly by Paul himself (see Gal 1:21). In this place Paul, who presumably had told his friends that his mind was filled with dark foreboding in regard to the outcome of his journey, was besought not to go to Jerusalem, and they who besought him thought that they had the sanction of the Holy Spirit for their counsel.

After a pathetic separation from the Christians of Tyre, Paul and his company came to Ptolemais, twenty miles further south, where they stopped one day and saluted the brethren; and then after a sail of twenty-five miles they reached the end of their sea-voyage at Cæsarea. Here they tarried some days with Philip the evangelist.

It is possible that Paul's arrival in Cæsarea was reported in Jerusalem, and that this report led the prophet Agabus to go down to Cæsarea to meet Paul. Doubtless this was the same prophet whom Paul had met in Antioch in the year 44 A. D. He now assured Paul that the Jews would deliver him into the hands of the gentiles. This dark prophecy led the companions of Paul and also the Christians of Cæsarea to urge him not to go to Jerusalem. But Paul withstood their entreaties and continued his journey, it having been arranged before leaving Cæsarea that Paul and his companions should lodge in Jerusalem with a Cypriote Jew by the name of Mnason.

§ 126. **Paul's Reception by the Church in Jerusalem.**—The account which Luke gives of Paul's reception by the church in Jerusalem is disappointing. It does, indeed, say that the brethren received him and his companions gladly, and also that the elders glorified God when Paul had rehearsed the story of his gentile ministry before them; but there is no word about the offering which he had long been gathering and which the brethren of various provinces had now brought up to the mother church. We are not told whether this ministration was acceptable to the saints, whether any expression of gratitude was sent back to the gentile churches, or whether the loving service tended to strengthen the bond of sympathy between the Jewish and gentile believers. It is suggestive of coldness that the Jerusalem church is not said to have expressed any sympathy for Paul during his troubles.

On the day after his arrival in Jerusalem, when he had told James and the elders about his work among the gentiles, it became manifest that he was regarded with suspicion by the majority of believers. They had heard that he was in the habit of teaching the foreign Jews to forsake Moses, and it is plain that they regarded this report as true. For James and the elders at once proposed that he should set himself right with the church by the public performance of a levitical ceremony. This step would have been unnecessary had not the report concerning Paul been widely accepted. The manner in which the proposition was made to Paul suggests that the elders themselves did not credit the report and expected that Paul would disavow it. The ceremony which they wished him to perform was that he should purify himself with four men who were under a vow, and that he should be at charges for their release. Paul consented to their wish, and on the following day began a week's participation with the four men in the ceremony made necessary by their vow.

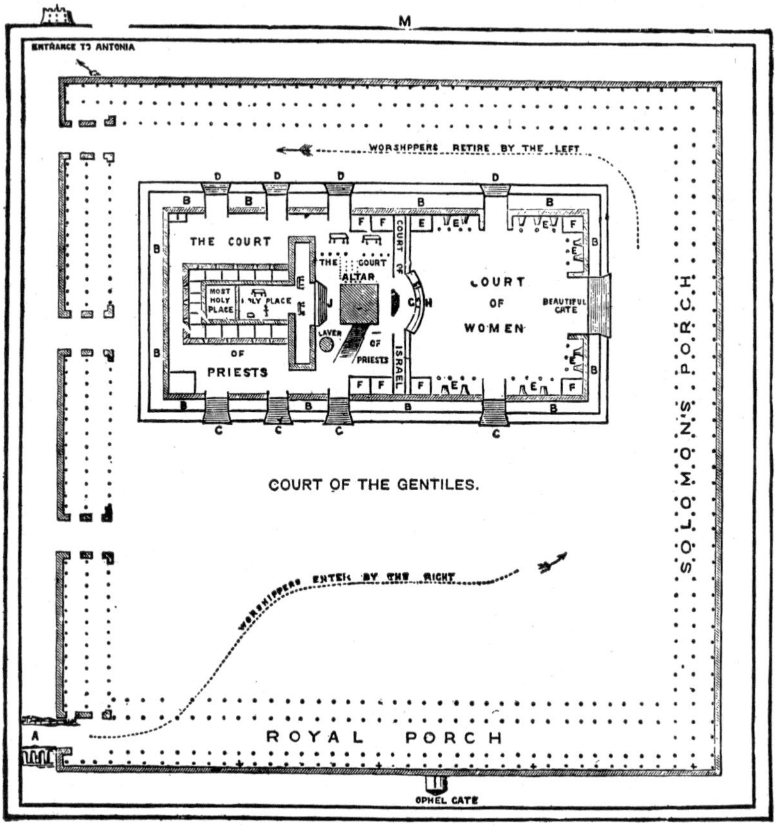

PLAN OF HEROD'S TEMPLE
[From Edersheim, *The Temple at the Time of Christ*]

It is important to keep clearly in view the aim of Paul in this ceremonial act, which was simply to declare the report untrue that he had taught the Jews to forsake the law of Moses. He had not done this thing. He had sought to lead Jews to faith in Jesus, and he had taught that salvation was by grace, not by works of the law; but he had not gone about denouncing Moses, or teaching that Jews ought not to regard Jewish rites. He himself had observed a Jewish rite in circumcizing Timothy, and again in shaving his head in Cenchreæ because of a vow; but he had not observed these rites as in any sense *necessary* to salvation.

His act in Jerusalem was not an admission that he considered the observance of the Mosaic law necessary even for a Jew. It was at most an admission that the observance of these rites might be a means of grace.

It appears, then, that Paul could take part in this ceremony in Jerusalem with a good conscience. It was in accordance with his principle "to become all things to all men." It is obvious, however, that his act might easily be misunderstood. It was misunderstood by the elders themselves if they regarded it as a proof that Paul continued to be an observer of all the requirements of the law. It was misunderstood by believing Jews in general if they thought, as was perfectly natural for them to do, that Paul, in keeping this ordinance, thereby con-

A TABLET FROM HEROD'S TEMPLE
Forbidding Gentiles to go beyond the Court of the Gentiles on pain of death

fessed that he held the common Jewish view of its importance. But of course the fact that his deed was liable to be misunderstood was not a sufficient reason why he should refuse to perform it.

§ 127. **Paul's Arrest in Jerusalem.**—What effect Paul's concession had on the Jewish believers we are not told. The time appointed for the purification had not passed before certain unbelieving Jews from Asia, perhaps old enemies of Paul from Ephesus, saw him in the temple, and raised a tumult against him. The charges against him were, first, that he taught men everywhere to disregard the law, and second, that he had defiled the temple. The former charge is not essentially different from the report that was in general circulation in Jerusalem, and which we considered in the last paragraph. The second charge had, according to Luke, no other foundation than the fact that Trophimus the Ephesian had been seen in the city in company with Paul. There may have been other grounds than this, but it is absurd to suppose that Paul took an uncircumcized man into the temple. He knew the law that a gentile who should go beyond a certain barrier[1] should be put to death (see *Jewish War*, 5. 5. 2; 6. 2. 4), and it would have been both sinful and foolhardy for him to transgress this law. There is not the slightest evidence that he did.

But the Jewish attachment to the temple was fanatical, and the multitude did not ask for evidence in support of the charges against Paul. They at once dragged him out into the court of the gentiles, and there sought to kill him. But he was saved by the prompt action of the Roman captain,[2] Claudius Lysias, who was in command of the temple guard stationed in the tower of Antonia at the northwest corner of the temple (*Antiq.*, 15. 11. 4; *Jewish War*, 5. 5. 8). This guard is spoken of as a "cohort," which was the tenth of a legion and so numbered from five to six hundred men. The intervention of Lysias was not out of sympathy for Paul, but only because he feared a tumult. He thought that Paul might be that Egyptian who had headed a revolt against the Roman rule, and who, when his followers had been cut down or scattered by Felix, had escaped (*Antiq.*, 20, 8. 6). Lysias commanded that Paul should be bound with two chains, and be brought into the castle.

§ 128. **The Address from the Castle Stairs.**—When Paul, surrounded by soldiers and separated somewhat from his foes, was being carried up the stairs of Antonia, he asked and secured from the captain permission to speak to the people. He beckoned with his hand, on which there was now a chain, and the excited crowd before him became quiet. Then he set out to explain and defend his course as a preacher of Jesus the Messiah. He told of his early Pharisaic

[1] One of the marble tablets bearing this notice to the gentiles has been discovered, and facsimiles may be seen in the museums, e. g., in the Haskell Oriental Museum in Chicago. A cut of it is shown on p. 185.

[2] While Judea was under Roman procurators, Roman troops were stationed in Jerusalem to maintain the authority of Cæsar. Other troops were located in Cæsarea, the official residence of the procurator.

training and his hostility toward the disciples of Jesus, then of his experience on the way to Damascus and of the Lord's commission to him to go to the gentiles. At this point, as he spoke of his mission to the gentile world, his audience interrupted him. They cried out that he was not fit to live—a Jew who claimed that the Messiah had come and had sent him to set up the messianic kingdom among the gentiles! This thought was intolerable to them.

When the tumult broke out afresh, the captain commanded that Paul be taken into the castle and scourged. He hoped in this way to ascertain the prisoner's offense. Evidently he had not understood Paul's address, which was in Aramaic, for if he had known what Paul had said he would have seen that the cause of the tumult was purely religious. By the declaration of his Roman citizenship Paul escaped the scourging, and also secured a certain power over the captain, who had exceeded his authority in commanding Paul to be scourged and was now "afraid." Thus matters stood at the close of the day, and Paul was kept a prisoner in the fortress.

Our report of the address from the castle stairs may be attributed directly to the author of the "we-passages," that is, to Luke. The numerous graphic details in the setting of the address favor the view that the narrative was by an eye-witness. And the impression of Paul which these details give us is in harmony with what we know of his character and career. For they present a man of marvelous self-possession, quickness of thought, and power of adaptation; a man so generous that he could address his would-be murderers without an allusion to their attempt on his life, and so self-forgetful that his own peril did not seem to come into his mind when there was an opportunity to work for his Lord.

§ 129. **Paul before the Sanhedrin.**—The next day after the attempt on Paul's life, the captain brought him before the Sanhedrin, hoping to find out in this way why he was accused. But in this hope he was disappointed. There was no examination of Paul; even the form of a trial was not reached. The Pharisees and Sadducees were stirred up against each other, and the dissension became so violent that the captain, fearing lest Paul should be torn in pieces, had him brought back into the castle.

The events of this meeting of the Sanhedrin are not free from difficulty. Paul had apparently begun his defense, and having made the statement that he had acted conscientiously in all that he had done, the high priest,[1] regarding this remark as worthy of censure, commanded those by Paul to smite him on the mouth. Paul, stung by the injustice of the priest, replied to this command with words fitted to make the trouble greater rather than to diminish it. He called Ananias a whited wall, accused him of acting against the law, and threatened him with the judgment of God. When Paul was called to account for this disrespectful speech to the high priest, he pleaded ignorance. He said he did not know that the one who had addressed him was the high priest. This implies that he would not have spoken as he had, if he had known with whom he was dealing. It is not an admission that his words were in themselves unjustifiable, but only that the man who had ordered him to be punished was shielded by his office. No explanation of Paul's ignorance regarding the speaker is satisfactory. It has been attributed to imperfect eyesight, or the language has been regarded as ironical, or the difficulty has been attributed to a misunderstanding on the part of the author of Acts.

The second event of the meeting is not less difficult of explanation than the first. We are told that when Paul perceived (we are not told how) that one part were Sadducees and the other Pharisees, he cried out that he was a Pharisee and was on trial because of his belief in the resurrection. It sounds strange at first to hear the Christian Paul saying: "I am a Pharisee;" but the strangeness disappears very largely when we remember the situation: it was said in relation to the Sadducees and their faith. On the doctrine of the resurrection, which Paul said had led to his trial, he classed himself with the Pharisees. It is plain that he could not have done otherwise. But how could he say that he was on trial because of his belief in the resurrection of the dead? He had been seized in the temple as one who sought to destroy the Jewish religion, and who had defiled the temple. His attitude toward the resurrection had been in no wise the cause of his arrest. What then did he mean? It is possible, as Knowling says in view of vs. 9 (see *The Expositor's Greek Testament*, "Commentary on Acts") that Paul had narrated his experience on the way to Damascus. If this was the case, then the difficulty in explaining Paul's word about the resurrection may be due, in whole or in part, to Luke's condensation of what was said. Vs. 11 has the same suggestion to make, for this speaks of some testimony which Paul had borne to Jesus; but no such testimony is found in Luke's report. Perhaps, then, a fuller record of what was said might clear up the difficulty of Paul's word. As it stands, it is not intelligible.

§ 130. **Paul's Removal to Cæsarea.**—Twice Paul had been saved by Claudius Lysias, and now a third deliverance followed close upon

[1] Ananias was made high priest by Herod, king of Chalcis, between 47 and 59 A. D. He was wealthy and covetous. See Schürer, *The Jewish People*, Div. 2, Vol. I p. 200.

these. On the day after the meeting of the Sanhedrin, more than forty Jews formed a plot to assassinate Paul. This plot may well have originated with those Jews from Asia whose attempt to kill Paul in the temple had been baffled by the Roman soldiers. The plan of the conspirators was to have Paul brought again before the Sanhedrin, and as he was being conducted to the place of meeting they were going to fall upon him and kill him. Apparently they anticipated that he would be sent with a very small escort.

This plot was frustrated through a nephew of Paul, who, having heard of it, went to Antonia and reported it to him, and then, at his request, reported it also to the chief captain. He at once took steps to have Paul removed to Cæsarea, the residence of the procurator. This course was more than the immediate danger called for. The cohort in Antonia could doubtless protect Paul from the conspirators. But the captain knew that the prisoner would be safer in Cæsarea than in Jerusalem, and he may easily have seen that as long as he remained in Jerusalem, there would be a liability of fanatical outbreaks on his account. Therefore he wisely decided to send him at once to Felix.

An escort of four hundred foot-soldiers and seventy mounted men was made ready, and at the third hour of the night, when the streets would be free, they set out with their prisoner. There was no time for him to see his friends and to say farewell. It is not improbable that Luke, or some other one of Paul's companions, was allowed to go with him, as was the case later when he set out for Rome. The entire escort went as far as Antipatris, forty-two miles from Jerusalem, which they probably reached the next afternoon, and for the remaining twenty-six miles to Cæsarea Paul was guarded only by the horsemen. The letter which was sent with the prisoner declared that he had done nothing worthy of death or of bonds, and that the accusers had been charged to present their case against him before the governor in Cæsarea.

§ 131. **Questions and Suggestions for Study.**—(1) When Paul was about to start from Corinth for Jerusalem how did he change his route and why? (2) For what purpose did he go to Jerusalem, and who went with him? (3) How long had he been engaged in collecting money for the poor in Jerusalem? What churches had contributed? What motive moved Paul in this work? (4) Describe the journey from Corinth to Jerusalem, giving the route and the main incidents of the journey. (5) How was the offering of the gentiles received at Jerusalem? (6) What had been reported in Jerusalem concerning Paul? (7) How did the elders propose that Paul should prove the falsity of this report? (8) Was there any truth in the report? (9) Was it consistent with Paul's life and teaching to participate in the ceremony? (10) How was his act liable to be misunderstood? (11) What motives influenced Paul to take part in this ceremony? Can you draw from his act a general principle applicable to many cases?

(12) What Jews made an assault on Paul in the temple? (13) What were their charges against him? (14) What was the foundation for the second charge? Why was it absurd? (15) How was Paul saved from the mob? (16) What was Antonia and where did it stand? (17) Who was in charge of it, and how many soldiers were under him? (18) Who did the captain think that Paul was, and why?

(19) What is the course of thought in Paul's address from the castle stairs? (20) At what point was he interrupted, and why? (21) For what purpose did the captain command that Paul be scourged? (22) How was he saved from this? (23) Why may we attribute our report of this address to Luke? (24) When and why did the captain bring Paul before the Sanhedrin? (25) What led to the interruption of Paul's defense? (26) What did Paul mean by saying that he was a Pharisee? (27) How may his statement that he was on trial because of his belief in the resurrection be explained?

(28) Who plotted against Paul's life, and how did they hope to accomplish their desire? (29) How was the plot frustrated? (30) Why did the captain send Paul to Cæsarea? (31) Describe the escort and the journey.

§ 132. **Supplementary Topics for Study and References to Literature.**

1. Write a chapter on Paul's last visit to Jerusalem. It may have the following outline: The step which Paul took to conciliate the Jewish Christians in Jerusalem; the cause and manner of his

arrest; his speech from the castle stairs; his appearance before the Sanhedrin; the plot against his life; his removal to Cæsarea.

2. On Antonia see:

Josephus, *Jewish War*, 6. 1, 2; Schürer, *The Jewish People*, etc., Div. 1, Vol. II, pp. 55, 56.

3. About how long, according to Acts, was Paul in Jerusalem on his last visit?

CHAPTER XX

PAUL'S IMPRISONMENT IN CÆSAREA

SYNOPSIS

§ 133. **Paul and His Accusers before Felix.**—The city to which Paul was brought a prisoner from Jerusalem was one of the chief works of Herod the Great, built on the site of an earlier town called Strato's Tower, and dedicated in Herod's twenty-eighth year. It had many palaces and public edifices of white stone, a temple on the water-front that was visible far out at sea, a large theater and amphitheater, sewers that were flushed by the tides, and a safe and commodious harbor which was beautifully adorned (*Antiq.*, 15. 9. 6; 16. 5. 1; *Jewish War*, 3. 9. 1). It was a city of considerable size. Josephus says that at the outbreak of the Jewish War in 66 A. D., the heathen population rose up against the Jews and put 20,000 to death. If this statement is even approximately correct, and if, as Josephus says, the greatest part of the inhabitants were Greeks, then the total population of Cæsarea must have been many thousands.

That there were Christian disciples in Cæsarea we have already seen. It was the home of Philip, who had established the church in Samaria, and the scene of Peter's triumph in the house of Cornelius. It was a place that Paul had visited at least three times since his conversion, the last occasion having been some two weeks before he was sent thither by Claudius Lysias. The word which Agabus had spoken to Paul in this very city, saying that the Jews would deliver him over to the gentiles, had been fulfilled with startling suddenness.

The procurator to whom Paul was delivered from Jerusalem was Antonius Felix, who, according to Josephus, was appointed by the emperor Claudius in the year 52 A. D. (*Antiq.*, 16. 5. 1). He had a Jewish wife by the name of Drusilla, daughter of Agrippa I,

THE MOLE OF CÆSAREA, LOOKING SEAWARD

whom he had alienated from Azizus, her husband, by means of a magician. Tacitus says that Felix had been a slave, and that when set free he retained a slave's temper. According to Josephus, he was a man of lust and blood, whose only remedy for the disorders of Judea was a campaign of force (*Jewish War*, 2. 13. 2. 7).

Within a week after Paul's arrival in Cæsarea, his accusers appeared before Felix, the high priest himself coming down and bringing a trained advocate, who, to judge from his name, Tertullus, was a Roman. The Jews, through Tertullus, brought three charges against Paul, viz., first, that he had created insurrections among the Jews everywhere; second, that he was a leader of the sect of Nazarenes, and third, that he had tried to profane the temple. To these charges Paul replied, when Felix had beckoned to him, and his reply contains four points. He declared that the charge of being an insurrectionist could not be proven, that belonging to the sect of the Nazarenes was not contrary to the law, that he had done nothing disorderly in the temple, and that the council at Jerusalem had found nothing against him. Felix having heard both sides refused to pronounce on the case at once, and said that he would wait until Lysias should come down. This may have been a device for turning the Jews away. At any rate they seem to have had no hope of securing a judgment against Paul from Felix, and apparently made no further attempt to do so. In the meantime their purpose was in a measure accomplished, for their enemy, so long as he was kept a prisoner in Cæsarea, could not carry on his work of destroying the law of Moses.

§ 134. **Paul before Felix and Drusilla.**—The two years spent in Cæsarea are an almost complete blank in the history of Paul. He had a good deal of liberty, was allowed to meet his friends and receive their ministrations, and doubtless was allowed exercise out of doors with a guard to attend him. We must suppose that he was active in the interest of the gospel, so far as he had opportunity, for this was his passion; but in what form of activity he may have been engaged we do not know.[1]

In the early part of Paul's stay in Cæsarea he was summoned to

[1] Some scholars hold that the letters to Philemon, the Colossians, and Ephesians were written from Cæsarea, but without sufficient ground.

speak of the faith in Christ before Felix and his Jewish wife. The procurator was impressed, as Herod Antipas had been impressed by the preaching of the Baptist, but the impression was not abiding. What Paul had said about righteousness and judgment did not deter Felix from seeking bribes from his prisoner. It would be interesting to know what gave Felix the impression that Paul could procure money to buy his liberty. We have no reason to think that Paul ever dressed as did the wealthy. On the contrary, as he was frequently dependent on the labor of his own hands for support, we are doubtless to think of his dress as extremely plain. It is possible that Felix was led to think of a large bribe by the number and means of those friends of Paul who visited him in his confinement.

§ 135. **Paul and His Accusers before Festus; the Appeal to Cæsar.**—Porcius Festus was appointed procurator by Nero in the place of Felix, whom the emperor recalled, very likely because his administration was not successful. The appointment of Festus is put with most probability between 58 and 60 A. D. (Schürer, *The Jewish People*, etc., Div. 1, Vol. II, pp. 182–84, note). We know almost nothing of the character of the man except what can be gathered from Acts. Josephus indicates that he was a good deal better than his successor, Albinus (*Jewish War*, 2. 14. 1), but this does not give us any very definite knowledge of him.

Festus visited Jerusalem almost immediately after landing at Cæsarea, and the chief priests and principal men, having laid Paul's case before him, asked that he might be sent back to Jerusalem for trial. This shows that they had by no means forgotten Paul, but were simply waiting for a favorable opportunity to destroy him. According to Luke, they did not now expect a judgment against Paul, but hoped to kill him on his way to Jerusalem. The reply of Festus to this request of the Jews was creditable to him. He had not yet heard Paul's side of the case, and it would therefore have been manifestly unfair to grant the request of his accusers.

Moreover, Cæsarea was his official residence, and Paul was there. It is also likely that Festus knew something of the inflammable character of the Jerusalem populace, and felt that it would be easier to dispatch the case at a distance from the storm center. Therefore he refused the request of the principal men, and said that they should come down to Cæsarea, and there make known their case against the prisoner.

From Luke's account of what Festus said to Agrippa (Acts 25:14-16), it appears that the Jews had asked either that Festus should give sentence against Paul on their testimony alone, or that his case should be transferred from the Roman to the Jewish bar for judgment. If this latter disposition of the matter was what they sought, it would agree very well with the plot to kill Paul on the way to Jerusalem.

As soon as Festus returned to Cæsarea, he gave a hearing to Paul and his accusers. The Jews presented many and grievous accusations, the nature of which may be inferred from Paul's reply. He declared that he had not sinned against the law of the Jews, the temple, or Cæsar, and therefore we judge that their charges had concerned these points. They were thus partly political and partly religious. The attitude of Festus toward Paul after he and his accusers had spoken was not altogether honorable. He asked Paul whether he would go up to Jerusalem and there be judged before him. This is the very thing which he had once refused to allow, and now, at any rate, there was nothing to justify such a step. It was plainly a proposition which Festus made in order to gain favor with the Jews. He himself, at a later day, told Agrippa that he had found nothing worthy of death in Paul (Acts 25:25), and indeed that he knew of no single valid charge against him to send to the emperor. It was his duty, then, to release Paul rather than to ask him if he would go to Jerusalem. Paul's reply to this question of Festus was the only one which he could give. He knew well that to go to Jerusalem meant death. If he did not wish to be put to death in Jerusalem on utterly false charges, the only thing now left him was to appeal to Cæsar. This, accordingly, he did, and when Festus had conferred with his councilors, perhaps to ascertain whether there was any legal hindrance in the way of granting Paul's appeal, he formally transferred the case to the supreme court in Rome.

§ 136. **Paul before Agrippa and Bernice.**—Agrippa II, son of Agrippa I who died in 44 A. D. in Cæsarea, was ruler over the small kingdom in Lebanon, which had been his uncle's, also over the region which had belonged to Herod Philip and over parts of that of Herod Antipas. His capital was Cæsarea Philippi. Like his father he was devoted to Rome, where he was probably educated and spent most of his life prior to about 53 A. D. (Schürer, *The Jewish People*, etc., Div. 1, Vol. II, p. 191). He took the side of Rome in the Jewish War, and remained in power until his death in 100 A. D. He left no heir. He had little of the ability which had characterized his grandfather, and rendered no worthy service to his people during his reign of a half-century. Bernice with whom he lived in an unlawful relation was his sister. Drusilla, wife of Felix, was another sister.

Agrippa and Bernice came to Cæsarea to welcome the Roman procurator, and while there, having become acquainted with Paul's case from Festus, Agrippa desired to hear him. This wish was of course granted, especially as Festus hoped that from a hearing before Agrippa he might learn something definite about Paul's case which he could send to the emperor. He evidently thought that Agrippa would have an understanding of the peculiarities of the case such as he, a Roman, could not hope to have. That Agrippa was well informed regarding Jewish customs and questions of the law, Paul acknowledged in the opening of his speech.

In his defense before Agrippa Paul went over the ground with which we have already become familiar. He spoke of his early life and education, his career as a persecutor of the Christians, his conversion on the way to Damascus, and his mission to the gentiles. His statement of the reason why the Jews persecuted him is notable. He said that he was accused by the Jews concerning the hope of the messianic promise. As no such charge had ever been brought against Paul, we may perhaps regard this statement as giving his analysis of the real underlying reason of the Jewish hostility. The promise made to the fathers was, for him, fulfilled in Jesus, as proven by his resurrection; and he, in obedience to the heavenly vision, had preached this Jesus as the Messiah. It was this fact—Paul's language seems to imply—which was the real cause of the hatred of his countrymen. The actual charges against him were merely superficial; this was the root of the trouble.

The apology before Agrippa does not appear to have furnished Festus any more definite information regarding his prisoner. Agrippa pronounced Paul innocent. Just what impression Paul's preaching of Jesus made upon him, it is difficult to say. If his reply to Paul's question (Acts 26:28) was not ironical, it was at any rate no more than half-hearted. As to Festus, he does not appear to have been touched at all by the apostle's message. He regarded Paul as a fanatic whose condition verged on insanity.

§ 137. **Questions and Suggestions for Study.**—(1) Describe Cæsarea—its location, notable features and population. (2) What Christians lived there? On what occasions had Paul been in the city? (3) When and by whom was Felix made procurator of Judea? 4) What was the character of the man and his administration? (5) What charges did Tertullus make against Paul? (6) Name the four points of Paul's reply. (7) What action did Felix take? (8) What was the nature of Paul's imprisonment in Cæsarea? (9) How deeply did his preaching affect Felix? (10) When and by whom was Festus appointed to the procuratorship of Judea? (11) What favor did the chief priests seek from him? (12) How did they hope to destroy Paul? (13) What answer did Festus give, and why? (14) Describe the hearing before Festus. (15) Show wherein the proposition which Festus made to Paul was dishonorable. (16) What was the only course left open to Paul?

Give the main facts regarding Agrippa II. (18) Why had he and Bernice come to Cæsarea? (19) Why was Felix glad to have Agrippa hear Paul? (20) How may the statement of Paul that he was accused concerning the hope of the Messiah be explained? (21) What effect did Paul's defence have on Agrippa and Festus?

§ 138. **Supplementary Topics for Study and References to Literature.**

1. Write a chapter on Paul's imprisonment in Cæsarea, having perhaps the following outline: the city; the nature of Paul's confinement; the Roman procurators Felix and Festus; Agrippa II; the charges against Paul; the apostle's defense; how he came to appeal to Cæsar.

2. On Cæsarea read:

Josephus, *Antiq.*, 15. 9. 6; 16. 5. 1; *Jewish War*, 3. 9. 1; Schürer, *The Jewish People*, etc., Div. 2, Vol. I, p. 84.

3. On the date of the appointment of Festus see:

Schürer, Div. 1, Vol. II, pp. 182–84, note; Turner, in Hastings' *Bible Dictionary*, article "Chronology of New Testament," II, 8.

4. The Herods of the book of Acts; their relation to one another and to the Herods of the Gospels.

CHAPTER XXI

THE VOYAGE TO ROME[1]

§ 139. **From Cæsarea to Fair Havens.**—In the latter part of August,[2] or early in September, of the year 58, 59, or 60 A. D., Paul with other prisoners embarked at Cæsarea to go to Rome. But the ship in which they embarked was bound for places on the coast of Asia. Probably there was no ship then at Cæsarea which was to sail directly for Rome, and as the season was advanced it was thought best to take this north-bound ship in hope of making a transfer at one of the large Asiatic ports.

The escort that conducted Paul to Rome consisted of a centurion by the name of Julius, and a considerable, though indefinite number of soldiers (Acts 27:31, 42). Julius appears in our narrative as a high-minded man, worthy to rank with the other centurions known to us from the New Testament (Matt. 8:5; Mark 15:39; Acts 10:1). Throughout the journey he treated Paul with kindness and consideration. He gave heed to the pilot and the owner of the ship in the matter of setting sail from Fair Havens, rather than to Paul, but this was quite natural, and argued no lack of kindness for his prisoner. He acted on Paul's advice when the sailors sought to escape from the ship, and ordered the soldiers to cut the ropes and let the boat fall into the sea. It was his regard for Paul that led him to oppose the counsel of the soldiers, when they proposed to kill the prisoners, lest they should escape as the ship went to pieces.

[1] Considerable portions of this chapter are taken from my *Student's Life of Paul*, with the kind permission of the Macmillan Company.

[2] An approximate estimate based on Acts 27: 9, taken together with the distance which they had then sailed, and allowing for the stops in Sidon and Myra. See Turner in Hastings' *Bible Dictionary*, article "Chronology."

As Paul was fortunate in being delivered to the care of Julius, so also was he fortunate in being allowed to have with him two old and tried friends, Luke the physician, and Aristarchus a Macedonian of Thessalonica, both of whom had accompanied him on his journey from Greece to Jerusalem two years before. These men not only made the voyage with him, but appear to have remained with him through his Roman imprisonment (Col. 4:10, 14; Philemon 24).

The second day from Cæsarea the ship touched at Sidon, and Paul was allowed to go ashore, and to be refreshed by the attention of Christian brethren. This little item is of interest because it gives us our first knowledge of a Christian community at Sidon, and shows that they knew and loved Paul. It is not at all improbable that they were his own converts, and that he had visited them some ten years before when he with Barnabas went up from Antioch to Jerusalem to confer with the elder brethren regarding the question which was troubling the church at Antioch (Acts 15:3).

The next port at which Paul's ship called was that of Myra in Lycia, about five hundred miles from Cæsarea. Here the prisoners were transferred to a ship of Alexandria which was bound for Rome. It had a cargo of wheat, and carried in all 276 passengers. The westward journey from Myra to Fair Havens on the south of Crete, a distance of about three hundred miles, was slow and difficult on account of strong head winds, and when they reached the Cretan harbor, they waited some days (Acts 27:9).

§ 140. **The Storm and the Shipwreck.**—While the ship lay in the harbor of Fair Havens, there was apparently much discussion as to the best course to be taken. Paul was strongly opposed to continuing the journey, feeling sure that in this case both ship and passengers would be lost. His counsel was probably based on his long experience of the Mediterranean (2 Cor. 11:25), and was wise, as the result showed, though in the matter of the loss of life his opinion was changed some days later (vs. 22). The centurion, who might have taken his prisoners ashore and wintered in Crete, was persuaded by the pilot and the captain, or perhaps the owner of the ship, to continue his voyage. It was not now expected that they could get to Rome before winter, nor were they disposed to attempt it. They wished only to reach Phœnix, some forty miles farther west, which had a better harbor in which to winter. Therefore, when the wind blew softly, they set sail, and kept as close to the shore as possible.

Soon after leaving Fair Havens a hurricane from the northeast struck the ship, and for fourteen days it was driven, partly unrigged and helpless. As no sun or stars appeared—the only compass which they had in those days—the sailors could not calculate where they were, or whither they were being borne, though they feared that they should run aground on the Syrtis off the coast of Africa west of Cyrene. As it proved, they were driven far to the north of this dangerous region.

The one bright incident during the hopeless days of the tempest was Paul's vision and words of cheer. As he had been assured two years before that he must bear witness in Rome (Acts 23:11), so now again an angel appeared to him in a dream and assured him that he should not only stand before Cæsar, but also that all other persons on the ship should be delivered from the storm. Paul added, as though on his own authority and not as a part of the angel's message, that they must be cast on a certain island. They were not destined to make a harbor, but at the same time they were all to escape from the sea. What effect these words of cheer had on the passengers we are not told.

In the last night on shipboard, after they had anchored, an incident occurred which showed that Paul, though a prisoner, was an important member of the ship's company. About midnight some of the sailors lowered the boat under pretence of laying out anchors from the foreship, but with the intention of pushing off and abandoning the vessel. They were probably convinced that land was near, and that it was safer to approach it in the small boat than in the ship. Paul saw the aim of the sailors, and immediately made it known to the centurion, who, without waiting to consult the captain, ordered the soldiers to cut the boat's ropes and let it fall into the sea. It is significant that Paul, though he had been assured in his dream that he should reach Rome, was on watch at midnight, and was quick to see what concerned the common welfare. Later in the same night we see Paul in another characteristic scene. He was confident that they were to reach land in safety, and besought all the passengers to take food. He himself began to eat, after he had given thanks to God, and his spirit communicated itself to the rest. They also ate, and were of good cheer.

In the morning, as they were seeking to bring the ship into a bay, it grounded, and soon began to be broken by the violence of the waves. The soldiers were in favor of killing the prisoners lest they should escape, for if the prisoners escaped, they themselves would be held responsible. But Julius chose to take the risk of the prisoners' escaping, for he wished to save Paul. His confidence appears to have been rewarded, for though all the passengers were separated, and each got to land as best he could, there is no record that anyone attempted to escape.

§ 141. **On the Island of Melita.**—The island of Melita, on which the shipwrecked people found themselves, has been almost universally identified with Malta, an island seventeen and one-fourth miles long and nine and one-fourth miles wide, lying south of Sicily about fifty-eight miles; and St. Paul's Bay on the north side of the island has been shown to answer in a remarkable way to the requirements of the narrative as the very place of the wreck. The direction of the wind which struck the ship off the coast of Crete points toward Malta. The fact that an Alexandrian ship wintered in one of the harbors of the island points to Malta, which had excellent harbors, rather than to *Meleda*, the only other island whose name allows it to be considered as the scene of the wreck of Paul's ship. This Meleda is far up on the coast of Illyria, and thus was not a likely place for a ship to winter that was bound from Alexandria to Puteoli and other ports on the *west* coast of Italy.

Paul and his fellow-passengers were obliged to stay in Malta about three months, until the opening of navigation. This may have been in the early part of February. The inhabitants of the island, descendants of a Phœnician colony or of a kindred people from Carthage, received the ship's passengers with kindness. The Roman magistrate, the highest officer on the island, entertained them for three days; and when they embarked in the spring, the people of the island provided such things as they needed for the journey. This kindness both of Publius, the magistrate, and the inhabitants in general Paul repaid richly, for he healed the father of Publius of a severe illness, and others who were sick with various diseases.

The incident of the viper contains various details that are characteristic of Paul. It was like him to be active for the comfort of others, as he was in gathering sticks for the fire. It was also like him not to make any ado over the bite of the viper, but simply to shake the reptile off into the fire. He had been in scores of perils equally great, and the Lord had delivered him.

The judgment of the barbarians when they first saw the viper on Paul was as natural as was their later judgment when they saw that he experienced no ill result. Paul was a prisoner, and when the people saw a viper on his hand, it was easy to think that this was a righteous punishment for some crime. But when he shook it off, and took no harm, they reasoned that he was a god, as did the Lycaonians when Paul healed the cripple.

§ 142. **From Melita to Rome.**—The ship which took the prisoners from Malta was from Alexandria, and had wintered in one of the harbors of the island. On its way to Puteoli it touched at Syracuse in Sicily, some ninety miles from Malta, and again at Rhegium in Italy, which was sixty-three miles farther. From there they came on the second day to Puteoli, two hundred and twelve miles from Rhegium.

In Puteoli, the principal port of southern Italy, where one of the first temples for the worship of Augustus was erected, Paul and his companions were refreshed by the presence of Christian brethren, at whose solicitation they remained a week. There had long been a Jewish colony in Puteoli (see Schürer, *The Jewish People*, etc., Div. 2, Vol. II, p. 241), perhaps because it was a flourishing seaport, but we know nothing of the founding of the church there. It is possible that the brethren had heard of Paul and his work, and therefore wished him to tarry a few days with them, or it may be that their invitation rested simply on the fact that he was a Christian and a prisoner.

From Puteoli Paul went the remaining 129 miles by land. It seems that word of his coming must have been sent to friends in Rome on his arrival at Puteoli, for when he at length reached the

Market of Appius, forty miles from Rome, he was met by a company of Christian disciples from the metropolis, and again, ten miles farther on, was welcomed by others at the Three Taverns. This

THE ARCH OF DRUSUS: ENTRANCE TO ROME FROM THE APPIAN WAY

was a happy omen for his arrival in Rome, and it is no wonder that Paul thanked God and took courage. In Jerusalem, when he had been seized and imprisoned, no effort had been made by the Jerusalem church to deliver him or to comfort him so far as our narrative informs us; but now from these brethren, chiefly gentiles, to whom he had written two years before, he receives tokens of the liveliest sympathy, though he comes as a prisoner.

§ 143. **Questions and Suggestions for Study.**—(1) When did Paul's voyage to Rome begin? (2) What was the plan of voyage as they left Cæsarea? (3) Describe Paul's escort both pagan and Christian. (4) Where did the ship touch first, and what interest attaches to the event? (5) Where did Paul change ships? (6) What sort of ship was the new one, and how many people were on board? (7) Why did the ship stop in Fair Havens?

(8) What was Paul's opinion in regard to leaving Fair Havens? On what was it based? (9) With what plan did they leave Fair Havens? (10) Describe the experience of the next fourteen days. (11) What was Paul's dream? (12) What plan of the sailors did Paul thwart? (13) What did the soldiers counsel regarding the prisoners, and why?

(14) Describe the island of Melita. (15) How long did Paul remain there? (16) How were the passengers treated? (17) Describe the incident of the viper, and its interpretation by the inhabitants. (18) How did Paul get away from Malta? (19) At what points did his ship touch, and where did he disembark? (20) Who received him in Puteoli? (21) How did he complete his journey to Rome? (22) At what places was he met by Roman Christians?

§ 144. **Supplementary Topics for Study and References to Literature.**

1. Write a chapter on the voyage of Paul to Rome. Illustrate with a diagram showing the route from Cæsarea to Rome, the places where Paul landed, and their distances from each other.

2. On this journey read:

James Smith, *The Voyage and Shipwreck of St. Paul.*

3. On Rom. 16:3–16 see:

McGiffert, *The Apostolic Age*, pp. 275 ff. for a statement of the view that it refers to the church at Ephesus; and for the view that it is part of the original letter to the Romans, see Sanday and Headlam, *Commentary on Romans*, Introduction, pp. xlxxv ff., and Gilbert, *Student's Life of Paul*, pp. 212–15.

CHAPTER XXII

PAUL'S ROMAN IMPRISONMENT AND THE CLOSE OF HIS LIFE

SYNOPSIS

§ 145. **The Scene and Nature of Paul's Imprisonment.**—The long and eventful voyage of Paul from Cæsarea to Rome is the last chapter of his career on which we have any fulness of information. After his entrance into the metropolis, though we do not wholly lose sight of him, we have henceforth but scant knowledge of his movements and fortunes.

It appears from Luke that he spent about two years in a very mild sort of imprisonment. One soldier only was detailed to guard him, to whom he was apparently bound by a chain (Eph. 6:20). He was allowed to have his own private lodging, where he was free to receive his friends and to preach the gospel. The expense of this lodging, which can not have been trivial, was doubtless borne by the many friends in Rome, if not by the companions of Paul.

If we regarded the letter to the Philippians as our only authority for Paul's residence in Rome, we might think that he was kept in the prætorian barracks (Phil. 1:13), which were on the east of the city, near the Viminal Gate. The language of the Philippian letter, however, is satisfied if, with Weizsäcker, we assume that Paul's lodging was near to the barracks. He would thus have easily become known to the guards. It seems that this lodging was found and hired almost as soon as Paul arrived in Rome, for he was settled in it and had a conference with the Jews within three days of that arrival.

§ 146. **The Conference with Jews in Rome and Other Activities of the Roman Imprisonment.**—At the earliest possible hour Paul called together some of the leading members of the Jewish community in Rome, which, confined at first to the region beyond the Tiber, was now found scattered through the city (Schürer, *The Jewish People*, etc., Div. 2, Vol. II, pp. 235 ff.). Paul seems to have asked for this conference that he might explain his situation, and, if possible, secure the sympathy of his Jewish brethren. The fact that the chief Jews came together at Paul's invitation indicates that his name was known among them, as we should naturally expect to have been the case. Their statement that they had received no letters from Judea concerning him, and that none of the brethren from the East had come with an injurious report, is limited to the recent events in Jerusalem, which had led to Paul's being sent as a prisoner to Rome. It does not imply that they had never heard about him at all.

THE EMPEROR NERO
(The Cæsar to whom Paul appealed)

The first meeting led to a second at the request of the Jews themselves, and this second meeting was numerously attended. The purpose of the Jews in asking for the second conference with Paul was that they might hear from him concerning the new "sect." Their language seems to imply that they had, as yet, no first-hand knowledge regarding it. It seems strange that this should, indeed, have been the case, since there had been Christians in Rome for years. But Rome was a vast city, and the believing Jews may, for a long time, have been quite separate from the synagogues. Moreover, it is possible that the Jews knew more of Christianity than they cared to avow; their statement may have been true, but not all the truth.

At the second meeting Paul discoursed the entire day, with the result that some believed the things which he spoke and some disbelieved. In view of the warning with which Paul closed, and in view of his general missionary experience among the Jews, we may probably think of those who believed as few in number.

Luke gives no other details of Paul's activity in Rome beyond what he says of these two meetings with the Jews. He only makes the general statement that the apostle spoke with all boldness to all who came to him. This statement suggests that Paul may have accomplished not a little, for always when he was able to speak freely to men concerning the Lord Jesus there were encouraging results; but it gives us no certain information regarding the outcome of his work.

Such information, however, is found in Paul's own letters to a limited extent. Thus he wrote to the Philippians that the gospel had been promoted in Rome by his experience (Phil. 1:12). His presence had encouraged others to preach the word without fear (Phil. 1:14). He was, indeed, a prisoner, but such was his influence on the soldiers that they considered him innocent of any crime. His bonds were regarded by them as due simply to his religious faith (Phil. 1:13). In his letter to the Colossians, written from Rome, he speaks of his activity in admonishing and teaching, and of the powerful inward energizing of God of which he was conscious (Col. 1:28, 29). This language suggests that his preaching and his influence in general was productive of manifest good results.

We know the name of only one person whom Paul converted while in Rome, and that was Onesimus, a slave belonging to Philemon of Colossæ in Asia Minor (Philem. 10). The saints of Cæsar's household (Phil. 4:22), since they do not appear to be referred to in the long list of greetings in Rom. 16, which was written between two and three years before Paul came to Rome, may have been a part of the fruit of his labor. Paul was supported in his work by various former colleagues. Aquila and Priscilla were in Rome before him (Rom. 16:3), Luke and Aristarchus had come with him from Cæsarea, Timothy and Mark were with him when he wrote to the Philippians and Colossians (Phil. 1:1; Col. 4:10). Material aid of some sort was received from Philippi by the hand of Epaphroditus (Phil. 4:10, 18), and the Ephesian Onesiphorus often refreshed Paul, whether by material or spiritual gifts, or both, we are not told (2 Tim. 1:16). But the letters of Paul from his Roman imprisonment not only give us information concerning his situation in Rome, but also enable us to gain most significant insight into the condition of affairs in the cities of Macedonia and Asia in which Paul had previously labored, or in which Christianity had been planted as the indirect result of his labors. We must pause here, therefore, to look further into these letters.

§ 147. **Progress of the Work at Philippi. Paul's Letter to the Church in the City.**—A little more than ten years had passed since Paul planted the church at Philippi, and from two to four years since he last visited that church. But the brethren at Philippi had not forgotten him. They contributed to his support while in Thessalonica and Corinth, and now after a considerable interval (Phil. 4:10), having heard that he was a prisoner in Rome, perhaps through Luke who seems to have been a Philippian, they sent and ministered to his need by Epaphroditus (Phil. 2:25–30; 4:18). This gift occasioned Paul's letter, and doubtless the information which Epaphroditus brought served in part as a basis for it.

The church at Philippi was now organized with bishops and deacons (Phil. 1:1), who are addressed in the opening of the letter, though not by name and only *after* "all the saints." The members of the church—five are mentioned by name (2:25; 4:2, 3)— are recognized by Paul as co-workers in furtherance of the gospel from the first day until the present (1:5). The letter implies that some of the membership were eminent for Christian graces. Thus it is said that they were undaunted by persecution, and though called to suffer as Paul himself suffered while in Philippi and now in Rome, they still remained faithful (1:27–30). Epaphroditus had hazarded his life as the messenger of the church to Paul (2:30). Even more significant in this connection is 3:17, for this verse implies that there were some Christians in Philippi who, in Paul's judgment, were worthy to be marked and imitated, persons in whose lives the spirit of the gospel was eminently manifested.

But at the same time, though Paul in his generous love spoke of the church as his joy and crown (4:1), there was clearly a decided lack of harmony among its members (see, e. g., 2:1–5; 4:2). From the single concrete illustration which is given, viz., the division between Euodia and Syntyche, we should hardly infer that the trouble was between the Jewish and the gentile element in the church, for these names are both Greek. But this evidence does not justify any positive statement on the point. The noteworthy fact is that women were prominent in the church, and were recognized by Paul as fellow-workers with him in the gospel. It is interesting to note that Paul, while writing about this somewhat unpleasant matter, could make a playful reference to the name of Synzygos,[1] the man whom he wished to act as a peacemaker between Euodia and Syntyche. Whether these women were officers in the church, and what the cause of difference between them was, are questions on which the letter throws no light.

§ 148. **The Situation in Colossæ, as Reflected in Paul's Letter to that City.**—One hundred and fifty miles east from Ephesus, on the road which Paul would have taken on his second missionary journey had he not been forbidden to preach the word in Asia, stood Colossæ. Twenty miles to the west, on the same great road, was Laodicea. The church in Colossæ may be called a Pauline foundation, though Paul was never there (Col. 2:1). It appears to have owed its origin to Epaphras, himself a Colossian, of whom Paul speaks as a beloved fellow-servant and faithful minister in Christ (Col. 1:7). He may also have established the church at Laodicea and at Hierapolis, the latter a famous city about twenty miles to the north from Laodicea (Col. 4:13). Epaphras was not unlikely a convert of Paul, having heard the gospel preached by him at Ephesus; in any case, he was a spiritual son of the apostle. If we suppose that the church at Colossæ was founded during or soon after Paul's work in Ephesus, it was some five years old when the letter was written.

[1] This word according to its etymology means yokefellow, or perhaps better mediator, peacemaker (Lipsius, Drummond). In saying "true" Synzygos Paul plays on the etymological sense of the word.

The letter was occasioned by a report which Epaphras had brought to Paul in Rome (Col. 1:8). He had borne the love of the Colossians to the apostle, and had doubtless told of the condition of the church. That he was extremely solicitous for their welfare, and for the churches of Laodicea and Hierapolis, appears from Col. 4:12, 13. The condition of the church as a whole, though threatened by serious error, was still sound. They had faith in Christ and love toward all the saints (Col. 1:4), the gospel was bearing fruit among them and increasing (Col. 1:6). The peril of false teachers was at hand, but had not yet seriously invaded the church.

Whether the church at Colossæ had a formal organization does not clearly appear, though the message to Archippus seems to suggest it.[1] The church seems to have met in the house of Philemon (Philem. 2). The fundamental doctrine of the false teacher or teachers at Colossæ was angel-worship (Col. 2:18), hence quite unlike the heretical teaching which we meet at Rome and Corinth. A necessary part of the worship of angels, that which prepared one for intercourse with them, was an ascetic severity to the body (Col. 2:23). This consisted in the avoidance of certain kinds of meat and drink (Col. 2:16, 21), in the observance of Jewish holy days (Col. 2:16), and perhaps also in circumcision (Col. 2:11; 3:11). The angel cult was apparently observed in order to secure visions and revelations of truth (Col. 2:18). It was perhaps claimed that this cult showed "humility," inasmuch as the worshiper did not presume to approach the most high God, but only an angel.

It does not appear that the teachers of this new cult brought any charges against Paul, though it is evident that they presented their doctrine as superior to his. Nor does it appear that they purposely lowered the dignity of Christ. Paul saw that this would be the inevitable result of the acceptance of their doctrine, and for this reason he opposed it with the utmost vigor. In Christ are all the treasures of wisdom and knowledge (Col. 2:3); therefore there is no need of seeking help from angels. By the cross of Christ have the principalities and powers been despoiled (Col. 2:14, 15), since their power over man lay in the bond which was nailed to the cross; and therefore there is no need to fear any angelic powers or to seek to propitiate them.

Whence the cult of angels with accompanying asceticism came can not be determined. It has a Jewish color from its reference to circumcision and feasts,

[1] Salmon, *New Testament Introduction*, p. 383, thinks that Archippus was at Laodicea.

but its doctrine of asceticism in meat and drink, and its use of the "rudiments of the world"[1] point rather to a gentile origin. But wherever it originated, whether at Alexandria, the home of the *Logos* speculation, or elsewhere, it was an early stage of that gnostic system of thought which attained its greatest influence in the second century.

§ 149. **Christianity in Other Cities in Asia; the Letter to the Ephesians.**—The so-called letter to the Ephesians was probably not meant for the Ephesians at all.[2] It seems clear that it was intended for readers with whom Paul was not personally acquainted (see, e. g., Eph. 3:2). The only suggestion of the New Testament in regard to the readers is that they may have been at Laodicea. In the letter to the Colossians the writer speaks of a letter "*from* Laodicea" which they are to read, presumably a letter which he had written to the Laodiceans (Col. 4:16). It is natural to identify the letter to the Laodiceans with the so-called letter to the Ephesians because it appears from Colossians that conditions in Colossæ and Laodicea were similar (Col. 4:16), and by the side of this fact stands the similarity, often very close, between the letter to the Colossians and our Ephesians (cf., e. g., Col. 1:3, 4 with Eph. 1:15; Col. 3:18—4. 1 with Eph. 5:22—6:9; and, in general, the teaching in regard to Christ). But whether the readers were at Laodicea or in some other city in the vicinity of Colossæ is of subordinate importance. The chief point for our present survey is the fact that a report of their condition had reached Paul in Rome, which report was of such a character that it inspired our letter. From the extraordinary character of the letter we may infer the extraordinary character of the report. It spoke of their faith in Jesus and their love toward all the saints (Eph. 1:15). So also had the report from Colossæ spoken of that church (Col. 1:3, 4). Yet the faith and love of the unnamed church seem to have stirred the apostle more deeply than the report

[1] On this expression see Gal. 4:3, 8. The reference is not to the principles of the Mosaic law, but to "angels who represent the elements" (von Soden).

[2] The words "in Ephesus" are lacking in certain of the oldest authorities for the text (see margin R. V.), and the character of the letter itself furnishes strong evidence that it was not written to a church with which Paul had sustained the intimate and long-continued relations which he had had with the church in Ephesus. Some have supposed that it was a circular letter addressed to a number of churches in Asia, of which Ephesus may perhaps have been one. See recent works on New Testatment introduction.

of Christian progress at Colossæ. The letter which that faith and love occasioned seems to have been written out of a heart overflowing with gratitude and triumphant joy. No other letter of Paul maintains throughout so lofty a plane of thought and feeling. No other letter is so poetical, so pervaded by serene hope and courage and gladness. Large sections of it have the exaltation and glow of the best hymns (e. g., 1:3–14; 2:4–10; 3:14–21; 4:11–16; 6:10–20).

The members of the unnamed church are not thought of as perfect. Some of them need to be warned against even such gross sins as falsehood and stealing, covetousness and drunkenness (4:25, 28; 5:3; 18). In the relationship of husbands and wives, children and parents, servants and masters, the ideal has by no means been attained. But in the church as a whole is manifested a genuine faith in Jesus and an incorruptible love. The letter makes the impression of a company of men and women whose eyes have beheld the vision of Christ, and in whom a new life is struggling mightily for complete mastery. The apostle goes before them as a leader in the Christian way, confident that his readers will follow even unto "the stature of the fulness of Christ." Such, in general, was the unnamed church to which the so-called letter to the Ephesians was sent. If this letter lights up the room in Rome where Paul was held a prisoner, it also sheds a glory upon the Christian estate of its readers. We do not know who planted the gospel among them, but it seems plain from the letter that it was planted deeply and well. It is probably true that the church to which this letter was sent, as also that at Colossæ, was, indirectly, a foundation of Paul, for he by his great work in Ephesus thoroughly established the gospel in the Roman province of Asia.

§ 150. **The Trial and Death of Paul.**

1. *Some fixed points.*—When Paul wrote to the Philippians and to Philemon, i. e., late in the second year of his imprisonment,[1] he was confident that he should be released (Phil. 2:24; Philem. 22). He asked Philemon to prepare a lodging for him, and told the Philip-

[1] Phil. 1:12–18 looks back over a considerable period. Phil. 2:25–30 involves four journeys between Philippi and Rome, besides a period of indefinite length in which Epaphroditus hazarded his life in ministering to Paul's needs. This passage therefore suggests that the letter can hardly have been written before the latter part of the second year.

pians that he trusted he should see them shortly. Now Paul was in a position to know something of the probable course of events. He had been in Rome a long time, and had Christian brethren in Cæsar's household. He doubtless had some good grounds on which to base his hope of release. His conviction is one of the fixed points which we have to guide our thought. And it may be noticed here that we have no reason to think that Paul's expectation was not realized. There is no evidence that this hope proved to be groundless. Of course, he may have been mistaken in thinking that he should be liberated, but there is nothing to indicate that this was the case. For —and this is another fixed point—there is evidence that Paul was put to death under Nero, but none that determines the year of his death. Clement of Rome, in his first letter to the Corinthians, which Harnack assigns to the period 93–95 A. D., testifies that Paul suffered martyrdom under the prefects. This connects his death with Rome, but does not indicate the year. If that was known in the time of Clement, it was afterward lost. Hence, as Nero did not die until 68 A. D., the martyrdom of Paul may have occurred in any one of a half-dozen years. The fact, then, that the apostle suffered in the reign of Nero does not have any bearing upon the other fixed point, that, in the second year of his imprisonment, he was confident that he should be released.

There is still another point to be taken into account. As far as Acts and the letters of Paul are concerned, if we leave out of consideration the letters to Timothy and Titus, there is no evidence that Paul's imprisonment terminated with a formal trial. True, he was sent to Rome *to be* tried, but Festus and Agrippa had admitted that there was no damaging evidence against him, and that he might have been set at liberty if he had not appealed to Cæsar. Further, there is no evidence that any accusers ever appeared against Paul in Rome, if we still disregard the letters to Timothy and Titus. Indeed, the fact that his case was not taken up for at least two years favors the supposition that his enemies did not follow him to the metropolis. We are at liberty, then, to think that when Paul wrote to the Philippians and Philemon, and expressed the hope of a speedy release, he expected that the case against him would simply be quashed.

2. *Some possible evidence.*—The letters to Timothy and Titus

can not, according to many recent scholars, be accepted as altogether genuine. They contain Pauline elements, and they contain elements (especially 1 Timothy and Titus) which, it is thought, can not have originated with Paul. It is generally agreed that there was no time in the life of the apostle up to the Roman imprisonment in which the letters could have been written. The situation of the writer in the respective letters is either to be brought down this side of that imprisonment, or is to be regarded as fictitious. Now the allusions to the movements of the author are a part of the letters which, it appears to me, can with least show of conclusive argument be regarded as subsequent to the time of Paul. But these allusions imply that Paul was set at liberty, that he returned to the East, that he visited Corinth, where Erastus who had been with him stopped (2 Tim. 4:20), Macedonia and Crete (1 Tim. 1:3; Titus 1:5), probably also Ephesus, to which place Aquila and Priscilla may have accompanied him (2 Tim. 4:19), that he visited Troas also, where he left a cloak with Carpus (2 Tim. 4:13), and Miletus, at which place Trophimus was left behind ill (2 Tim. 4:20). While at Ephesus, Paul may have carried out his purpose to visit Philemon at Colossæ (Philem. 22). He purposed to spend the winter in Nicopolis, perhaps the city of that name in Epirus (Titus 3:12). The letters do not enable us to determine the course which Paul took on this eastern journey. Since he planned to winter in Nicopolis, and then in the second letter to Timothy urged him to come on to the place of his imprisonment before the winter, it may be surmised that his arrest took place in or near Nicopolis. These allusions to a journey among the churches of Achaia, Macedonia, and Asia—a journey for which there is no place in the record of Paul's life prior to the Roman imprisonment—accord with the purpose which we know Paul cherished at the time when he wrote to the Philippians and Philemon.

There is nothing in 2 Timothy that necessarily points to Rome, even as there is no clue given regarding the grounds on which Paul was again imprisoned. Yet since trustworthy tradition puts the martyrdom of Paul in Rome, and since in this letter he speaks as though anticipating death in the near future, the only probable supposition regarding the imprisonment and trial of which the letter speaks is that they were in Rome. The difference between Paul's condition according to 2 Timothy and that which is reflected in Philippians and the last verses of Acts is very marked. Then his friends were with him; now one and another has deserted him. Then he looked for speedy release; now he looks for speedy death. Then there was no allusion whatever to any hostility of the government toward him; now he speaks of being delivered "out of the mouth of the lion." Then there was no indication that accusers had appeared against Paul in Rome; now he speaks of his "defense," and also of the evil done him by a certain Alexander, who, as Timothy is warned against him, may be regarded as a native of Ephesus, possibly the same man who attempted to speak in defense of the Jews in the theatre during the tumult raised by Demetrius (Acts 19:33).

It appears according to 2 Timothy that Paul had been put on trial, but that the evidence brought against him had not been strong enough to secure his immediate conviction. It may be supposed that his enemies were given further time to summon witnesses, or to procure other evidence. It is obvious, then, that he can not have been on trial simply for being a Christian. He would not have defended himself against that charge, but would at once have frankly confessed that it was true. If the accusation against him was that he had long been a disturbing element in the empire, and that his preaching had led to riots, doubtless it was capable of being established. But beyond the general fact that he suffered martyrdom in Rome in the reign of Nero nothing is definitely known about the close of his great career.

151. **Questions and Suggestions for Study.**—(1) Describe the Roman imprisonment of Paul. (2) What indication have we of the location of his lodging? (3) Why did Paul seek a conference with the Jews of Rome? (4) Had they any knowledge of him? (5) Why did the Jews seek a conference with Paul? (6) What was the result of this conference? (7) What details regarding Paul's Roman activity are found in the letters to the Philippians and Colossians? (8) What old helpers were with Paul in Rome, and what special aid did he receive? (9) What was the general condition of the church at Philippi at this time? What officers did they have?

What occasioned the letter to them? (10) What indication does the letter contain that there was a vigorous Christian life at Philippi? (11) Locate Colossæ; describe the origin of the church there and its condition when the letter was written to it. (12) What false teaching threatened the church at Colossæ? (13) What effect would its acceptance have had on the doctrine of Christ? (14) Whence did this false teaching come? (15) What was the probable destination of the letter to the Ephesians? (16) What does the letter suggest about the Christian estate of the readers?

(17) When was Paul confident of release, and what is the significance of this fact? (18) What is the tradition concerning the time and place of Paul's death? Does it fix the year? (19) What facts suggest that Paul may have been released without trial? (20) What letters may throw some light on the close of Paul's life? (21) What allusions are there in these letters to an eastern journey and a second arrest? (22) What differences are there between Paul's imprisonment according to 2 Timothy and that imprisonment which is reflected in the last verses of Acts and in Philippians? (20) What suggestions has 2 Timothy regarding a trial of Paul?

§ 152. **Supplementary Topics for Study and References to Literature.**

1. Write a chapter on the Roman imprisonment of Paul and the close of his life.

2. On Nero and his persecution see:

Gibbon's *History of the Decline and Fall of the Roman Empire*, chap. 16; and Weizsäcker, *The Apostolic Age*, Vol. II, pp. 141 ff.

3. On the origin of the letters to Timothy and Titus consult such recent works on New Testament Introduction as Godet, Jülicher, Zahn, Holtzmann, and Salmon.

4. On the carrying out of Paul's plan to visit Spain see:

McGiffert, *The Apostolic Age*, pp. 415 ff. and Findlay in Hastings' *Bible Dictionary*, article "Paul the Apostle." The student will have noticed, in the course of the last chapter, that when Paul was in prison at Rome his thoughts turned back to the East. If he still planned to go to Spain, he had postponed the visit.

PART V

CHRISTIANITY IN THE LATTER PART OF THE FIRST CENTURY

CHAPTER XXIII

THE LIFE OF A JEWISH-CHRISTIAN CHURCH AS SEEN THROUGH THE EPISTLE TO THE HEBREWS

SYNOPSIS

§ 153. **The authorship and date of the Epistle to the Hebrews.**
§ 154. **The spiritual condition of the church to which the Epistle to the Hebrews was written.**

§ 153. **The Authorship and Date of the Letter to the Hebrews.**—This can be determined within certain broad limits, but not precisely; and for our present purpose this indefiniteness is not important. That the author was a Jew and a Hellenist is the common belief of scholars, and as to the date of composition, it is plain that Hebrews was not written until the second Christian generation (Heb. 2:3; 13:7), but yet before Clement, *Epistle to the Corinthians* (93–95 A. D.).

It is, however, more important to ask after the readers of the Epistle to the Hebrews. These have been sought in Jerusalem, Alexandria, Rome, Antioch, and elsewhere. Some scholars have supposed that they were Jews, others that they were gentiles, and yet others that they were all Christian believers without regard to nationality. The question need not here be discussed at length, but we will briefly indicate the reasons for holding that it was addressed to the church at Jerusalem. First, the title "to the Hebrews" (πρὸς Ἑβραίους), though not a part of the original letter, represents the only tradition of the early church in regard to its destination, a tradition found both at Alexandria and Rome. As this early tradition points to Jewish-Christians exclusively, it points to Palestine, for we know of no church elsewhere that was exclusively, or even predominantly, Jewish-Christian; and if it points to Palestine, then most naturally to the church at Jeursalem.

Again, the argument of the epistle from the first chapter throughout seems much better adapted to Jewish than to gentile readers. The author seeks to show that the Christian revelation is superior to that which was made to the fathers, and here and there he turns aside to exhort his readers not to drift away (Heb. 2:1), that is, away from the truth that the revelation in Christ is superior to that of the Old Testament. Now this method of argument is perfectly intelligible if the readers were Jews; but it is not plain why an author should address gentile readers on this wise, since there was no gentile church in the first century, so far as we know, that exalted the Old Testament revelation above the revelation in Christ. The only people who actually did that made their headquarters in Jerusalem; they were judaizers, the extremists of the Jewish-Christian church. The only church in which there was a tendency to place Moses above Christ, or on the same level with him, was the church in Palestine.

Finally, there is a passage in the epistle itself that seems to point to Jerusalem as the home of the readers, viz., 13:10–14. The author exhorts his readers to go forth with him "without the camp," for they "have not here an abiding city." The meaning of this figurative language is obvious if Jerusalem stands in the background.

§ 154. **The Spiritual Condition of the Church to Which the Epistle to the Hebrews Was Addressed.**—The church at Jerusalem, to which, on the basis of the above evidence we may believe this letter to have been written, was a church with a good record. Its members had endured a great conflict of suffering (Heb. 10:32); they had taken joyfully the spoiling of their possessions (Heb, 10:34); they had before them the example of rulers who had nobly ended their lives (Heb. 13:7). Nor was their present estate wholly without praiseworthy features. There were some members who ministered to their brethren (Heb. 6:10; 13:1), as had been done in time past. There were still some who assembled together for worship (Heb. 10:25), and who strove against sin, even though their striving was not unto blood (Heb. 12:5). But the church as a whole was losing its earlier spiritual vigor, and was tending toward a judaizing formalism. They were dull of hearing (Heb. 5:11), satisfied with the first lessons of truth (Heb. 6:1); they wavered in the confession of their hope (Heb. 10:23); their hands hung down and their knees were palsied (Heb. 12:12); they were becoming unmindful of the claim of love (Heb. 13:2, 16), and open to divers strange teachings (Heb. 13:9); and they were inclined toward the service of the tabernacle (Heb. 13: 9, 10). Their doctrinal error was a failure to hold fast the beginning of their confidence in Christ, and at the same time an exaltation of the imperfect revelation of the law; and their practical defect was a loss of love.

Such was the general condition of the church which had been founded at Pentecost, and in which, during its earlier years, the apostles had labored.

§ 155. **Questions and Suggestions for Study.**—(1) What reasons are there for thinking that the Epistle to the Hebrew was addressed to the church at Jerusalem? (2) What had distinguished this church in the past? (3) Describe its condition when this letter was written. (4) What did the writer seek to accomplish by his letter?

§ 156. **Supplementary Topic for Study.**—On the basis of the preceding discussion and of a careful reading of the Epistle to the Hebrews write a paragraph on the condition of the church addressed.

CHAPTER XXIV

THE INNER LIFE OF THE CHURCHES OF CRETE AND ASIA AS SEEN THROUGH THE LETTERS TO TIMOTHY AND TITUS, THE LETTERS OF JOHN, AND THE REVELATION

SYNOPSIS

§ 157. **General condition of the churches.**
§ 158. **Errors in doctrine.**

§ 157. **General Condition of the Churches.**—The letters to Timothy and Titus and the first three chapters of Revelation make a strong impression that the condition of the churches with which they deal was very unsatisfactory. This is much less noticeably the case with the letters of John, though they speak of *many* antichrists and *many* false prophets, to whom the world gives heed (1 John 2:18; 4:1, 5). But the letters of Timothy and Titus certainly did not aim to give a general survey of church conditions, and accordingly their data can be used for such a survey only with great caution. The first three chapters of Revelation purport to reflect the general state of Christianity in the churches of Asia (seven by name, but this number doubtless used representatively), and their picture makes a more favorable impression than is made by the letters of Timothy and Titus. The letters of John, which also are doubtless to be associated with the churches of the province of Asia and the first of which appears to be general in character, contain still more of light and less of shade.

In the churches of Crete the unruly men and vain talkers were "many," and they overthrew the faith of whole houses (Titus 1: 10, 11); but these men were would-be teachers, such, apparently, as sought the office of leader, and hence their number is not to be regarded as large in comparison with the entire church. The letters to Timothy, so far as they directly concern the Christian state of the church in Ephesus, deal with a fraction of the community, and that fraction is seemingly a small minority. "Some" had made shipwreck concerning the faith, but only two names are mentioned (1 Tim. 1:19). "Some" were profane babblers, and said that the resurrection was already past, but here again only two names are mentioned (2 Tim. 2:17). In the "grievous times" when evil men and imposters waxed worse and worse, the author speaks of the folly of these evil men as destined to be made manifest to "all," as though they were but a small fraction of the Christian community.

According to the first letter of John, the great majority of the Christian circle which the author addressed were "children of God," who had an anointing from the Holy One (1 John 3:1; 2:20); they had not been led astray (1 John 3:7), they believed in the name of the Son of God (1 John 5:13), they shared the great and precious knowledge of him and the Father (1 John 5:18–20). In the individual church into which 2 John gives us a glimpse, if there were some who were in danger of going onward and not abiding in the teaching of Christ, there were also those who walked in truth; and the third letter introduces us to a church in which, if there was a Diotrephes who loved the pre-eminence, there was a Gaius whose soul prospered and a Demetrius who had the witness of all and of the truth itself.

The survey of Asiatic Christianity, which is given in the Revelation, discovers but one church that is deserving of no praise (Laodicea), and over against this we may place another that receives praise unmingled with any word of blame (Philadelphia). Even in the one church which is said to be dead (Sardis) there are a few members whose spiritual garments are undefiled. Of the other four churches, there was one whose past was brighter than its present (Ephesus), another whose present was brighter than its past (Thyatira), one that was spiritually "rich" and prepared for the approaching tribulation (Smyrna), and another in which Christian faithfulness had received the martyr's crown (Pergamum). The pictures of three out of the four are not without shadows, but notwithstanding these shadows we cannot fail to recognize in them living churches in which the gospel was bearing genuine fruit.

§ 158. **Errors in Doctrine.**—In three of the churches of Asia (Ephesus, Pergamum, Thyatira)—the only ones in which any doctrinal error is specified—we hear of the teaching of Balaam, which consisted of two articles, viz., that Christians might (or should) eat sacrificial meat and commit fornication. This teaching was also characterized as "Nicolaitan," possibly from some Nicolas who was its originator or more eminent exponent. It was formally set forth in Thyatira by a woman who claimed the name of prophetess.

This doctrine reminds us at once of the articles of compromise which were proposed at the conference in Jerusalem and accepted by the church at Antioch. The eating of sacrificial meat and the practice of fornication (intermarriage with near relatives) were there named as two things from which gentile Christians should abstain in order to have fellowship with their Jewish brethren. The association of just these two practices in Revelation suggests, indeed, some connection with the compromise of the early day, but that was probably not the case. The comparison of the error in the church at Pergamum with the practice of Balak (see Num. 25:1, 2) shows that the word "fornication" was meant to be taken in its literal signification, but it is impossible to take it thus in Acts 15:29. It is possible that the practice of eating sacrificial meat in some of the Asiatic churches had existed from the time of Paul, or that it appealed to some word of his. We know that he allowed the practice subject to one condition, viz., the brother's welfare. Why the author of Revelation looked on the practice as Satanic (Rev. 2:24) we do not know. We are equally uninformed on what grounds any persons who called themselves Christians sought to justify unchastity. It may have been a perversion of Paul's doctrine of sin and grace, analogous to that which is alluded to in Romans (Rom. 3:8; 6:1). But however the doctrine arose, the fact of the practice itself is significant.

The letters of John combat an error which is new, not being found in any New Testament writings of earlier date. It concerned the person of the Savior. Some Christians held that Christ was baptized, but denied that he was crucified. It was Jesus only who was crucified, the Christ having departed from him. Hence the emphasis with which the letter affirms that Jesus is the Christ (1 John 2:22), and that Jesus Christ came not in water only, but also in blood (1 John 5:6). The false doctrine plainly destroyed the unity of Christ's person, and therefore it was opposed with the utmost earnestness. The author of the letter considered that it was nothing less than anti-Christian, a practical denial of both the Father and the Son. But they who held this speculation regarding Jesus Christ thought that they had gone onward from the simple doctrine of the church to something higher (2 John 9). This speculation was part of Gnosticism, and may have been set forth by Cerinthus, who, according to Irenæus (*Heresies*, 3. 3. 4), was a contemporary of John and lived in Ephesus.

Of the forms of error alluded to in the letters to Timothy and Titus nothing definite can be made out. There were persons who said that the resurrection was past (2 Tim. 2:17); there were others who opposed marriage and the eating of meat (1 Tim. 4:3); there was a teaching of endless genealogies and fables (1 Tim. 1:4; 2 Tim. 4:4). But these references are all vague. One thing, however, is clear from a survey of the writings which we are now considering, viz., that many forms of error arose within the church in the last quarter of the first century, threatening both its fundamental doctrines and the purity of its life.

§ 159. **Concerning Organization.**—The first letter to Timothy and the letter to Titus contain certain very noteworthy features in the matter of ecclesiastical organization. Titus is represented as having authority to appoint elders in the cities of Crete, as well as to set in order other things that were wanting (Titus 1:5). Timothy, in a like manner, is clothed with authority superior to that of bishops. The sending to him of a list of qualifications for the office of bishop implies that he would make use of this information in the examination of candidates (1 Tim. 3); and again, his position is clearly indicated when he is told not to receive an accusation against an elder unless it is supported by two or three witnesses. Thus he is evidently thought of as presiding over the elders.

Here, then, we have a significant fact, viz., that Timothy and Titus are assumed to have authority from Paul supeiror to that of bishops. But of such a transfer of authority by Paul or any other apostle there is no trace in Acts or in other New Testament writings with the exception of 1 Timothy and Titus. Moreover, the letters of Paul do not once indicate that he himself assumed to appoint an elder on his own authority. He and Barnabas together, according to Acts (Acts 14:23), appointed elders in the churches of Pisidia and Lycaonia, though it is doubtful whether they did this without church action (χειροτονήσαντες). Since, then, there is no evidence that Paul himself appointed elders, it seems altogether unlikely that he delegated authority to others to appoint elders. This feature, therefore, seems to point to a time considerably later than Paul.

Again, in 1 Timothy and Titus it appears to be taken for granted that every church had one or more elders (Titus 1:5; 1 Tim. 3:1); but we have already noticed that the church at Corinth, of which we have fuller knowledge than of any other Christian community in the apostolic age, appears to have had no elders at the time when the letters were written to it, and also that we have no trace of formal organization in the church at Rome at the time of Paul's letter. This point also suggests, at least, that these passages in 1 Timothy and Titus reflect the practice of an age subsequent to the life of Paul.

Once more, 1 Timothy refers to a body of elders, a presbytery (1 Tim. 4:14), by the laying-on of whose hands Timothy was supposed to have some "gift." But the organization of elders into a body that performed certain official acts can not have taken place until the appointment of elders had become general, and presumably, it was not a little later than that.

Finally, the elaborate statement of the qualifications necessary to fit one for the office of elder or deacon is not only wholly without parallel in other writings of the New Testament, but in itself is suggestive of a time when these offices were thoroughly established. At the appointment of the Seven, it was sufficient to find men who were of good report and full of the Spirit and of wisdom (Acts 6:3). Very different from this simplicity is the elaborateness of specification in 1 Tim. 3 and Titus 1:5–9.

Thus in four particulars these letters point to an age in which the organization of the church had become, or, at least, was in *process* of becoming, thoroughly solidified.[1]

§ 160. **Questions and Suggestions for Study.**—(1) What is the general impression regarding the state of the church which is made by the letters of Timothy and Titus? (2) The impression made by 1 John? (3) The impression made by Revelation 1–3? (4) What reasons are there for thinking that the "unruly talkers" and "profane babblers" in Crete and Ephesus were only a small minority of the church? (5) How did the author of 1 John describe the majority of the Christian community to which he wrote? (6) Give details regarding the churches of Asia as seen in Revelation 1–3.

(7) What was the doctrine of the "Balaamites"? (8) Was there any connection between it and the articles of the Jerusalem compromise? (9) What new error do the letters of John combat? (10) Name some of the errors referred to in the letters to Timothy and Titus.

(11) What authority are Timothy and Titus represented as having? (12) Why does this suggest a time later than the life of Paul? (13) Specify three other features of organization in 1 Timothy and Titus which seem to be post-Pauline.

§ 161. **Supplementary Topics of Study and References to Literature.**—

1. On the basis of the preceding discussion and of a careful reading of the letters to Timothy and Titus, also the letters of John and the first three chapters of Revelation, write a short chapter on the condition of the churches of Crete and Asia in the latter part of the first century.

2. On Gnosticism see:

Harnack, *History of Dogma*, Vol. I; Headlam in Hastings' *Bible Dictionary*, article "Gnosticism."

[1] If the widows of 1 Tim. 5 are regarded as a distinct order in the church—a view which there is little to favor—this, too, would better suit the end of the century than the times of Paul (see Bennett in Hastings' *Bible Dictionary*, article "Widows").

CHAPTER XXV

THE ABIDING SIGNIFICANCE OF THE APOSTOLIC AGE

We have now completed our survey of the short but momentous period in which the Christian religion was first promulgated. The details of this movement, so far as our fragmentary records have preserved them, have been passed in review. We have had glimpses of strong heroic men and women intent on the fulfilment of what they felt to be a divine mission. We have seen little fires of the new faith kindled in the greater cities and towns on the east and north of the Mediterranean Sea. Various results of the Christian movement on individual character have been noticed, also its reaction on the synagogue and its relation to the Roman government.

Looking away now from the details of the apostolic history, let us seek, in conclusion, to form some estimate of its abiding significance as a whole.

§ 162. **The Apostolic Age in Relation to Jesus.**—We have seen that the period which is called the apostolic age began with extraordinary manifestations of spiritual power within a few weeks after the death and resurrection of Jesus. There had been no interval in which legends regarding him could have grown up to obscure the sharp outlines of his brief ministry or to blur the plain sense of his words. Such legends may have sprung up at an early day, but not between the close of the earthly ministry of Jesus and the creative beginning of the apostolic age. Nor does that age itself, if we regard it as practically closed with the death of Peter and Paul, reveal to us the origin of any important legend affecting the outlines of the historical Jesus. If any such legend took definite shape during those years, the fact lies beyond our knowledge.

The record of the apostolic age is then an unimpeachable witness to the reality and power of Jesus of Nazareth. Its record does not mirror to us, in large number, the separate details of Jesus' life and the words he spoke, but rather his personal spiritual power over human life. If we had no gospel according to Mark with its vivid picture of the manner in which Jesus wrought on the physical condition of the sick and suffering, the record of the apostolic age would supply its essential truth. If we had no gospel according to Matthew with its priceless collection of the Master's words, the record of the apostolic age would not only convince us that these words or such as these had been spoken, but would give us a fairly distinct idea of their scope and spirit. If we had no gospel according to Luke with its perception of the tenderness and comprehensiveness of the sympathy and love of Jesus, the record of the apostolic age would constrain us to infer that these qualities existed in him in a superlative degree.

Thus the events and incidents of the apostolic age, antedating as they do the composition of our gospels, affirm with many clear voices that just back of them, in the then immediate past, lived and acted a man of immeasurable spiritual resources. They witness not only that Jesus was able to win adherents who would gladly die for him, but they witness what is vastly more significant, that there proceeded from him a subtle power by which the characters and lives of men were marvelously transformed, and that this power gave promise already of an entirely new social order—a kingdom of righteousness and peace and joy.

§ 163. **The Apostolic Age and the Christian Faith.**—The record of the apostolic age not only brings us near to the historical Jesus, and thus possesses an abiding value for all Christians, but its conception of the religion of Jesus is also of permanent importance. This importance grows mainly from two facts—the nearness of the apostolic age to the historical events on which the Christian religion was based and the exceptional ability of its leading representatives.

Nearness to the underlying historical events gave to the Christianity of the apostolic age an eminently vital and practical character. Some of the first preachers had been personal companions of Jesus, all of them were men of his generation. The force of the historical facts gave to the new religion an atmosphere of intense reality. It left little room for speculation and theorizing. This force impelled believers to be missionaries rather than theologians. It stirred the human mind profoundly, it is true, and as nothing before had stirred it; but this quickening was still controlled and directed by the most practical considerations. In short we may say that the nearness of the historical facts made the Christianity of the apostolic age eminently Christian, that is, made it revolve around the personality of the historical Jesus.

Then, in the second place, the exceptional ability of the leading believers in the apostolic age gave to its conception of the religion of Jesus exceptional value. The men who stood at the head of the Jewish section of the new society—Peter and James and John—and those who led in the greater work among the gentiles—Paul and Barnabas, Silas and Timothy, Luke and Titus, Aquila and Prisca and Apollos with many others, were people of eminent endowments. Of this statement the establishment, the geographical expansion, and the spiritual development of the Jewish and gentile churches within the life-time of these men and women, beset as the work was with great peril and difficulty on every side, are brilliant and conclusive proof. The foregoing pages have furnished indirect evidence of this claim in the case of several of the leading characters.

This combination of exceptional ability with exceptional historical position gave to the conception of the religion of Jesus which prevailed in the apostolic age very great significance. There is but slight foundation for the claim that the Christianity of the apostolic age should be regarded as normative because of the *official* relation which the leaders of that age sustained to Christ. It will be remembered that only three of the original apostles appear in our record of the work of the early church,[1] and their labors were practically confined to the Jews. Of those who led in the work among the gentiles even Paul, though spiritually an apostle, can hardly be called an apostle in the official ecclesiastical sense of the word. His apostleship did not conform to the conditions laid down in Acts 1:21 ff., for he had not been a witness of the earthly ministry of Jesus. Our claim, then, that the Christianity of the apostolic age has peculiar

[1] It must be remembered that the original apostles, of whose work we know so little, were probably of greatest significance as the fashioners, and largely also the source, of the oral tradition of the life and work of Jesus.

significance rests not upon any outward and official relationship, but upon more stable facts.

§ 164. **Limitations of the Apostolic Age.**—As Christians we do not seek our Golden Age in the past. Judaism out of which Christianity sprang was a religion of the future, and still more was this true of the new faith. It anticipated a glorious consummation when the will of God should be done on earth as it is done in heaven. This hope was not realized in the apostolic age. They who lived in those intense years and wrought with Peter and Paul, with Barnabas, Clement, Epaphras, and their co-workers, saw only the brilliant beginning of its realization.

While, therefore, we look back across the centuries to the apostolic age with peculiar admiration and with deep gratitude, and while we place at least one of its great heroic names above all those of the intervening generations, it is not our Golden Age. That lies before us, and far above both our level and that of the apostolic age.

The Christianity of the present day is without doubt of a more perfect sort than was that which sprang up out of heathenism under the ministry of Paul and his fellow-laborers. Could the men of that time have had a clear vision of the church and the Christian civilization of the twentieth century, they might have thought that the consummation of the ages was not far beyond what they saw. The close of the apostolic age saw a company of believers which, though considerable, was yet unknown to the great mass of people in the Roman empire; now their successors dominate the world. Then there were but few agencies in operation for the spread of the kingdom, now the agencies are numbered by thousands. Then the means of attaining a knowledge of the facts of Christianity and of the Old Testament revelation were, for the larger part of believers, limited to the evangelists who went about from place to place teaching and preaching; now these means are most diversified and ample. Then the body of believers were but poorly educated, when educated at all, and though they might have an intense and pure Christian life in the heart, they were not able to attain a broad and intelligent grasp of the new religion; now the body of believers in Christian lands are educated, and relatively free from gross superstitions.

Then the church felt no upward pressure from the past. Gathered mainly out of heathenism, the hereditary tendency among converts was downward rather than upward. Now each generation has behind it the accumulated momentum of a long Christian civilization. Its environment is the product of centuries of toil and suffering, and brings home to the individual, as was not possible in the apostolic age, the importance of Christian ideals and the power of the Christian spirit.

In these fundamental respects, not to mention others, we have advanced beyond the apostolic age, though the advance has been far less than it ought to have been. This advance, it may be noted, has not been evenly distributed through the eighteen and a half centuries since the death of Peter and Paul. On the contrary, it belongs mainly to the last four centuries. The Christianity of the apostolic age was not maintained in the subsequent generations. There was a decline from the first century to the sixth, and thereafter for eight centuries the church, as regards vital apprehension of Christ, simplicity of faith and worship, and the evangelization of the world, was but a far-off echo of the apostolic age. A forward movement began with the Reformation, and the church has been gradually getting into line and sympathy with its high creative beginning. Large sections of it, as has been said, have now advanced in many particulars beyond that beginning.

That this advance is in a measure offset by other points in which we still fall short of the apostolic age can not be denied. Thus it is certain that the outlines of the historical Jesus have become obscured, and certain also that with this loss has gone a lessening of the church's sense of his reality and a diminution of the spirit of earnestness. Moreover, it can hardly be doubted that with the growth of complexity in organization and in religious ceremonies there has come to be an importance attached to these things in themselves which hinders the progress of the Christian religion. The trend away from simplicity and reality which we see in the history of Judaism and, indeed, in the history of every other great religion, is to be seen also in the history of Christianity. If it is less marked here than elsewhere, and if at times there has been a partial recovery of the primitive sense of the reality of Christ and the primitive simplicity of faith, this has been due in no slight degree to the mighty object-lesson on the fundamental truths of the gospel furnished by the record of the apostolic age.

§ 165. **Questions and Suggestions for Study.**—(1) What gives to the apostolic age peculiar significance as a witness to Christ? (2) To what does it witness regarding him? (3) What two facts give to the Christianity of the apostolic age peculiar significance?

(4) What was the effect of the nearness of the historical facts upon the thought and life of the apostolic age? (5) What general proof have we of the exceptional ability of the leaders of the apostolic age? (6) Can we base the significance of apostolic Christianity upon any official relation of its leaders to Christ?

(7) Did the apostolic age realize the ideal of Christ? (8) Name some particulars in which the Christianity of the present is in advance of that of the apostolic age? (9) When has this advance been made? (10) Name some points in which apostolic Christianity is still in advance of the church.

APPENDIX

IMPORTANT POLITICAL EVENTS OF THE APOSTOLIC AGE

TIBERIUS CAESAR, emperor 14 to 37 A. D.

- 34 A. D. Death of Philip, tetrarch of Iturea, Trachonitis, and Gaulonitis. His territory made part of the Roman province of Syria.
- 36 A. D. Pilate, procurator of Judea (in which was also included Samaria), removed from office, and sent to Rome for trial—succeeded by Vitellius.

CALIGULA, emperor 37 to 41 A. D.

- 37 A. D. Herod Agrippa I is given the territories of Lysanias and Philip, with the title of king.
- 39 A. D. Herod Antipas, tetrarch of Galilee and Perea, deposed and banished to Lugdunum.
- 40 A. D. Herod Agrippa I receives also the territory of Antipas.
- 41 A. D. Herod Agrippa I receives also Judea and Samaria, formerly ruled by procurators.

CLAUDIUS, emperor 41 to 54 A. D.

- 44 A. D. Herod Agrippa I dies at Cæsarea (Acts 12:20–23).
- ? Jews expelled from Rome (Acts 18:2).

NERO, emperor 54 to 68 A. D.

- 52–62 A. D. Antoninus Felix and Porcius Festus, in succession, procurators of Judea. Cf. pp. 195, 198.
- 66 A. D. The Judeo-Roman war begun.

GALBA, OTHO, and VITELLIUS, in succession, emperors, their combined reigns lasting from 68 (June) to 69 A. D. (Dec.).

VESPASIAN, emperor 69 to 79 A. D.

- 70 A. D. The destruction of Jerusalem.

TITUS, emperor 79 to 81 A. D.

DOMITIAN, emperor 81 to 96 A. D.

NERVA, emperor 96 to 98 A. D.

TRAJAN, emperor 98 to 117 A. D.

INDEX OF NAMES AND SUBJECTS

THE CONSTRUCTIVE STUDIES

The Constructive Studies comprise volumes suitable for all grades, from kindergarten to adult years, in schools or churches. In the production of these studies the editors and authors have sought to embody not only their own ideals but the best product of the thought of all who are contributing to the theory and practice of modern religious education. They have had due regard for fundamental principles of pedagogical method, for the results of the best modern biblical scholarship, and for those contributions to religious education which may be made by the use of a religious interpretation of all life-processes, whether in the field of science, literature, or social phenomena.

Their task is not regarded as complete because of having produced one or more books suitable for each grade. There will be a constant process of renewal and change—the possible setting aside of books which, because of changing conditions in the religious world or further advance in the science of religious education, no longer perform their function, and the continual enrichment of the series by new volumes so that it may always be adapted to those who are taking initial steps in modern religious education, as well as to those who have accepted and are ready to put into practice the most recent theories.

As teachers profoundly interested in the problems of religious education, the editors have invited to co-operate with them authors chosen from a wide territory and in several instances already well known through practical experiments in the field in which they are asked to write.

The editors are well aware that those who are most deeply interested in religious education hold that churches and schools should be accorded perfect independence in their choice of literature regardless of publishing-house interests and they heartily sympathize with this standard. They realize that many schools will select from the Constructive Studies such volumes as they prefer, but at the same time they hope that the Constructive Studies will be most widely serviceable as a series. The following analysis of the series will help the reader to get the point of view of the editors and authors.

KINDERGARTEN, 4–6 YEARS

The kindergarten child needs most of all to gain those simple ideals of life which will keep him in harmony with his surroundings in the home, at play, and in the out-of-doors. He is most susceptible to a religious interpretation of all these, which can best be fostered through a program of story, play, handwork, and other activities as outlined in

Religion in the Kindergarten (Bertha Marilda Rhodes). This work is designed to help the thousands of teachers who have not had special training in kindergarten methods to present religion to little children in a concrete, simple, and dramatic way. Plays, pictures, and music are used extensively, with material gathered from the Bible, from the fund of story, from nature, and particularly from the activities of the children themselves.

The Sunday Kindergarten (Carrie S. Ferris). A teachers' manual giving directions for the use of a one- or two-hour period with story, song, play, and handwork. Permanent and temporary material for the children's table work, and story leaflets to be taken home.

PRIMARY, 6–8 YEARS, GRADES I–III

At the age of six years when children enter upon a new era because of their recognition by the first grade in the public schools the opportunity for the cultivation of right social reactions is considerably increased. Their world still, however, comprises chiefly the home, the school, the playground, and the phenomena of nature. A normal religion at this time is one which will enable the child to develop the best sort of life in all these relationships, which now present more complicated moral problems than in the earlier stage. Religious impressions may be made through interpretation of nature, stories of life, song, prayer, simple scripture texts, and handwork. All of these are embodied in

Child Religion in Song and Story (Georgia L. Chamberlin and Mary R. Kern). Three interchangeable volumes, only one of which is used at one time in all three grades. Each lesson presents a complete service, song, prayers, responses, texts, story, and handwork. Constructive and beautiful handwork books are provided for the pupil.

Stories of Shepherd Life (Elizabeth Miller Lobingier). A Sunday-school project consisting of thirty-six lessons built around the life-activities of the early Hebrew shepherds. Through the use of this material the teacher is able to bring to the child an appreciation of the lives of a considerable group of the human family and inspire an interest in the elemental virtues of such a group.

JUNIOR, 9 YEARS, GRADE IV

When the children have reached the fourth grade they are able to read comfortably and have developed an interest in books, having a "reading book" in school and an accumulating group of story-books at home. One book in the household is as yet a mystery, the Bible, of which the parents speak reverently as God's Book. It contains many interesting stories and presents inspiring characters which are, however, buried in the midst of much that would not interest the children. To help them to find these stories and to show them the living men who are their heroes or who were the writers of the stories, the poems, or the letters, makes the Bible to them a living book which they will enjoy more and more as the years pass. This service is performed by

An Introduction to the Bible for Teachers of Children (Georgia L. Chamberlin). Story-reading from the Bible for the school and home, designed to utilize the growing interest in books and reading found in children of this age, in cultivating an attitude of intelligent interest in the Bible and enjoyment of suitable portions of it. Full instructions with regard to picturesque, historical, and social introductions are given the teacher. A pupil's homework book, designed to help him to think of the story as a whole and to express his thinking, is provided for the pupil.

JUNIOR, 10–12 YEARS, GRADES V–VII

Children in the fifth, sixth, and seventh grades are hero-worshipers. In the preceding grade they have had a brief introduction to the life of Jesus through their childish explorations of the gospels. His character has impressed them already as heroic and they are eager to know more about him, therefore the year is spent in the study of

The Life of Jesus (Herbert W. Gates). The story of Jesus graphically presented from the standpoint of a hero. A teacher's manual contains full instructions for preparation of material and presentation to the class. A partially completed story of Jesus prepared for the introduction of illustrations, maps, and original work, together with all materials required, is provided for the pupil.

In the sixth grade a new point of approach to some of the heroes with whom the children are already slightly acquainted seems desirable. The Old Testament furnishes examples of men who were brave warriors, magnanimous citizens, loyal patriots, great statesmen, and champions of democratic justice. To make the discovery of these traits in ancient characters and to interpret them in the terms of modern boyhood and girlhood is the task of two volumes in the list. The choice between them will be made on the basis of preference for handwork or textbook work for the children.

Heroes of Israel (Theodore G. Soares). Stories selected from the Old Testament which are calculated to inspire the imagination of boys and girls of the early adolescent period. The most complete instructions for preparation and presentation of the lesson are given the teacher in his manual. The pupil's book provides the full text of each story and many questions which will lead to the consideration of problems arising in the life of boys and girls of this age.

Old Testament Story (Charles H. Corbett). Also a series of stories selected from the Old Testament. Complete instructions for vivid presentation are given the teacher in his manual. The pupil's material consists of a notebook containing a great variety of opportunities for constructive handwork.

Paul of Tarsus (Louise W. Atkinson). The story of Paul which is partially presented to the pupil and partially the result of his own exploration in the Bible and in the library. Much attention is given to the story of Paul's boyhood and his adventurous travels, inspiring courage and loyalty to a cause. The pupil's notebook is similar in form to the one used in the study of Gates's "Life of Jesus," but more advanced in thought.

Right Living. A Discussion Course for Girls and Boys (Maurice J. Neuberg). The problems of boys and girls presented in a manner and vocabulary adapted to their interests and needs.

HIGH SCHOOL, 13–17 YEARS

In the secular school the work of the eighth grade is tending toward elimination. It is, therefore, considered here as one of the high-school grades. In the high-school years new needs arise. There is necessary a group of books which will dignify the study of the Bible and give it as history and literature a place in education, at least equivalent to that of other histories and literatures which have contributed to the progress of the world. This series is rich in biblical studies which will enable young people to gain a historical appreciation of the religion which they profess. Such books are

The Gospel According to Mark (Ernest D. Burton). A study of the life of Jesus from this gospel. The full text is printed in the book, which is provided with a good dictionary and many interesting notes and questions of very great value to both teacher and pupil.

The First Book of Samuel (Herbert L. Willett). Textbook for teacher and pupil in which the fascinating stories of Samuel, Saul, and David are graphically presented. The complete text of the first book of Samuel is given, many interesting explanatory notes, and questions which will stir the interest of the pupil, not only in the present volume but in the future study of the Old Testament.

Paul, Son of Kish (Lyman I. Henry). A narrative reconstruction of the life of Paul that will appeal not only to the twentieth-century boy, but to his parents as well.

The Life of Christ (Isaac B. Burgess). A careful historical study of the life of Christ from the four gospels. A manual for teacher and pupil presents a somewhat exhaustive treatment, but full instructions for the selection of material for classes in which but one recitation a week occurs are given the teacher in a separate outline.

The Hebrew Prophets (Georgia L. Chamberlin). An inspiring presentation of the lives of some of the greatest of the prophets from the point of view of their work as citizens and patriots. In the manual for teachers and pupils the biblical text in a good modern translation is included.

Christianity in the Apostolic Age (George H. Gilbert). A story of early Christianity chronologically presented, full of interest in the hands of a teacher who enjoys the historical point of view.

In the high-school years, also, young people find it necessary to face the problem of living the Christian life in a modern world. To meet this need a number of books intended to inspire boys and girls are prepared or in preparation. The following are now ready:

Problems of Boyhood (Franklin W. Johnson). A series of chapters discussing matters of supreme interest to boys and girls, but presented from the point of view of the boy. A splendid preparation for efficiency in all life's relationships.

Lives Worth Living (Emily Clough Peabody). A series of studies of important women, biblical and modern, representing different phases of life and introducing the opportunity to discuss effective womanhood in the modern world.

The Third and Fourth Generation (Elliot R. Downing). A series of studies in heredity based upon studies of phenomena in the natural world and leading up to important historical facts and inferences in the human world.

Young People's Projects (Erwin L. Shaver). There are six separate projects and a leader's guide.

ADULT GROUP

The biblical studies assigned to the high-school period are in most cases adaptable to adult classwork. There are other volumes, however, intended only for the adult group, which also includes the young people beyond the high-school age. They are as follows:

The Life of Christ (Ernest D. Burton and Shailer Mathews). A careful historical study of the life of Christ from the four gospels, with copious notes, reading references, maps, etc.

What Jesus Taught (A. Wakefield Slaten). This book develops an unusual but very stimulating method of teaching college students and other Christian association groups and the many thoughtful people to be found in young people's societies and in churches. After a swift survey of the material and spiritual environment of Jesus this book suggests outlines for *discussions* of his teaching on such topics as civilization, hate, war and non-resistance, democracy, religion, and similar topics. Can be effectively used by laymen as well as professional leaders.

Great Men of the Christian Church (Williston Walker). A series of delightful biographies of men who have been influential in crises in the history of the church.

Christian Faith for Men of Today (E. Albert Cook). A re-interpretation of old doctrines in the light of modern attitudes.

Religious Education in the Family (Henry F. Cope). An illuminating study of the possibilities of a normal religious development in the family life. Invaluable to parents.

Christianity and Its Bible (Henry F. Waring). A remarkably comprehensive sketch of the Old and the New Testament religion, the Christian church, and the present status of Christianity.

It is needless to say that the Constructive Studies present no sectarian dogmas and are used by churches and schools of all denominational affiliations. In the grammar- and high-school years more books are provided than there are years in which to study them, each book representing a school year's work. Local conditions and the preference of the director of education or the teacher of the class will be the guide in choosing the courses desired, remembering that in the preceding list the approximate place given to the book is the one which the editors and authors consider most appropriate.

PRINTED IN THE U.S.A.

Date Due

DESK RESERVE PL			
DESK RESERVE P. L.			
My 6 47			
MAY 9 '50			
DESK RESERVE			
Se 52 Chr Ed 37			
OPEN RESERVE			
OCT 14 1955			
MAY 20 '57			
MAY 15 '62			
MAY 25 '62			